ASSESSING PROBLEM CHILDREN

Assessing Problem Children

Issues and Practice

MASUD HOGHUGHI

in collaboration with

CAROLINE DOBSON

JOHN LYONS

ANDREW MUCKLEY

MICHAEL SWAINSTON

BURNETT BOOKS

in association with ANDRÉ DEUTSCH

First published 1980 by
Burnett Books Limited
in association with
André Deutsch Limited
105 Great Russell Street London WC1

Printed in Great Britain by
Ebenezer Baylis & Son Ltd
The Trinity Press, Worcester, and London

British Library Cataloguing in Publication Data

Hoghughi, Masud S
Assessing Problem Children

1. Problem Children
I. Title
326. 7′4   R J 506. P63

ISBN 0 233 97244 7

ISBN 0 233 97269 2 PbK

For John Gittins
and generations of Aycliffe staff

Contents

Preface

EVERY YEAR THOUSANDS of children go through a variety of processes glorified by the term 'assessment'. The outcome is used to justify actions which frequently serve to exacerbate the children's original difficulties. This is mainly because there is little coherence in the approaches adopted by one profession or institution compared with another, even when the same child is the subject of scrutiny.

Because of this fragmentation of approaches, there is little common sense or focus in the identification and alleviation of children's problems. We at the Aycliffe School deal every day with the often profoundly damaged products of this costly process. Our work with these severely disordered children, and indeed, our experiences of assessment in a wide variety of other settings with different populations, does not persuade us that the present confusion and muddle-headedness is either necessary or desirable.

This book is the result of an attempt to create a coherent, integrated conceptual model of assessment and its associated practices. It offers a relatively comprehensive classification of children's problems and shows how these problems may be identified. It is intended to be a practical handbook for use by everyone who has the difficult task of assessing a problem child. It is hoped that, by specifying the evidence on which assessment of problems may be based, it will help to remove divisive professional boundaries and provide the basis of a common approach.

We are grateful to the Managers and Trustees of Aycliffe School and the many professional and academic colleagues who have encouraged and supported our empirical approach. We also wish to thank Ken Cornwall, John Gittins, Trevor Groom, Fran Lyons, Richard and Susan Nethercott, Garth Pattison, Chris Raistrick, Jim Wheatley and Len Wilson who read and commented on portions of this book.

As always, the Librarian and his staff at the School of Education of Newcastle University have provided an exceptional service. Without their help our task would have been much more difficult to accomplish.

It would not bode well for our future welfare if we did not also acknowledge the good grace of our permanent companions who not only put up with our aggravations while we were writing the book but also helped with its progress. This book is as much the product of Doreen Kipling's good-natured persistence with chaotic manuscripts and variable demands as it is the work of the authors. Without her, it would not have been written.

We hope this book will provide a modest start to an empirical, evidence-based discipline of assessing and treating problem children. 'For us, there is only the trying. . . .'

Part I: Issues

1 / What is Assessment?

EVERY SOCIETY'S PRIME TASK is to survive. It develops, accordingly, a social order which is most likely to achieve this end. Those who upset this social order and pose a threat to its survival are identified as 'problem people' and dealt with according to that society's standards and resources. The process of determining who these problem people are and what should be done with them can be termed 'assessment'.

The book is about children as problem people, how they are assessed, and the issues surrounding such a process. Although attempting to control and predict problem behaviour is as old as man, 'assessment' as a systematic activity is very new. The main meaning assigned to assessment in standard English dictionaries and continued to this day has instead to do with 'the determination of amount, or scheme of fixing the value for the purpose, of taxation'.

The newer professional meaning is 'evaluating personality in which an individual, living in a group under partly controlled physical and social conditions, meets and solves a variety of lifelike problems, including stress problems, and is observed and rated by a team of observers' (English and English, 1958). The word has come to be used by social agencies to mean 'determining the characteristics of an individual or group' for such purposes as school selection, protection of children from non-accidental injury, suicide prevention and any such matters that fall within their professional purview.

Although the conception of assessment as an integrated, purposive activity is new, the practice has important historical antecedents. The oldest of these is medicine, which in the course of its development has paid increasing attention to the exact description of signs and symptoms of illness and detailed recording of treatment measures. This empirical approach, that is one based on producing and evaluating evidence, combined with advances in biological and natural sciences has ensured the development of medicine into the most scientific discipline dealing with one category of human problems.

Concern with madness and 'badness' is also old. The former has become, accidentally, the province of psychiatry which draws mainly on the scientific prestige and, occasionally, the rigour and empiricism of medicine. 'Badness' is mainly a matter of explicit personal moral judgment; but collective judgments have become codified in law and the breach of particular laws in turn defines the 'criminal'. Relatively recently, work with offenders has extended to determining their characteristics as a prelude to allocating them to appropriate facilities.

Along with medicine, the most important contribution to the assessment of human beings has been made by psychology. From its beginnings in the nineteenth century, it has been centrally concerned with the development and evaluation of methods of making relatively stable generalisations about individual human behaviour. Applications of psychology to problems of living, understanding of human development, and the effect of environmental variables on behaviour now form a major element in any integrated and comprehensive assessment system.

Recent Developments

Assessment as an integrated institutional activity is a peculiarly British notion and seems to have its roots in the positivist approach to the treatment of young offenders in the 1930s. It originated in the attempt to find appropriate placements for boys sent to approved schools and borstals. The 'scientific turn' of what had been purely subjective commentary on youngsters owed much to the development of remand homes and 'Classifying Schools'. These brought together for the first time on one campus a variety of professionals, including medical officers, psychologists, field and residential social workers, to systematically observe a child in a group, record their observations, and use their assessment findings as a basis for allocating that child to a particular type of facility (Gittins, 1951). The historical evolution of this form of residential assessment and the prestige attached to it stimulated the development of smaller local facilities, such as reception homes, and 'observation and assessment' centres.

The 1969 Children and Young Persons Act abolished the

Approved School Order and brought together within the Community Homes system all provisions for children. Section 36(4) of the Act reads:

> 'Every regional plan shall contain proposals –
> (a) with regard to the nature and purpose of each of the community homes for which the plan makes provision;
> and
> (b) for the provision of facilities for the *observation* of the physical and mental condition of children in the care of the relevant authorities and for the *assessment* of the most suitable accommodation and treatment for those children.' [our emphasis]

It appears from this text that observation relates to the condition of the children, and assessment to that of a facility suitable for them. The mention of both 'observation' and 'assessment' in the same sentence, without defining either, is suggestive of confusion and uncertainty about what they entail. The juxtaposition of the two words in the Act is responsible for the name 'Observation and Assessment Centre' given to facilities which carry out certain tasks related to this objective. The same confusion and ambiguity pervades other documents (*e.g.* Assessment of Children, Scottish Home and Health Dept., 1971). If local authorities have a duty to provide facilities for the assessment of children, it would seem essential that they should share a common notion of what assessment means and what activities are associated with it. But this is evidently not the case.

This is the major cause for anxiety about the mushrooming of numerous 'O & A Centres' around the country. Their activities are diverse and unrelated, and lack a common core apart from their concern with problem children. The necessarily confused and damaging outcome has led to widespread, often misguided, criticism of assessment as an activity and has turned it into yet another ideological battlefield about the social processing of problem children (see e.g. Hoghughi, 1978b, Ch. 8).

And yet, considering the increasing range and severity of children's problems, it is necessary to differentiate the children in terms of the type of intervention they require and to justify allocation of scarce resources and the considerable cost to them and to society. They present problems whose origins and significance are profoundly affected by their transient developmental characteristics and environmental conditions. They, therefore, require a specialist orientation which takes note of these in the assessment of their problems. Rather than take up space by criticising the criticisms of assessment (see for example Hoghughi, 1979a), it may be more profitable to proceed to defining assessment and its concomitants.

The Concept of Assessment

In the present context, assessment is defined as a continuous 'process of identifying problems and determining what should be done about them'. This is a minimal definition which is open-ended and allows for the adoption of a wide variety of approaches and settings in which the assessment may be carried out. The continuity and interdependence of assessment and treatment may be best seen in the following conceptual model (Hoghughi, 1979c):

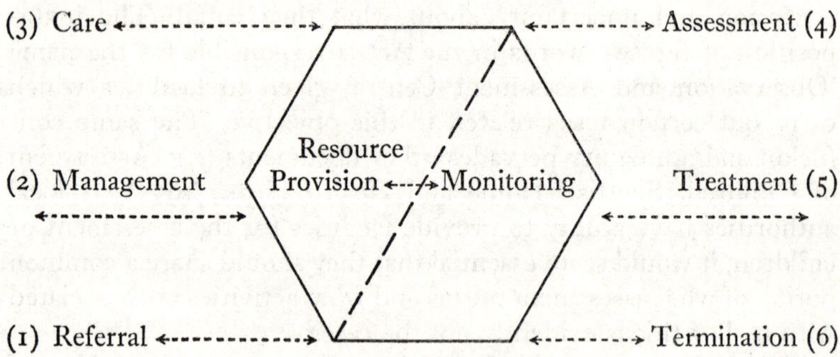

Tasks with Problem Children
A Conceptual Model

The core components of the model are as follows:

Referral. No child becomes subject of intervention unless he presents (negative) characteristics which, in a particular setting, are deemed to justify intervention.

Management. Nothing can be done with the child until the impact of his problems on the agency have been reduced to tolerable levels and he and the agency can coexist without undue threat to each other.

Care. Physical, emotional and social succour are necessary to ensure the survival of the child and make it possible for a specialist agency to carry out the two major professional tasks of assessment and treatment.

Assessment. This is concerned with the description of the child's problem and the determination of what should be done to alleviate it.

Treatment. Having discovered what should be done to ameliorate the problem, treatment is concerned with determining how the aims should be achieved and implementing the necessary measures.

Termination. When treatment has been achieved, and the problem is no longer outstanding, intervention is terminated. As new problems emerge, the involvement with the child can take new turns through the continuous process of monitoring and re-referral.

Because the determination of treatment measures is largely shaped by the environment in which it takes place, it is more appropriately the subject for a book on treatment. This book is concerned primarily with the determination of children's problems although, as will become clear in Chapter 2, the particular approach adopted has immediate and direct relevance to indicating appropriate treatments.

Any assessment relates only to a time and a place. It is, therefore, limited in its predictive potential. In a purely logical sense, assessment can only be made of *past* behaviour which may help point to future trends. However, the logical and empirical limitations of the predictive value of assessment does not reduce its indispensability as a basis for undertaking future action. Any *rational* intervention must be based on an assessment of the problem with which it is inextricably bound (Haynes 1978, Hoghughi 1979b).

Philosophical Aspects

Assessment is what philosophers call a 'polymorphous' concept. It is a term, the meaning of which depends on its particular context and content. Watching people play a game can be called as much an assessment activity as is measuring their skin conductivity, seeing how they react to provocation or asking about their private lives. Because of this diversity it is neither possible, nor particularly useful, to attempt to exhaustively define assessment. Rather, it is more worthwhile to regard assessment as a continuing process aimed at providing information about a person or situation as a guide to undertaking the most appropriate action. Whether what is done is called 'assessment' or not depends on the explicitness of the process and the purpose to which its products are put.

It is commonly assumed that actions following a 'formal' process of assessment have been prescribed by that assessment, but a link between the assessment and the actions that follow from it is a matter of fact and degree rather than of logical necessity. The same assessment may have diverse treatment implications, depending on the theoretical orientation and resources of the treatment agent. For example, a child with problems of self-control may be seen to be in need of counselling, behaviour therapy, or both. In practice, the link between such assessment and its treatment implications for children remains suspect (Reinach *et al*, 1976, Hoghughi, 1978b).

In terms of philosophy of science, the process of assessment is like that of any other inferential system (Popper, 1972). It starts with the perception of a problem which disturbs the observer. The observer has a *hunch* or an idea of what may be wrong and sets about collecting the relevant information. The 'causal' hunch and the attitude (moral or otherwise) determines the kind and quality of information obtained with which to *describe* or delineate the problem.

The description of the problem leads to greater *understanding* by the observer who may be sufficiently satisfied with his understanding to regard what he has learned as *the explanation* of what has gone wrong. This, however, is an additional logical step. For its validation, it relies on some form of testing *predictions*. But such testing is impracticable and often technically impossible in the case of human beings, because there are numerous possible explanations for the same piece of behaviour. Although some may be more probable than others, there is logically no way for anyone to be certain.

When a behaviour is explained and predicted, *control* may be exercised over the behaviour. But just explaining something does not imply that it can be controlled; nor does the ability to control a behaviour imply that it is understood. Successful measures of control deriving from and theoretically related to the explanations increase the probability that the explanation may be right.

The major problem with applying a logical analysis of the concept of assessment to practice is that human beings do not behave logically or consistently. They engage in measures of control which do not follow from adequate descriptions or tested explanations of problems. Further, the same set of problems are currently explained by very different and often contradictory hypotheses. And to confound the confusion, the same explanations permit wholly different and often incompatible modes of control. One result of this is a perceptible degree of scepticism about the utility of any form of assessment among those who deal with problem people. At the same time, those very people, by virtue of the fact that they treat different human beings differently, engage implicitly in some form of assessment. It would, therefore, seem more useful to try and systematise the process rather than to give up any attempt at doing differential assessment and then proceed as if it had been carried out.

In view of these limitations, it is essential to remember the hypothetical status of assessment statements. These statements and the treatment prescriptions to which they lead are limited to the 'here and now' and the circumstances under which the statements were made. Before much can be done to evaluate any assessment in part or as a whole it is necessary to know the assessment agency, whether an individual or a group. Such knowledge helps to determine the limits of reliability and validity of the information provided and the degree to which its assessments can be trusted to stand up to changes in time, place and circumstances. In the light of this it is evident that no assessment is ever conclusive. It is, at best, a probable indicator of the state of the person under a particular set of circumstances. This is not to say that assessment does not remain the major source of predictively valid statements but rather that its predictive validity cannot be taken for granted as either absolute or self-evident.

Need for Assessment

As awareness of and concern for problem people has grown, various forms of assessment have come into an increasingly central position. Professions which have developed to identify and deal with problems have in turn identified difficulties which make the existence of the professions necessary. A whole social welfare industry has come into existence, of which assessment is the cornerstone. This symbiotic relationship of problems and their identifying agencies has political, economic, social and professional aspects which are complex, profound and beyond the scope of this book.

In the last resort, however, they cannot be wholly divorced from the processes and products of assessment.

In a society with contending priorities, the asssessment of problem people, their need for, and 'right to' resources, has become complex and dependent upon specialised knowledge. Despite massive increases in what might be broadly termed 'social welfare' expenditure in the recent decades, the demand for these resources has outstripped their supply. This makes assessment of problem people and their corresponding needs a matter of critical importance.

The necessity to allocate scarce and shrinking resources rationally and efficiently to the most deserving places great demands on assessment. The definition of the 'most deserving' is fraught with political complexities and preferential definitions which may never be resolved beyond dispute. But a democratic society, through the interaction of its political and professional agencies and the operation of 'market' forces, eventually establishes a broad spectrum of criteria which enable allocation of resources to be made with a large measure of public acceptability.

The expenditure of resources is only part of the total 'cost' and its justified use part of the 'benefits' of assessment. Increasingly important is the consideration of the price paid by society if problem people are mismanaged. This involves both the notion of risk to the social fabric and damage to those individuals who become subjects of official intervention.

This topic has received considerable attention and is likely to remain a major source of social concern (Hobbs, 1975; Rosenheim, 1976; Hoghughi, 1978b). An assessment process based on comprehensive information which takes account of its own limitations, the damages and benefits that may accrue from it, and is open to public scrutiny is the most rational and ethically acceptable instrument for legitimising official intervention in the lives of other people. At a fundamental level, no rational action can be taken to alleviate a problem unless the extent and intensity of the problem and its place in the wider context of the individual and society are known. Only when an assessment of the original problem has taken place does it become possible to evaluate the results of intervention. In this, assessment is the cornerstone of accountability and due process, and is essential to the development of a systematic, evidence-based approach to tackling social problems.

Ultimate evaluation of an assessment can only be done sensibly in relation to a particular outcome. Obviously, some assessments are not worth the effort, and, equally obviously, some others handsomely reward the resources expended. Which is which depends on the circumstances, the potential of the assessment to guide action, and the importance attached to rational intervention. Some of the issues involved in such evaluation are elaborated in the following chapters.

Criteria for Evaluating Assessment

There are many different types of assessment. To separate the good from the poor, a number of criteria may be applied. These are central concepts in scientific methodology and are treated at length in relevant texts. They do, however, merit a brief mention here.

Reliability

Reliability is the first evaluative criterion applied to any form of measurement. It is primarily an estimate of the dependability, stability and consistency of the actions and their results. Reliability is a matter of degree; every assessment has some degree of error and it is this error which prevents it from being totally reliable. The more 'factual' and descriptive the assessment, the more reliable it is likely to be. As simple descriptions begin to be superseded by more complex ones and interpretations become ever more abstruse, their reliability becomes more suspect. Reliability forms the necessary core of assessment without which no trust can be placed in its outcome.

Different forms of reliability apply to the assessor, tests and measurements, the children, and the conditions under which they are assessed. These are elements of a total assessment, each of which has its own reliability value but in turn contributes to the reliability of the whole process. Even when a reliable test is used by a reliable tester, the eventual outcome may be unreliable because the test has been used in inappropriate circumstances (Kerlinger, 1964; Haynes, 1978).

All behaviour is inherently variable and the more complex the behaviour becomes the more variable it is (Fiske, 1971). In view of this, the degree of reliability of a whole assessment process or any individual stage within it should be related to the purpose of assessment. The less important the possible outcome of assessment the less attention needs to be given to the reliability of the judgment. In more important cases, such as whether a child should be removed from home or not, the reliability of judgment becomes of paramount importance.

In most practical settings, however, it is not feasible at the present stage of development of techniques and resources for assessment to carry out the necessary work to establish the reliability of a total assessment process. For this reason, the most practical immediate solution appears to be the monitoring of the consistency of the results of a particular tool or part-process of assessment over a period of time with a view to determining its reliability in due course. The reliability of the total process can be established incrementally over a period of time, as in medicine, when a disciplined approach to assessment has been adopted by practitioners.

Validity

The notion of validity is the most central, complex and controversial in assessment. This is because validity is about 'truth' and the nature of 'reality'. As there is no single truth and there are many realities, it is difficult to establish validity (Kerlinger, 1964; Haynes, 1978; Livingston, 1978).

Validity is the answer to such questions as, 'How do you know you are assessing what you think you are assessing?'; 'How far is an IQ a measure of intelligence?'; 'How much weight can we place on certain emotional expressions as possible predictors of future maladjustment and depression in children?' As these examples indicate, the validity of any element or process of assessment can be looked at in terms of its content, how much it corresponds with other established facts and truths about a person, the degree to which it fits into an acceptable theory, and its ability to predict certain outcomes.

The difficulty of establishing the validity of any element or the total process of assessment is related to its complexity. It is easy to establish that a child who is unhappy, does badly at school, or that a truant may be afraid of school. These elements can be validated in a reasonably straightforward manner. On the other hand, to suggest that difficulties in establishing relationships and maintaining personal equilibrium are symptomatic of a 'borderline' psychotic personality is more difficult to validate. Validity is a matter of degree and depends for its final weight on every element of the assessment process: the assessment tool, its relevance to the subject's condition, the circumstances under which the assessment is carried out, and variables related to the assessor. Although any one of these elements may be valid, ultimate judgment of validity must be based on the criteria of validity being met in the case of each individual element.

Numerous studies of tests, measures and specialised skills of different professional groups have shown validity to be a much more elusive quality than normally assumed. If rigorous criteria of validity were to be applied, few tests, measures or assessment processes and agents would pass muster. This is no reason for giving up assessment but rather a stimulus towards sharpening up each element of the process.

For the present judgments of validity must relate to the degree of consensus which they command among groups of people who, for a variety of reasons, are deemed to be knowledgeable. The judgments they make, however, should be regarded as tentative and of unknown validity. Because the validity of assessment in the vast majority of circumstances is not adequately established, assessment agents should ensure that their comments are not treated as infallible and that any potentially damaging consequences of their uncertain assessment, such as negative labelling, are minimised.

Efficiency

This criterion relates to the judgment of the costs and benefits of assessment. Costs include financial outlay, expenditure of resources in terms of manpower and materials, as well as the inevitable price that has to be paid by the child, society, and the assessment agent in order to achieve the benefits of assessment. The efficiency of assessment increases as the cost, in relation to the final outcome, is reduced. The point frequently made by critics of present assessment facilities, such as local authority O & A centres, is that because they do not have the appropriate resources and organisation they take an inordinately long time to assess a child and thus the payoff is particularly poor in relation to the price paid by the parties involved (Reinach *et al*, 1976).

Relevance

This is a more ambiguous notion and one that is not frequently considered in evaluating assessment. Pertinence to the matter in hand as a definition of 'relevance' is a matter of subjective judgment and one which is shaped by the professional training of the assessment agents. Clearly, it is expected that professionals concerned with assessment of children's problems should advance the knowledge of the problem and point to ways of achieving its amelioration. On this basis, much assessment is not relevant and, often through a reordering and renaming of the difficulty, sidesteps the issues of why the child has been found problematic and what should be done with him. A complicating factor is that what is relevant from the viewpoint of the referral agent, may not be so from the assessment agent's viewpoint or those of the child and his parents. Bearing in mind such a diversity of views, it makes sense to ensure that assessments are sufficiently comprehensive as to cover legitimate demands made on them by those centrally concerned with the child.

Usefulness

All the above considerations are subservient to the usefulness of assessment. Ultimately, assessment may be carried out at the highest level of reliability, validity, relevance and efficiency, but if it is not useful to the person who sought the assessment or the child who was deemed to need it, then the effort expended on it would have been wasted. As people make different uses of assessment, different criteria of usefulness are employed. In the case of a problem child, the objective is to alleviate his problems and it, therefore, becomes possible to gauge the usefulness of an assessment according to the degree to which it facilitates such alleviation.

The usefulness of an assessment results from the interaction between it and the competence of those who use it. This raises the possibility that the potential of an assessment, however good, may not be realised simply because the people for whom it is intended cannot use it. Although in operational terms such an assessment is no better than a less advanced one, it nevertheless has the potential which enables more advanced use to be made of it. If it has met the criteria previously suggested, then obviously it reflects more closely the state of the child than a less rigorous assessment. To that extent it can become the basis of the development of appropriate treatment. The sensible reaction is not to derogate advanced assessment (DHSS, 1977) but to try to match up the capability of users to it, provided a deliberate attempt has been made to keep the prescriptive implications of assessment realistic and practicable.

Constancy and Variability of Behaviour

Empirical assessment is concerned not only with the description of present problem behaviour, but also with predicting how that problem may develop and what should be done to change its course. This concern presumes the predictability of human behaviour. In turn, the need for predicting behaviour arises because human beings do not act in ways which are either wholly constant or wholly variable.

Ideas of constancy and variability are at the core of human behaviour and its assessment (Mischel, 1968; Fiske, 1971). Logically, no talk of constancy would be sensible other than by contrasting it with some variability (Passmore, 1961). If human behaviour were totally constant it would be totally predictable. On the other hand, if behaviour were wholly variable and at the mercy of chance events, there would be no possibility of predicting it. As it is, different behaviours and personal characteristics can best be construed as falling somewhere along the continuum of constancy and variability. Under variable conditions, people can still be differentiated because they tend to behave more one way than another. People also show individual differences in the face of identical environmental circumstances. These differences persist over time and the degree of variability enables predictions to be made.

All behaviour results from the interaction of personal and environmental characteristics. In order to discover relative constancies and variabilities of behaviour, the ideal would be to systematically vary the environment in which the individual is placed to see whether the behaviour is significantly changed. If, for example, a child behaves aggressively at school, it may be profitable to place him in other settings to see whether, and how much, he continues to behave aggressively. If the behaviour can then be judged (with appropriate safeguards for reliability and validity) as 'aggressive', then it is legitimate to regard that child as aggressive.

The more important it is to make accurate predictions about a person's behaviour, the more essential it will be to systematically determine how much of his behaviour is due to environmental pressures and how much due to personal tendencies. Because individual characteristics cannot be manipulated, for a whole variety of ethical and technical reasons, the environment should therefore be changed. A child who engages in extensive self-injury while at home may have to be removed to another environment. This would enable comparisons to be made between that child and others. His behaviour can be observed in order to discover whether the tendency to self-injury is the reaction to immediate and proximal environmental pressures or rather the result of certain personal characteristics which produce that reaction in other, apparently unstressful, settings.

Criticisms of Assessment

Such an idea leads naturally on to one of the most frequently voiced criticisms of assessment. It is said that since most formal assessment takes place outside the natural setting of the child, in a hospital, clinic, or residential facility, it is invalid and, therefore, by implication, useless. As has been indicated above, if the interest of assessment goes at all beyond the description of the present circumstances, then it is not only desirable but indeed necessary to remove the child from his 'natural' setting into a maximally different one in order to discover the degree of variability of his behaviour. Of course, caution should be exercised in evaluating the effects of the new environment on behaviour, but this does not reduce the importance of changing the behavioural setting. Nor is this to minimise the importance of evaluating the costs and benefits of such a removal, as will be discussed later.

The criticisms of the setting of assessment are sometimes extended to the idea of assessment itself and such criticism gets caught up in notions of objectivity versus subjectivity (e.g. Gray, 1978). At its simplest, the argument suggests that all assessment is to varying degrees subjective and dependent upon the prevailing circumstances and that, therefore, its results cannot be used legitimately as an objective basis for decision-making. This argument, at its most fundamental, is an epistemological one relating to the problem of acquiring and communicating knowledge and information. With human beings, objectivity-subjectivity can be regarded as a continuum denoting the degree of actual or potential agreement among individuals about a piece of information. A pulse rate, though obtained by an individual person, may be regarded as a fairly objective measure, as can an EEG or ECG reading. Such information can be called 'objective' not only because a record is available which can be interpreted by a variety of people but also because the parameters of interpretation are fairly clearly defined. On the other hand, the labelling of a piece of behaviour as 'immoral' or 'aggressive' is subjective because the behaviour is defined in terms of variable and not universally acceptable criteria. Some assessments are more objective than others by virtue of the instruments used to obtain the information. Some people produce more objective assessment than others because they use criteria which are more easily defined and command wider consensus than do others. Ultimately there cannot be any such thing as absolute, objective assessment. It is, therefore, misguided to criticise it for this reason. The best that can be done is the adoption of such assessment measures as are acceptable to knowledgeable and critical users of assessment.

A more serious criticism of assessment of problem children is that it results in labels which exceed, in the damage they do to the child, the benefits to him or to those who want to know what can be legitimately done to help him (Rains *et al*, 1975; Mercer, 1975; Hoghughi, 1978b). This argument is powerful and cannot be refuted in general terms. Undoubtedly some forms of assessment produce labels such as 'immoral', 'psychopathic', 'personality disordered', 'delinquent', 'aggressive', which determine significant people's behaviour to the child for an important part of his life.

At a logical level, every act of perception implies a form of classification or taxonomy which in turn involves an act of 'naming' or 'labelling'. The sociological perspective of labelling, however, regards it as an act of stigmatisation which legitimises certain negative acts towards the person so labelled (Becker, 1963; Rains *et al*, 1975). Also, any adjective and name given to a person may lead to illegitimate negative action. As it is not possible to avoid using such words or their equivalent perceptual taxonomies, logically the charge of labelling cannot be disproved. In this sense, the argument becomes metaphysical and devoid of any but moral value.

The act of referring for assessment may itself cause the child to be regarded as abnormal. But formal assessment is not the only source of labelling of problem children, though it may lend power and legitimacy to such labels according to the status of the agency from which the labels originate. However, the process of labelling goes back a long way; a child would not be referred for assessment unless he had already presented problems which, in the eyes of some responsible person, warrant intervention.

Ethics of Assessment

Most of the above arguments are also related to the ethics of assessment. As a formal coherent activity or indeed as an informal and haphazard one, assessment is undertaken for a purpose and has consequences both for the assessor and the assessed. Because the assessor is usually an adult in a position of power and the child is relatively powerless, this puts the latter in a minority position. It is, therefore, necessary to safeguard the interests of the child against inappropriate use or process of assessment. These safeguards do not only relate to questions of whether a child should be referred for assessment in the first place and what methods of assessment should be deployed, but also to the consequences of assessment in terms of outcome and prescriptions and the way they are carried out. It is necessary to be satisfied that a child is presenting serious enough problems which, unless curbed, would deteriorate so as to justify assessment in the long run anyway. If a child is problematic and warrants intervention, the most ethical course of action may be some form of objective assessment which is open to public scrutiny and on which intervention in the child's life may be based.

The methods of assessment may involve subjecting the child to practices which are not justified in relation either to the outcome or to the prevailing ethics of the community. To subject a child to strong electric shocks, for example, to determine his pain threshold could not be justified in terms of the use which could be made of the information.

The consequences of labelling have already been briefly discussed. Suffice it to say that labels have a power which transcends the immediate circumstances in which they are made and are frequently used as shorthand ways of legitimising further action which may not be in any way justified by evidence available.

Clearly, every effort should be made to minimise the use of labels with judgmental overtones with children. The development of empirical assessment and alternative approaches to the classification of children's disorders may make the use of labelling unnecessary (*see* Chapter 2). To counteract the effect of labels, not only is it necessary to engage in minimal labelling in the first place but also to ensure that all the labels bear qualifications of time and place which limit their use and applicability.

Much of the information obtained through a process of formal assessment will have come to light for the first time. Like other information, it is subject to the same requirements of confidentiality and safeguarding of privacy of individuals. There is the added constraint that such information can be used to justify measures which may have profound long-term consequences for the child and his family. Considerable caution should, therefore, be exercised in disseminating confidential information about a child and his family.

2 / Approaches to Assessment

THERE ARE MANY PROFESSIONS – such as medicine, psychiatry, education, psychology and social work – concerned with human problems. They use a wide range of approaches and instruments which vary in their formality and objectivity. Although all of them deal with human beings who have problems, their approaches are so dramatically different from one another that it is frequently not possible to see that they are all concerned with the same human beings.

Medicine has developed the most systematic approach, based on rigorous, increasingly empirical techniques. It encompasses the total bodily functioning of man. Although there are margins of error in its empirical operation and although it is subject to fads, fashions and foibles, it nevertheless remains the most objective, formal and universally accepted approach to one particular set of problems. Paediatrics is the branch of medicine most concerned with development and adaptive difficulties of young children. Its methods of assessment are wide-ranging and advanced. The outcomes of its intervention are non-stigmatising and readily accepted by not only the parents but also related professionals. Sadly, most paediatricians are not called on to extend their skills to the older child and adolescent, for whom no comparable medical specialist is available, despite the fact that the body undergoes dramatic physiological and psychological changes during puberty and adolescence.

In the absence of such a specialty, psychiatry has taken on the concern with problems of psychological adaptation of children and adolescents. It encompasses many facets and orientations and it is not useful to talk of it as if it were a unitary discipline. Certain aspects of it, such as the assessment and treatment of conditions which are suspected to have a physical basis *and* are responsive to physical treatment, are in the mainstream of medicine. Into this category would fall such disorders as psychoses or epilepsies.

The larger part of child and adolescent psychiatry utilises what is known about normal and abnormal developments in young people as a basis for making diagnoses. Such diagnoses and the classifications on which they are based are of varying complexity, rigour and utility (c.f. Philips *et al*, 1975; Rutter, 1976). They also raise a number of logical and empirical problems which renders their scientific status and usefulness suspect (Feinstein, 1977; Hoghughi, 1978a; 1978b; 1979b). Setting aside problems of dubious diagnoses, psychiatrists fulfil a major function in the screening of seriously problematic children by ruling out the possibility of major psychiatric disorders such as depressions and psychoses, susceptible to pharmacological intervention. Additionally, child and adolescent psychiatrists possess specialised knowledge of children's problems and, frequently, skills which are of enormous value in a wider process of assessment and counselling of those who have to deal with difficult children.

Education has succeeded in establishing relatively objective measures for the assessment of the abilities and aptitudes of children and methods for discovery of particular sources of educational difficulty. Educational assessment is limited to fairly narrow areas of human functioning which are increasingly seen to be at the mercy of other, wider aspects of social structure, family and personality. However, teachers, by virtue of their intensive contact with the child, close attention to classroom behaviour and ability to use the wide range of observational contexts, are particularly valuable and necessary contributors to assessment of problem children.

Much of educational assessment has been stimulated by the availability of methods for the determination of individual differences developed through the use of psychological techniques. Such techniques range from the use of objective physical measurements, as in psychophysics, to the most attenuated subjective assessment, as in determining 'ego' through interviewing. Psychology as an applied science encompasses a large proportion of human behaviour ranging from physiological aspects of individual behaviour to dynamics of groups. In its present state it is highly rigorous in some areas such as intellectual functioning, which provide reliable and valid information, but it also contains other areas such as assessment of personality through interview techniques, which are pitted with difficulties. Given its theoretical and empirical foundations it is potentially capable of integrating most of the activities related to the assessment of individual behaviour. Highly developed specialisms of clinical and educational psychology drawing on a range of rigorous techniques are of special value in the assessment and, increasingly, treatment of children's problems.

Social work, as an applied activity, has not yet acquired the status of a discipline. It derives its basic methods both of assessment and amelioration of problems from those developed by other professions. This is largely because social work still does not possess an integrating conceptual basis or empirical body of evidence on which it can draw. Perhaps because of its relative youth and its concern with the materially and politically disadvantaged, social work tasks are more at the mercy of shifting political fashions and definitions than are those of other helping professions. There is some evidence of attempts being made to introduce a more empirical element into social work (e.g. Pincus and Minahan, 1973). Despite the limitations of social work, however, social workers are concerned with identifying and providing appropriate and continuing help to the child and his family. Not only because of their legal responsibilities and central co-ordinating role in providing services, but also because of their presumed familiarity with the child's family and social context, they should be centrally involved in any comprehensive assessment of the child.

Underlying all the above approaches to assessment, there is the basic need for obtaining information which differentiates individuals or groups in terms of certain important characteristics which point to different treatment prescriptions. This problem of 'telling between' cuts across all disciplines. Each area of enquiry has its own adherents, jargon and preferred style of assessment. Among them, they isolate one functioning part of a person from the rest of him and fragment what is an integral human being. While this is understandable and possibly inevitable at the highest level of specialty, it negates the interdependence of human functions and problems. It can also limit the usefulness of the contribution of one group of specialists to the wider understanding of the child's problems by others.

Criteria for Evaluating Classifications

The primary merit of any approach to assessment – and the classifications that underlie it – is the degree to which it can act as a guide to what should be done to alleviate the particular cause for concern. This general requirement can be broken down into more specific criteria against which any classification system should be judged (c.f. Hobbs, 1975; Philips *et al*, 1975; Rutter, 1976; Hoghughi, 1978b). A good classification of children's disorders should:

- Present maximum, comprehensive information.
- Be capable of as many forms of validation as possible.
- Be based on systematic, validated information and remain open to changing personal and social circumstances of the subject.
- Be usable by persons both inside and outside a profession and thus make sense to a wide audience.
- Allow for fine gradations of judgment according to specialised needs and competence of its users.
- Be capable of incorporating new empirical findings regarding childrens' disorders.
- Not be a disguise for personal or cultural derogation.
- Take account of fundamental differences between adults and children and different cultural milieux and give due weight to the different significance of disorders according to the social context.
- Take account of different levels of response from normal to the seriously disordered in different functional areas: it should be 'multi axial'.
- Allow for developmental and organic changes. Note relative constancy and variability of individual behaviour to interaction with different environments.
- Not give prominence to one aspect of functioning at the expense of presenting a picture of the organic whole.
- Not be so theory-bound as to exclude its use by those who do not subscribe to the theory.
- Have direct and clear implications for treatment but allow for the use of a variety of methods.
- Be recordable in detail to allow research, refinement and use for teaching.

Attempts have been made to devise systems which satisfy all the above criteria. None has been particularly successful. It is evident that in the present state of knowledge, only the simplest *descriptive* systems which do not postulate a particular theoretical orientation or adduce any particular aetiological relationships are likely to command any sort of consensus (c.f. Prugh *et al*, 1975). Other aspects such as explanations must remain strictly tentative until more is known about the origins and development of disorders.

The Problem Profile Approach (PPA)

In the light of the foregoing comments, a descriptive classification has been developed (Hoghughi 1969, 1976, 1977, 1978b) and subsequently adopted in both the assessment and treatment of disordered youngsters at Aycliffe School. Its applicability, however, ranges over all school age children and, with suitable modifications, to adults. It has had a long period of exposure to multi-disciplinary teams of professionals, children and their parents. This book presents an elaboration of this approach.

The core of this approach is the concern with evaluating and alleviating problems. The reason for adopting problems as the focus of approach is that youngsters come to the attention of social agencies and go through particular forms of social processing because they present or are subjected to difficulties which are unacceptable to those around them. A number of other investigators, particularly in medicine and psychiatry (Weed, 1969; Ryback, 1974), have adopted similar approaches. However, their concern seems to have been primarily with developing good recording systems rather than evolving problem-based classifications for use in the assessment of problem children.

What is a problem?

In this context, a problem is simply defined as an 'unacceptable condition'. Unacceptability implies 'undesirability' under a particular set of circumstances of time and place, taking into account that what is unacceptable and undesirable in one context is not necessarily so in another. It is, for example, normal and acceptable for a child who has lost his mother to weep without provocation, but not so for another child who is not subject to such obvious stress.

The definition implies that there is a person or a group on whom the condition impinges who regards it as unacceptable. Simply put, an undetected problem is no problem at all, though the possibility of its existence can be considered and investigated. Problems can be presented in many areas, but only those which occur in critical areas warrant intervention. Critical areas are those which arouse strong evaluative reactions in terms of good or bad. As social and personal values change, so does the perception of what is critical. Furthermore, judgments of right and wrong or good and bad are not absolute or black and white. Rather, they are relative and a matter of degree. Each individual and society has a latitude of tolerance. It is only when the condition falls outside this band of acceptability that actions are precipitated. Indeed, the critical degree of departure from this tolerance determines the mode and the intensity of social intervention.

The concept of 'profile' encapsulates the idea that the pattern of problems perceived differs according to the particular viewpoint and that as the child and his circumstances change, so do the relative weight and intensity of his problems.

The definition of a condition as unacceptable implies that something should be done about it. This is sometimes made explicit, as in a court order. What the 'something' is depends on the rights and responsibilities of those who have defined the problem. The person who has defined the problem also needs 'power' to do something about the problem. Such power may be that of a headmaster who takes action against a truant, that of a mother who refers a child to social services because he is 'beyond control', of a police officer who apprehends an offender or a psychiatrist who says a child's attributes make him 'dangerous'.

It is possible to construe 'unacceptable conditions' from many points of view, leading to quite different classifications. In this approach the orientation is towards problems manifested or experienced by children in different functional areas. Because even disordered children are integrated entities, functional areas frequently overlap and invariably interact with one another. This simply reflects the human condition; problems in one area impinge on the total being and affect a wide range of functions. A classification that takes account of this fact is preferable to one that distorts reality for the convenience of the classifier. This classification of problems is comprehensive, although it allows for the use of specialised taxonomies within each functional area. Knowledge of the unacceptable condition is obtained from diverse sources. These will be described in greater detail in the next chapter.

The close scrutiny of information provided in each of these areas reveals why the particular condition has been found problematic: in what ways the child's functioning is considered to deviate from normal variations or society's latitude of tolerance. This accords with another important requirement of a classification of disorders – that it should indicate areas of normality or non-problematic attributes. The functional attributes covered by each problem area are only set out in summary form. The detailed Master Code is presented in Chapter 5.

Physical This area includes all disorders, dysfunctions and deficits to do with the body as a whole or any of its subsystems, whether hereditary or acquired during the child's lifetime from, say, colour deficiency and epilepsy, through diabetes and poor hearing, to undescended testicles. It also includes the psychoses, as well as psychophysiological, autonomic and visceral disorders.

Cognitive This category is concerned with the ability of the child to cope with the intellectual demands made on him in his daily life, particularly in school and work settings. The area also encompasses cognitive problems such as illiteracy, which may not have arisen as a result of intellectual defect but out of persistent truancy. In this sense, not being able to read and write fall within the cognitive problem area and are functionally equivalent to difficulties arising from intellectual deficit. The problem can be general, such as subnormality, or specific, such as difficulty in synthesising words. Supernormality may be a problem if it is ascertained that inadequate demands are made on the adolescent in relation to his capacity, which lead to undesirable modes of seeking intellectual satisfaction.

Family This is the largest and the most complex category of problems associated with disordered youngsters. In tackling such a large area there is a danger of infinite regress and, therefore, the limits of how far and wide the problems should be described depend on the specific requirements of the investigator. Problems can be traced back and sideways as far as necessary if they seem to be part of the present reality of the family.

Family problems encompass the background of the parents; their socioeconomic status; the neighbourhood they inhabit; the home; their individual characteristics at a variety of levels of analysis; the pattern, content and emotional tone of their interaction with each other and with their children, both together and singly; the style and method of upbringing of children including methods of control; existence of affective bonds; and children's relationships with their parents and one another.

Social Skills These encompass the difficulties and conflicts of the child in coping with the growing demands of social interaction with both peers and adults. They refer to perception of social cues and the ability to relate to others, reciprocate and engage in cooperative activity, amenability and response to social pressure.

Anti-Social Behaviour This is perhaps the area which causes the most anxiety about the total functioning of problem youngsters. It includes all infractions of laws, rules, customs and rituals of behaviour in the wider social (as opposed to small group) settings. It comprises chiefly all offences and encroachments against person and property as well as 'reflexive' offences such as drug taking and soliciting. In addition, it includes acts which, although not strictly offences – self-destructive gestures, temper tantrums, truancy and absconding – are nevertheless seriously disruptive and frequently provoke dramatic intervention by social agencies.

Personal This area covers three distinct but closely interrelated aspects: deviation in personality structure; and relatively stable personal attributes; emotional development, tone, adaptation, and control; identity or self-concept, best described as a child's difficulty in answering such questions as 'Who am I?', 'What am I?', 'Who cares for me?', 'What am I worth?', etc. Traditionally, most clinicians have confined themselves to the first two categories. The third, however, is regarded as crucial in the understanding of the way children see themselves and make sense of their lives, not only because it completes the picture of the child but also because it acknowledges that a child's behaviour results from the interaction of his perceptions and expectations with environmental conditions.

Dimensions of Problems

Children differ from one another in the number, type and quality of problems they present. At least four evaluative dimensions are essential in evaluating any problem child for purposes of distinguishing him from others and drawing up a treatment plan:

Extent refers to the number of problems listed for a particular child. The more problems listed, the more problematic the child is. A child with physical, family, behavioural and personal problems presents a larger area of 'unacceptable conditions' than does one with, say, only physical and personal. The range of problems within each area also contributes to the judgment of the extent of problems. Evaluation of extent is carried out by simple counting of problems.

Intensity relates to the depth of the problem. The more intense the problem, the more severe it will be. For example, a severely aggressive father is a more serious problem than a mildly aggressive one; the girl who mopes and says 'I am fed up' is less of a problem than one who is suicidally depressed. Evaluation of intensity can be done either subjectively by an individual, through consensus by an assessment group, or the development of an objective scale in any of the generally accepted ways.

Duration can be seen as a major contributor to judgments of intensity. It refers to the length of time a problem has been manifested. The supposition, broadly accepted, is that the longer a problem has existed the more difficult it will be to alleviate, if for no other reason than it will have become part of the child's total adaptation. This dimension takes note of the fact that in the course of a child's development one problem usually generates another without the former having been resolved. This aspect of evaluation may be expanded to differentiate between problems which are *manifest* (symptoms and signs) and those which are regarded as being at the *core* of the difficulty.

Urgency allows the assessment agent to rank problems in order of priority warranting intervention. Different criteria may be used for this type of ranking, such as the social impact of the problem or its consequences for the child. Whatever other criteria are considered, 'urgency' is likely to be the most influential in determining priorities. This involves subjective judgment, whether individual or group based, regarding the possible consequences of *not* taking certain measures. It can also be based on an understanding of the hierarchical order of problems, such as 'unless we reduce her anxiety, we cannot bring the rest of her behaviour under control'.

Evaluation of the Problem Profile Approach

The PPA was developed in a multi-disciplinary setting concerned with the assessment and treatment of severely disordered youngsters. It is an attempt to establish a rigorous, non-stigmatising, generally acceptable system for the description of children's problems. With its associated concepts it provides a systematic guide to those areas of a child's functioning which warrant intervention.

By eliciting reliable, broadly based and potentially validated information, it enables the development of complex typologies of children's attributes and of their responsiveness to particular treatments, both for single elements and sets of problems. It does not remove the eventual need for diagnostic systems but provides a basis on which they may be developed (see also Spitzer *et al*, 1977; Feinstein, 1977). Over the period of time the PPA has been in use, its advantages, compared with other commonly available classifications of children's disorders, have become evident. It may be worthwhile to set these out, particularly in relation to the previously presented criteria.

The six problem areas encompass the totality of difficulties experienced or presented by the child. Each area can be treated at the level of detail and comprehensiveness that the complexity of the child's problems and the resources of the assessment agency warrant. An individual social worker on first acquaintance with a child may use it as a handy checklist for a superficial scanning of the range of the child's other possible problems. Equally, a specialised agency may probe each element of the same checklist or an expanded one at high levels of specialism until the full complexity of the child's problems has been established.

Information is derived from three main sources (see Chapter 3). Because the information obtained relates to the same problem areas, such as physical functioning or social skills, it becomes possible to determine the consistency and weight of opinion regarding the child's problems. Reliance on multiple sources of information ensures that, even at its lowest level, it is likely to be more reliable and valid than alternative approaches which use a narrower range of information.

Unless the assessment agent is omniscient, his reliance on multiple sources of information encourages participation of others in the child's assessment, and hence decision-making about what to do with him. As will be argued later (Chapter 4), the more serious the child's actual or potential problems, the more necessary it will be to carry out team, as opposed to individual, assessment. This classification is particularly appropriate to a team or multi-disciplinary approach. This is especially important in the case of a threatening minority, such as disordered children, who may be given questionable labels which legitimise empirically and ethically marginal treatments. The wider the decision-making base, the less idiosyncratic it is likely to be.

The approach uses a language of problems which is almost universal and enables easier communication than can be achieved with any other classification between different levels of expertise and professional points of view. Because learning about functional areas is part of any normally intelligent citizen's upbringing, *everybody* can contribute usefully to the determination of each of the problem areas. The descriptive language is common English (or Hebrew or Cantonese or whatever) and as such demystifies the disorder of the child. This is an important consideration, bearing in mind that most classifications achieve professional status at the expense of making sense to the many non-specialists who are likely to be concerned with the welfare of the child and anxious to understand his problems.

The definition of 'problem', on which this approach is based, relates to the interaction of the child and his environment, including the time and the place in which the condition is found to be unacceptable. Thus, the approach is dynamic and allows for the fluid nature of the child's condition. Such fluidity results not only from the ebb and flow of the child's problems but also the shifting perspectives of those who deal with him.

The PPA does not depend on the use of derogating and empirically questionable labels such as 'psychopath'. The detailed description of problems transmits maximum information with minimum distortion and makes such labels unnecessary. The description provides the profile of a unique individual whose similarity with another individual is only to the extent of overlapping problems. This is quite different from the use of syndromic labels such as 'psychopathic' which suggest, at least superficially, that all who bear the label are alike, when this is at best dubious and a matter for empirical enquiry.

In this approach, the description of disorder does not assume common aetiological factors. This is one of the major limitations of diagnostic classifications, arising from the paucity of any established and accepted evidence regarding the roots of disorders. The present approach allows for wholly different aetiologies to be associated with the same pattern of disorder. This is in keeping with common clinical experience. For example, one girl's wrist-cutting may be a guilt reaction to incest with her father and her mother's suicide attempt, another's a learnt, manipulatory ploy.

Each of the 'causal' inferences here would themselves *constitute*, and be described separately, as problems, if they are ascertained as such.

An associated advantage is that the PPA is not bound to any particular theoretical orientation such as the psychoanalytic or the behaviourist. It leaves open the possible use of such orientations but only in so far as they enable the identification of particular problems which open them to detailed description and evaluation.

And, likewise, the approach makes diagnoses largely redundant. The function of diagnosis is to differentiate and facilitate relevant treatment. The configuration of one child's problems, particularly against the evaluative criteria of extent, intensity, duration and urgency, amply differentiates him from other children. Going beyond such a description is not necessary other than for purposes of developing an empirical typology. That activity can be carried out separately as research and should not, ethically, become mixed up with the alleviation of the child's problem. This is related to a more fundamental point. Bearing in mind the dynamic nature of most adolescents' problems and the multiplicity of changing circumstances associated with those problems, it may be argued that diagnosis of adolescent disorders, with its implications of permanence, is not only unnecessary but may be irrelevant and potentially against the best interests of children because it limits the possibilities of treatment.

Because diagnoses are not necessary, there will be no search for syndromes accompanied by the attempts to collect together as many syndromic signs and symptoms as possible. As few individuals present 'textbook' pictures of disorders and many fall uncomfortably between several syndromes, it may make more sense and be more true to human diversity if an attempt was not made to squeeze them into a few doubtful categories, but rather allowed each their unique configuration of attributes. In this sense, the PPA allows for a more complex and sophisticated view of human problems than a syndromic one. Because individuals are not diagnosed in terms of syndromes, this obviates the need to change diagnoses in the course of treatment. Treatment is instead geared to each element, as it emerges, of the configuration of problems.

This is not to say that certain collections of attributes are not regularly present and thereby lead to the identification of syndromes, such as 'simple schizophrenia'. Rather, the contention is that, in each human being, the diversity of problems is at least as great as the similarities and, unless empirically established broad spectrum treatments are available (as, for example, in schizophrenias), it may be more productive to concentrate on the differences in the problem profile than on the similarity of particular elements.

The acid test, ultimately, of any classification system, is the degree to which it guides action, in this case the treatment of problem children. Despite the formal connection between diagnosis and treatment, rarely, even in physical medicine, is total configuration of problems susceptible to only one form of treatment. Rather, in almost all cases, there is the need for a variety of approaches not only to deal with a particular problem but also to mobilise diverse resources to cope with side effects of treatment and related issues. Traditional approaches to children's problems are beset by doubts and ambiguities about how to bridge the gap between assessment and treatment.

By contrast, the PPA has direct pointers to treatment. Because the approach is elemental rather than holistic, it focuses attention on the use of methods of treatment suitable to each problem, though it does not rule out the use of one medium or method which may have a wider impact, such as the use of anti-anxiety medication which may alleviate several problems in one stroke. The treatment options are not foreclosed by diagnosis – they are left open in all their diversity – and, therefore, allow a multimodal approach to a disordered youngster. For example, family problems may indicate the use of intensive casework, while the youngster's aggressive behaviour may be modified by operant techniques and his anxiety reduced by appropriate psychotherapy or use of medication. If a specific technique does not work with its particular problem, then only that one technique needs to be changed rather than the whole treatment. While this approach demands greater sophistication in treatment, it is likely to be more efficient than any holistic approach and lead to more successful long-term alleviation of problems.

The PPA is particularly useful for purposes of training in the field of problematic children. The small number of problem areas and comprehensive nature of the classification makes it easy to remember and use even by the least experienced practitioners. At succeeding levels of sophistication, more complex description of children's problems can be provided without recourse to specialist barriers to acquisition of such knowledge.

Traditional classifications of children's disorders are partial and frequently holistic. They emphasise one aspect of the child's functioning and, by implication, underplay the importance of other functional areas in the genesis of the child's disorders. They are also difficult to record in adequate detail other than in research settings. For these reasons, it is currently difficult, with a few exceptions, to adduce rigorous and methodologically sound evidence regarding how children's problems change and respond to treatment in the inescapable context of their total functioning. The elemental and comprehensive nature of the PPA, on the other hand, is specially suited to recording and research. Through relatively straightforward research designs it is possible to determine changes in the extent and intensity of children's problems and the efficacy of particular treatment measures in relation to single (and clusters of) problems. Such an approach enhances the possibility of establishing an empirical discipline of treatment of problem children.

This approach has been put forward throughout as 'descriptive' rather than explanatory. This is because knowledge of the origins and circumstances associated with the development and continuation of problems is scant, patchy, inconsistent and inadequately established. There are, therefore, no generally acceptable explanations. Rather, there are many theories, typologies and sets of explanations each with their adherents. Because of the difficulties, both ethical and practical, of controlling human behaviour and the circumstances that impinge on it, certain critical forms of external validation remain logically and technically impossible.

In view of this it is more rational and ethical if all treatment were to be tied to a rigorous and detailed description of problems rather than to any inevitably hypothetical explanation that might be given for the problem. The choice of a treatment technique may presume an explanatory hypothesis on the part of the treatment agent, but in a multi-disciplinary team, it would remain limited to one functional area of one child, and could be tested as a short-range hypothesis.

In two important treatment applications, the potential of the PPA for complex, individual treatment of severely disordered children has been recognised and utilised (Hoghughi *et al*, 1977; 1978a; Nethercott, 1979). The early results confirm the conceptual soundness and operational utility of the system.

It is hoped that the PPA, with its potential for comprehensive, multi-disciplinary assessment and action-orientation, will form the basis of a new discipline of empirical assessment and treatment of disordered children and, when suitably developed, of other subject groups.

A Note on Positive Attributes

The definition of problem adopted in this book – an 'unacceptable condition presented or experienced by a child' – is deliberately negative. It may, therefore, suggest that the assessment of a child entails only the description and evaluation of his negative interactions with the environment. In an important sense this is true.

But, like all other human beings, problem children possess a mixture of positive and negative characteristics. In coping with them and enhancing their potential for self-help and improvement, it is crucial to know as much about their strengths as it is to know about their difficulties. Positive characteristics also fall under the same functional headings as do the problems. For example, a child can be described as a strong gymnast; particularly good at a school subject; having concerned and competent parents; capable of generating good feelings in others; socially adept or particularly resilient.

However, children warrant intervention in their lives because of the problems they present or experience rather than because of their strengths. Also, the evaluation of a child's strengths are of greater concern in planning how to ameliorate their problems. In any such treatment planning a wide range of resources should be evaluated of which the child's own competencies and strengths are a major element. But, since this book limits itself to assessment only, the evaluation of positive attributes will not be separately treated.

3 / Sources of Information

THE AMOUNT AND KIND OF INFORMATION and the way it is used is the major determinant of the quality of assessment carried out. 'Information' is a general term which covers everything that is or may become known about a person. Information is communicated and set out in the form of statements, whether 'opinions' or 'facts', which describe persons or events and have different probabilities of being false. The significance of this qualification is that no statement about a human being, however objective and rigorous, can be said to be 'certainly' true. Statements are made about one set of people by another who, given their different backgrounds, education, orientation and interests, are likely to be more or less off the mark. It is possible to evaluate information and determine its degree of error according to the same criteria as assessments in general, mainly reliability and validity.

In general terms, sources of assessment information fall into one of three areas: *referral*, *proximal* and *specialist*.

Referral sources include all those persons and agencies who have identified and defined a child as having problems which warrant intervention. The referral agency, whether a parent, the police, family doctor or anyone else, must have perceived an unacceptable condition (for example, temper tantrums, offending, unexplained injuries) to have referred the child. This 'unacceptable condition' can be further defined by the official agency which processes the child according to standard procedures and can often provide additional information about the history and development of the child from its own particular viewpoint. This information may relate not only to the child's contact with that particular agency, but also other aspects of background and current status. The amount and quality of information available from referral sources is dependent on the degree and quality of prior contact between them and the subject as well as their willingness to part with that information.

Proximal sources refer to all other agencies and persons who have had contact with the child and who may be able to provide information about specific areas and contexts of functioning. These persons and agencies are potentially numerous though the depth to which any one may be explored can vary from the simplest to the most complex. In assessing the child, his family, both nuclear and extended, neighbours, school, the police, clergy, voluntary and statutory agencies which have been involved, as well as friends of the family and any other concerned persons, may be asked to provide information regarding his development and express their views regarding the extent, depth, source and the course of the child's problems. Information from parents and schools is of particular significance in highlighting a child's problems. A search should also be made to find out whether there is a person or an agency which has had particularly close contact with the family and who may be able to provide a different perspective on the child's problems.

Specialist sources include all those persons who may be available for providing information regarding one particular area of functioning in which they have some form of expertise. Physicians and allied personnel would provide information about aspects of physical functioning; psychologists and specialist teachers would provide information about cognitive performance; social workers, experienced case workers, and those who work with families provide information about the family's structure and dynamics; psychologists and others, trained to observe and assess small group behaviour, can evaluate social competence; a wide range of people who work with problem children, but particularly psychiatrists and psychologists, can provide a measure of the child's potential for committing anti-social acts and present an appropriately complex picture of his personality structure, levels of emotionality and control, as well as aspects of his self-image.

It is important to remember that even the most expert specialists using the most rigorous techniques operate within a margin of error. The size of the error varies according to individual competence and the potential of the methods used to obtain the information. This should be borne in mind in making pronouncements about the child. However, despite any ambiguities that may surround information about a particular child, the risk presented by or to him may be so great that even dubious information has to be treated as if it were 'certain fact' but such a situation should only arise in exceptional and emergency conditions. As soon as the crisis has been dealt with it should be possible to try and establish the limits of the acceptability of information.

Children's Perceptions

People do not see the world and what happens in it in uniform ways but, rather, perceive events according to their own background and expectations. Although these may be similar, they may also be divergent from each other in important details. A person caught up in a stressful situation is likely to perceive the event differently from another who is watching the event from afar. Further, a particular person's reasons for committing an act may be different from the reasons perceived by someone else. It is not possible to establish the truth of one set of perceptions against the other in any very satisfactory way other than through the use of 'consensus'. But consensus reflects power and authority, whether individual or collective, rather than necessarily the validity of what has happened.

In the context of assessment, children's views of what has happened to them are rarely sought and are frequently discounted on the grounds that children have neither the maturity nor the intellectual competence to make valid judgments about their experiences. But aside from the relative validity of such observations, it is important to discover children's views of both their past and current state because these are additional and central sources of information regarding the child's reasons for behaving in particular ways. A variety of techniques can be used to help the child give an account of those aspects of reality that impinge on him and shape his life space.

Observation of Behaviour

All the information on a child can only be obtained through one or more of three activities (c.f. Cattell, 1965). The information is obtained through observing and noting events (life data); asking questions of the child and a whole variety of other persons (questionnaire data); and the use of specialised tests and measures (test data). These three types of activity – watching, talking and testing – provide all the information that may be used for constructing a comprehensive picture of the child and his problems.

Observation encompasses the full range of activities concerned with witnessing the behaviour of another person, directly or otherwise, and under a variety of circumstances with varying degrees of predetermined structure. Much observation takes place incidentally and without particular purpose. Deliberate observation, however, is undertaken in an attempt to identify, describe, explain and suggest possible solutions for problems presented or experienced by a youngster. Behaviour to be observed covers the full range of speech, mannerisms, moods, interactions and acts towards the self and others; in other words, everything that the individual does (Wright, 1960). In the end, even the most powerful questionnaires and tests have to be validated against what a child *does*. As such, observation is the cornerstone of all assessment.

In the present context, observation can be seen as ranging on a continuum from the external and the visible to the internal and the inferred (e.g. Cox and Rutter, 1976). All human behaviour is or can be watched and then described by an adverb, such as 'intelligently' or 'selfishly'. The adverb is then used as a basis for attributing a quality to the person ('intelligent', 'selfish'), which in turn becomes the basis for inferring a general characteristic of the person such as 'intelligence', 'selfishness' (Fiske, 1971).

Observation implies no theoretical bias in that it can be used as a basis for explanations and interventions which range from psychoanalysis to behaviour modification. However, it has received its major impetus from the development of behaviour therapy and other forms of behavioural intervention based on learning theory (Hersen and Bellack, 1974; Cone and Hawkins, 1977; Haynes, 1978).

Haynes *(op. cit)* has described the characteristics of behavioural observation as follows: a close association between assessment and intervention; emphasis upon specification of variables; emphasis upon quantification; emphasis upon current environmental causality; individual differences in behavioural characteristics and determinants; emphasis upon public events; emphasis upon observation of behaviour in the natural environment; evaluation of assessment procedures; behaviour therapy as a cybernetic system.

Though many of the elements above apply to all observations, Haynes' particular emphasis links behavioural observation to behaviour modification. This link is not necessary. It is, however, an important and necessary corrective to the tendency of dynamically orientated professionals who claim to 'notice', or in some other way infer unobservable characteristics of their patients or clients. Against Haynes' formulation, it should be stated that such detailed, highly specific observations require extensive skilled resources which are available only in either research projects or highly specialised settings where the treatment sophistication warrants the necessary effort.

The Behavioural Environment

The focus of all observation is behaviour, and all behaviour occurs in an environment. The reality of that environment includes all those elements which impinge on a child and to which, at any given time, he responds. This reality has a number of components each of which, depending on circumstances, may assume particular importance. The more important of these are:

The Self. This is the collection of experiences, expectations and attitudes of the child, his particular make-up, previous experiences of stress and coping, his perceptions of what is happening to him now and expectations of what is likely to happen if he behaves in particular ways (Bandura, 1969; Cottrell, 1969; Rotter, 1971).

The Peer Group. Much research evidence (e.g. Polsky, 1962; Buehler *et al*, 1966; Hargreaves, 1967) suggests that in group settings children are affected much more profoundly by their peers than they are by adults. The composition of the peer group, its dynamics and the way it impinges on a child at any given time, the norms for group behaviour and his perception of these norms and how they may be enforced, affect the way he is likely to behave in that particular environment (Sherif and Sherif, 1964). Problem behaviours are generated and maintained by peer group pressure, just as the reverse may become true depending on the prevailing circumstances. Children, because of their diverse 'selves' respond differently to prevailing group climates. In assessing the child it is, therefore, important to allow for the effect of the group in which he operates.

The Adults. Adults are in a position of authority and control much of the (more obvious) rewards and punishments that a child is likely to receive from his environment. They are, therefore, powerful determinants of a child's behaviour. Additionally, the child's past experiences of adults, and current perceptions and expectations of them, determine how he is likely to respond to them which, in turn will affect adult behaviour toward him. Frequently, adults in a position of observing children are unaware of the image they project to the child, the complexity of their interaction, and the degree to which this determines the child's behaviour towards them and the wider environment.

Another aspect of an adult's interaction with a child is his view of himself, his task in relation to the child and his personal values. An adult who is threatened by and intolerant of variations in a child's behaviour is more likely to behave in an oppressive and derogatory fashion towards him and provoke antagonistic behaviour which he will describe as the child's problem.

The Physical Environment. There is little systematic knowledge about the effect of physical environment on behaviour (c.f. Barker, 1968). Apart from certain features such as temperature, humidity, amount and quality of space and particular colours, the most that can be said is that the effect of the environment depends on the child's past associations with it and his current perceptions of its purpose and impact.

This aspect is usually given little prominence in evaluating children's (or for that matter, adults') behaviour. Increasing research, however, shows that certain factors, such as overcrowding and with it the invasion of the child's life space, are important determinants of behaviour, though to what extent and in what manner is not yet established. In the present state of knowledge, little can be done other than looking at the physical environment and noting any unusual environmental features which *may* be associated with problem behaviour.

Assessment in Structured Environments

Most children, even when they present problems, live in their natural home environment. Their problems can be investigated while they continue to live there. Most workers who visit the family or see the child on a day basis, are carrying out an assessment of this sort. However, specialised staff are in short supply and the economics of organisation frequently dictate that the child should be taken to them. Any environment in which specialists operate – school, clinic, or day centre – is of necessity a 'structured environment'.

The term 'structured' is ambiguous. It is not always clear whether those who use it intend to denote physical limits to and regulation of behaviour or the formality of relationship with the child and the process to which he is subjected. In this context a structured environment means one which is not open-ended or variable according to the wishes of the child and others who live with him, but one that is intended to fulfil a particular task and produce a specified end product. In this respect a child guidance clinic, a surgery, a day or residential assessment centre, are all instances of a structured environment.

The reasons for seeking a structured environment are often that the appropriate personnel are not available to carry out the assessment in an unstructured setting (such as the child's home); a child's behaviour cannot be systematically assessed in his natural environment; the target behaviour may not be manifested frequently enough in a natural environment to warrant the expenditure of resources and, therefore, the child is assessed in a structured setting in which the target behaviour, such as temper tantrums or aggressiveness can be precipitated; or the effects of the natural environment on the behaviour cannot be appropriately evaluated unless environmental characteristics and stimuli can be systematically varied and controlled.

In the social services area, however, the major reason for the removal of the child from his natural environment to a structured one is that the child presents or is subject to a risk which renders his continued stay in his normal setting inadvisable. Such 'risk' arises if the child is likely to be injured or suffer other physical or psychological harm if he stays where he is. Alternatively, the child may present the public, his family or other children with such risk that for others' protection he may warrant removal from his normal setting. In such cases, removal to a structured environment is not for the sake of better assessment but rather because of these other overriding reasons (Hoghughi, 1979a).

'Structure' is a matter of degree and as such it can be varied to resemble more or less the child's natural setting, depending on the requirements of the assessment. The important consideration is to ensure that the new environment is sufficiently sensitive and flexible to be able to discriminate between relatively stable behavioural characteristics of the child and those which are stimulated by the new environment.

Numerous studies of children and their parents in a variety of structured settings have shown that such settings do not hinder good assessment (*see* Haynes, 1978). In general terms, there is little research or other evidence to suggest that the requirements of assessment and structure are incompatible or that the results of such assessment are less reliable and valid than they would be elsewhere. Validity of assessment in structured settings is particularly difficult to determine as such settings must elicit the same range of behaviours as appears in the normal environment of the child. Because the range of behaviour in the latter is not known, it is not possible to see how such a requirement may be satisfied. If the child's behaviour is significantly different in the two settings, all that can be inferred is that the child's behaviour is more responsive to environmental stimuli than to stable personality characteristics. Such an inference would not mean that the assessment in one setting is more valid than the other. According to the purpose and desired rigour of assessment, it may be worthwhile to vary environmental features systematically to discover which features stimulate what behaviours.

The behavioural environment is a complex of elements which interact and which together control a child's behaviour. Each factor needs to be taken into account both separately and in interaction with others in order to allow an understanding of the child's behaviour. In theory, this would be so onerous both conceptually and practically that no useful observations would be made. In practice, however, this is not as difficult as it sounds because a competent practitioner or agency dealing with the assessment of children is likely to build up a store of knowledge, intuitive or empirical, of the baselines of behaviour of a variety of children which have emerged from the random interactions of all the above factors. It then becomes possible to make statements with varying degrees of probability, implicit or explicit, that for example 'this child is more aggressive than the normal run of children' or 'this child is more withdrawn than others in the same circumstances'.

Observer Variables

The meaning that an observer places on a child's behaviour enables him to make sense of that behaviour, and thus some interpretation is involved in all observation. The observer's own predispositions and expectations through training and role perception are the major determinants of what interpretation he will place on the observed behaviour. These expectations provide the structure and format of his observations. Who observes the behaviour is determined by considerations of economy, efficiency, involvement, reliability and validity of the outcome. A person who knows the child has obvious advantages in the ease with which he can observe familiar behaviour which might possibly change in reaction to an unfamiliar observer. But the closeness of an observer to a child does not necessarily increase the reliability or validity of his observations. Indeed, particularly in the case of problem children, those who are most familiar with them (such as parents) provoke and perceive behaviours which are part of a continuing interaction and do not make much sense other than in relation to them, even though the information they give is an essential part of the total assessment. It is useful to remain aware of the effects of interpersonal perception on behaviour and its observation and arrive at an acceptable balance of familiarity and distance.

The observer is like a measuring instrument, liable to make either constant or variable error. As such, the observer is likely to interpret a child's behaviour too leniently – where 'bullying and intimidation' are described as 'teasing' – or too strictly – where a mild scrap is described as an 'act of violence'. One way of overcoming this is through the use of non-interpretive, micro-descriptions of behaviours as well as a wide range of observers.

An extension of observer error is termed the 'halo effect'. The behaviour of a child who is *said* to be 'aggressive', 'depressed', or 'attention seeking' is more likely to be interpreted as falling into these categories than if he were not so labelled. The 'halo effect' cannot be eliminated, though it can be much reduced by having multiple observers, because most professionals take their interpretive cues from one another. The only satisfactory solution is to be aware of the force of such haloes and be ready to counteract them through seeking independent corroboration.

The point has already been made that every observation must be placed in a frame of reference of the assessor who is operating against a disciplined background. Physical signs such as seizures and dilation of pupils are unusual because they are often involuntary and unpurposive and, therefore, their interpretation is relatively straightforward. In social behaviour, on the other hand, there is little that is unpurposive and even less that is 'irrational'. What may be regarded as such by the observer may have a perfectly sound explanation, if the subject could or would give it. Furthermore, perceptions of intention, purpose and outcome of the same behaviour can be dramatically different according to who is the observer and who the observed.

All these factors are part of the complexity of human behaviour, which, though inconvenient from the viewpoint of scientific rigour, give it its unique fascination and flavour. The difficulties in categorising behaviour cannot be logically overcome. However, the use of uniform frames of reference by groups of observers with uniform training, frequent cross-checking of the frames of reference, and shared cultural values by the observer and the observed can reduce the divergence to acceptable levels.

Sampling

Although attempts have been made to observe the totality of a child's behaviour, these have had to be restricted to short periods because of the tremendous demands made on the observer. In any case, no such observation, however comprehensive, can be said to be exhaustive, because it is always possible to give examples of behaviours which had not been observed. All observations, therefore, relate to samples of behaviour. Such samples or portions of behaviour should be as representative as possible to enable appropriate inferences to be made about the child's behavioural characteristics. Representativeness is a matter of degree, and can only be evaluated in relation to the time, duration, place and circumstances of the observation.

Sampling can be done according to either time periods during which the number of occurrences of a particular behaviour is noted or the specific behaviour which can be observed as it occurs in due course. Each form of sampling has its own advantages and disadvantages (Kerlinger, 1964; Haynes, 1978). In general, time sampling is more useful where the target behaviours are relatively frequent and resources of a trained observer are available to record the occurrences of the behaviour.

Event sampling is more appropriate when the target behaviours are relatively infrequent and are not likely to occur at predetermined intervals. Most of the more serious problem behaviours of children, such as self-destructiveness, aggression, depression and anti-social behaviour, are of the latter variety. Event sampling demands that a child's behaviour should be watched sufficiently closely so that such occurrences can be noted. In this respect, residential facilities where children can be closely observed for longer periods and under a wider set of conditions obviously have a more useful role to play than non-residential ones.

The frequently noted 'behavioural slopes', or systematic changes over time of a particular behaviour, can be regarded as resulting from the habituation or adjustment of the subject to the observer and his methods. In order to ensure that behaviour is adequately sampled the child must be observed in a variety of situations and in comparison with other children so that the relative frequencies of behaviour can be established.

Observation Frames

Observations can be carried out either in general terms and subsequently divided into specific areas, or *vice versa*. As observation of behaviour can potentially cover the totality of human acts, it is not possible to provide an exhaustive list of categories of behaviour. Depending on the observer's frame of reference, particular behaviours will be observed. Specific observations related to the assessment of individual attributes will be presented in Part Two of this book. At this stage it may be worthwhile to set out two different general formats of observation which encompass the larger part of a child's behaviour and which may be found to be of particular value in observation of a child's behaviour in groups (Frame I: Hoghughi 1976; Frame II: Porteous 1976).

Frame I

GENERAL BEHAVIOUR:

Facial expressions, mannerisms, gait, manner of speech; Reaction to frustration, ability to tolerate frustration, reaction to levels off rustration; Expressed fantasy, day dreams, expressions of goals and ambitions, any role play; Particular fears, unusually strong interest or avoidance in some particular activity, striking habits which appear peculiar or out of the ordinary; How much control over behaviour? Does control break down under certain conditions? What are the conditions? What is his self-image? What does he think are his assets and liabilities? What does he see as his biggest problem? What do you think of these? How often does he express and cope with hurt, anger, sadness, joy? Is he on the whole a happy or sad child? Is his anger shown by irritability, blow up, or is it kept in check?

RESPONSE TO PEERS:

What sort of response does he seek from peers? What does he do to get it? How successfully? How does he react when he gets the response he has sought? What does he do when response is denied? Does he seek dominance or popularity or is he unconcerned about/untouched by the group? To what types of peers does he seem closest? Which does he avoid? How friendly is he with the others? How does he express friendliness? Whom does he come into conflict with? How does he express it? Is he good at judging the other children and regulating his own behaviour towards them? Does he seem to need the other children? Is he content to be alone? How often and under what conditions? How do the other children react to him? Is he popular, respected, disliked, feared, ignored? Is there a consensus of opinion about him? Is there any sexual interest in peers? How is it expressed? Attracted to any particular sub groups? What are they like? How good is he at getting on with the other children? Does he get on better in large or small groups?

RESPONSE TO ADULTS:

Which of above observations with peers also apply here? How often does he seek help, encouragement, affection? What form does it take? Does he get on with particular kinds of adults better or worse – male, female, older, younger, tougher, softer? Generally obedient or defiant? How does he show it? How often does he show aggression and in what form? How often sulky, worried, hostile, friendly, etc.? How do adults here feel about him? Can he manipulate adult reactions? How accurately does he understand adult intentions and instructions?

RESPONSE TO MANAGEMENT:

What management techniques seem to work best to get him to comply? Which seem to reduce defiance? How does he respond to insight-giving discussions? Is he interested in discussions? What is his reaction to threat or implementation of sanctions? Does discussion or peer group pressure help regulate his behaviour? How does he respond to limits set? Does it make a difference whether limits are obeyed by the rest of the group? In general, how does he respond to the structure of the day: rules, routines and activities? Do any particular rules, routines or activities give trouble?

Frame II

PHYSICAL:

Brief physical description: noise level, shouts a lot? Quiet?
Activity level: never sits still; Very lethargic?

HYGIENE AND DRESS:

Observation of what he does in this area, how much prompting needed to wash, how fussy about clothes; does he complain about clothes? does he mind what clothes he wears? Does he seem able to make his bed and keep his space tidy? Sleeping and eating – anything unusual?

INTELLECTUAL:

Thoughtful or not? Does he read much, and what does he choose to read? Does he produce ideas and suggestions which seem independent from the crowd or does he simply echo what has been said? Does he give constructive solutions to problems which arise or does he withdraw and look to others for the answer? What comments does he make about school work and classroom sessions? How does he react with games which require longer periods of concentration?

LANGUAGE:

Is speech clear and distinct? Does he appear to have a reasonable vocabulary for his age? Can he describe his ideas adequately? Does he resort to cliches and meaningless verbal substitutes? Can he converse? What about? Is there much repetitive content in his conversation?

GROUP BEHAVIOUR:

Has he proved constantly appealing to others? What does he do to gain popularity? Is it important to him to get group acceptance? What does he do when he feels left out of things? Does he make friends quickly? What kind of children does he associate with? Does he restrict or ration his friendship? Does he help to introduce people to each other, or help with other children? Does he appear strongly attached to a peer group culture and, as such, opposed to staff or adult ideas? If he falls out with a friend what follows on? Does he prefer to remain on his own? If influenced by peers will his behaviour change from previous characteristic levels of self-control, obedience, maturity, etc.? Can he be seen imitating other children?

AGGRESSION–SUBVERSION:

Does he fight much? What prompts him to hit others? Does he seek to establish a position of dominance? Does he swear at others or call them names? Does he plant stories, etc. and stir up conflict between others? Does he refuse to back down voluntarily from conflict situations? Are other children frightened or wary of him? Is he deliberately slow to carry out or understand staff instructions? Does he set up other children to annoy staff? Does he answer back a lot? Does he play up in front of others? Does he refuse to do as asked? Does he show overt aggression to adults and under what circumstances?

SEXUAL:

Does he show special interest or embarrassment when sexual topics are discussed? Has he engaged in any mutual sex play? Does he discuss girl/boy friends or sex? Is he shy when undressing?

SOCIAL CONFORMITY:
Does there appear to be deliberate over-conformity to staff wishes? Does he volunteer too much? Is he always too prompt in doing as told? Does he frequently mention reports and adults' views of him? Does he seek confirmation about how well he is doing?

HANDLING AND AUTHORITY:
What is his reaction to various kinds of handling? Does he take advantage of slackness? Does he respond aggressively to authoritarian treatment? Does he succumb to threat of sanctions? Can he function acceptably if treated as an 'adult'? Do environmental factors enter into his response to handling in a noticeable way? When surrounded by peers, or in an outside environment, does his response differ? Does he seem to respond well to a sympathetic approach? Is he easily reduced to tears, and if so, how? Does he appear to play adults off against each other? Does he actively try to get adult decisions changed by persuasion or non-cooperation? How far does he push his resistance, and how does this vary from person to person?

EMOTIONAL:
Tearful? Easily upset? Initial mood on first contact or arrival? How about mood changes? Does he get angry quickly? Does he calm down quickly? Does he laugh much? Is his mood infectious to other people? Is his face expressive of his feelings or is everything hidden behind a mask? How does he react when he is clearly upset? Does he become hostile? Does he seek support and if so from whom? Does he appear to forget about the problem and divert his attention elsewhere? Does he have temper tantrums?

GENERAL SELF-PRESENTATION:
Does he avoid being looked at? Does he look at people when he is talking? Is he secretive? Does he seem concerned about what people think of him? Is he unusually careful about his possessions? What are his reactions to self-criticism?

In evaluating the information in the above areas, it is necessary to recognise that individual behaviours form an integrated complex and are triggered off by simple or complex stimuli. The stimuli may be observable or not. The behaviour may be recurrent or episodic, intense or low level with varying degrees of self-control exercised by the child. It is as important to note what terminates a particular behaviour as it is to note what triggers it off. In general terms, it should be noted that all behaviours have an antecedent and a consequence which determine the duration of the particular behaviour.

The behavioural environment in which a child is observed is capable of manipulation in order to determine the constancy or variability of the child's response to particular circumstances. Frame I's section on management is one illustration of this. The child is deliberately subjected to various forms of management from soft to hard, fair to unfair, firm to indecisive, in order to note particular reactions. Such systematic variation of the behavioural environment is often not practicable in natural situations unless the adults are able and willing to adopt such roles.

Observational information is only as good as the accuracy with which it is communicated, placed in context, and used for formulating problems and modes of alleviating them. It may, therefore, be necessary to develop and use specific observation sheets coded for particular children and/or specific behaviours as a way of providing reliable information. A number of general observation schedules are available in print or may be available from publishers (e.g. Jones, Reid and Patterson, 1975).

Questionnaires and Interviews

Talking is the most distinctive human activity. Questions can be the most efficient way of eliciting information from a person about those aspects of his life of which he can be expected to be aware. Talking can be structured in a form which ranges from paper and pencil questionnaires (a substitute for asking questions out loud) through formal interviews to free floating conversation in a natural setting. The criteria applied to all forms of assessment such as reliability, validity, usefulness and rigour, are relevant to the form that such questioning may take and the degree of structure that may be imposed on it.

In order to elicit the most factual information, questionnaires may be developed which are applied under standard conditions so that comparable data may be obtained. The design of questionnaires and responses to them is a complex subject (e.g. Oppenheim, 1966) which will not be pursued here. It is, however, important to point out that the greater the structure in the form of questioning, the more easily it can be validated. There are numerous questionnaires available which cover various fields. In the subsequent chapters we have mentioned these where widely available and appropriate.

Interviews. Interviewing has been described as 'conversation with a purpose'. The purpose of the conversation is normally to obtain information which relates either to facts about the child such as his age and school history, to highly interpretative accounts and evaluations such as attitudes to the police and the importance of peers in his life. The degree of interpretation involved applies both to the subject and to the interviewer and accounts for the large margin of error in both the reliability and validity of interviewing as a technique (Yarrow, 1960; Cannell and Kahn, 1968; Shouksmith, 1968; Morganstern, 1976).

Interviews can be conducted either on the basis of an 'interview schedule' – a predetermined format and wording of questions – or in an unstructured manner. On the whole, interview schedules are more satisfactory because they ensure that an area is totally covered and the questions are asked in a standard fashion which enables the comparison of one child to others and the refinement of the whole interviewing situation by the interviewer. Interview schedules can be geared to factual information ('How many children were there in your last family group home?'), fixed alternative questions ('Do you like your father?'), or open-ended questions ('What do you feel about your chances of keeping out of trouble?').

As with all other forms of assessment, the questions asked in an interview are shaped by their setting and purpose. These aspects also determine the level and complexity of the interview situation and the degree of rigour brought to bear on it. Thus, the interviewing of a young person for purposes of certification under the Mental Health Act would be more exhaustive and rigorous (one hopes) than one which seeks to establish whether a child wishes to return home from a residential facility.

The advantages of interviewing lie in the fact that it is the easiest and most natural form of obtaining information from and about children. It is flexible, capable of being adapted to individual circumstances of particular children, and can produce information about areas of a child's functioning, such as his hopes and anxieties, which may not be open to scrutiny by other methods. As such it is a particularly useful tool for the assessment of children, especially those who are put off by formal situations. It also has the advantage of allowing direct comparison of the statements about a child among the various assessors, and enables probing into reasons and contexts of a child's behaviour without which both observations and test results are deficient and arid.

The difficulties of interviewing lie in achieving adequate levels of reliability and validity, reducing the ambiguity in the perception of both questions and answers, and the inherent variability of these answers according to a child's mood, circumstances and expectations of the outcome of the interview. Interviewing requires high levels of training, skill and other personal characteristics such as sensitivity, warmth and empathy (Truax and Mitchell, 1971). It is costly in terms of both time and specialised personnel. As such there are also restrictions on who can use it to advantage.

With the importance attached to verbal communication, its currency among all groups of people concerned with problem children, interviewing is the most immediately appealing and culturally acceptable method of obtaining information and one that can be placed on a rigorous footing (Shapiro, 1979). Its advantages can be maximised through the use of interview schedules which, at the same time, take account of the unspoken words such as silences, facial expressions and emphases with which speech is interspersed.

Tests

Tests are collections of standardised items or measures intended to yield quantitative data. Their purpose is to differentiate between human beings in a structured repeatable manner which reduces observer variability and subjective judgments.

There is a wide array of tests covering many aspects of human behaviour (e.g. Buros, 1972). There are numerous tests covering most aspects of physical functioning, intelligence, attainment, vocational aptitudes, social relationships, personality, attitudes and values.

The merits of tests lie in their relative objectivity: different users are able to get roughly the same response from the same subject. They can be specific to particular aspects of functioning such as creativity or anxiety reaction; they are easy to validate against not only other tests but observable events; and they yield numerical results which can be easily computed and communicated. The disadvantages lie in their tendency to glorify and lend weight to some highly dubious conclusions, their susceptibility to distortion by the subjects can be high, their tendency to reify the characteristic they measure, their openness to vagaries of both tester and subject, their assumption that significant words in a test mean the same to all children, and frequently poor validity against external criteria.

From a practical point of view, they have the advantage of structuring observations and yielding a great deal of information about a child. Their major limitation lies in the amount of training and skill needed in the administration of tests and interpretation of results and the consequent restrictions on their use. Frequently, the more valid and potentially significant a test, the greater are the restrictions on its use by unqualified personnel. Both the British Psychological Society and the American Psychological Association classify availability of tests according to the kind of persons who can use them. Most of the better tests fall into the most restricted category which can be used only by specially trained and accredited psychologists.

These limitations severely restrict the use of tests in the majority of assessment situations where the appropriately qualified persons are not available. For this reason, we have not given particular prominence to tests for the assessment of problem areas. We have, however, indicated, where appropriate, those tests which are relatively widely available and may be used by persons who are not specifically trained in their administration. An exhaustive list of tests available may be obtained from test publishers such as National Foundation for Educational Research and from other sources (Mittler, 1970; Johnson and Bommarito, 1971; and Buros 1972).

Personal History

The information from the above sources contributes to a full description of the major influences and events in the development of the child from his infancy, and describes comprehensively his present circumstances and condition in order to arrive at decisions regarding what should be done about him.

Because of the continuity of the circumstances impinging on the child from his birth up to time of assessment, it may not be possible or particularly useful to separate out the background from the present state of the child in his environment. This can be set out in the form of a personal history with appropriate dates of significant events in the life of the child. 'Significant' in this context is defined as any event which is felt to have had an important bearing on the child's life or those of other members of his family who will have indirectly affected his behaviour. What is important depends on cultural, professional and personal biases and orientation of the assessor. On the whole, dynamically orientated practitioners place greater emphasis on early life and patterns of affective bonding than those who are behaviourally inclined. A personal history would include details of birth, all major events such as changes of address and factors of the home situation, changes in school, accidents, offences, contact with specialised agencies, placements, other forms of intervention and anything else which appears important.

History taking can be carried out either through a questionnaire to referral and proximal sources or through conducting structured interviews which are intended to reveal the full picture of the child's development and the events that have impinged on him. History taking techniques are highly developed in medicine and psychiatry and provide an important source of information for clinical judgment. One important aspect both of personal history taking and of the provision of background information is to ensure reasonably accurate pinpointing of the time, circumstances and course of development of particular problems and attempts made to alleviate them. This is crucial in evaluating what has been done and with what effect, so as to choose the most appropriate new mode of intervention.

Background information on the child could be usefully set out in the following form:

FAMILY LIST

Members of the immediate family as well as other persons in the home.

FAMILY SETTING

Geographical setting, physical state of home and neighbourhood; economic status, standing in the community.

FATHER

Background: Origin, family life, education, job, employment stability.

Personal characteristics and behaviour: Intelligence, personality features, attitudes to authority and society; personal problems.

Father's attitude and behaviour towards child: Involvement with child; attitude to problem behaviour: methods of coping with the problem behaviour; quality and degree of support, guidance and affection.

MOTHER
As for Father.

PARENTAL RELATIONSHIPS
Stability of family life, strength of emotional bond, harmony, dominance and decision making patterns; modes of coping with each other's problems; separations.

SIBLINGS
Incidence and patterns of problems including offences; significant features; influence on child; rivalry and scapegoating; quality of emotional bond.

CHILD'S DEVELOPMENT AND BEHAVIOUR
Though main focus is on the onset, source and development of problem behaviour, it is also important to describe any notable positive events and characteristics.

Each section should bring out the response by the relevant people to child's problem behaviour and his reaction to intervention. Each section, therefore, comprises two parts, the second one of which will be devoted to the child's account and interpretation of *what happened and why*. This will emerge from comprehensive interviews with the child. Such interviews can be usefully structured in the following manner:

AT HOME
Child's view.

AT SCHOOL
Child's view.

IN THE COMMUNITY
Child's view.

OFFENDING (with dates and some indication of seriousness)
Child's view.

SPECIALISED INTERVENTION AND ITS EFFECTS
This deals with the child's view of referrals to and action by specialised agencies, such as a Child Guidance Clinic, School Psychological Service, medical and psychiatric services, court, probation, social services, and others.

These sections provide comprehensive information from referral and proximal sources to which specialist comments can be added as a result of the use of interviews, observations and questions.

4/Organisation of Assessment

Assessment is a coordinated, purposive activity which involves different people and requires diverse resources. In order to meet its objective of providing assessments efficiently, it requires an organisation of its tasks and resources.

Material Resources

These comprise, broadly speaking, buildings and equipment. Little is known about the specific building requirements for residential or centre-based day assessment by practitioners or planners and architects. It is, therefore, unlikely that buildings for this purpose would be very different from many others designed to house children and their caretakers. In the face of this, the major consideration should be to provide an environment for the adequate management and care of children. These include facilities for living (and sleeping), working and recreation. Adequate provision is now usually made for meeting these needs in warm, comfortable and attractive surroundings. Additionally, care considerations demand that while the child should be at all times observable, he should also be able to withdraw from group pressure in order to replenish personal reserves. A range of environments from open to closed areas, multi-purpose spaces such as common rooms, and factors such as diversity of colours, textures and spatial complexities are required to stimulate a range of behaviours which considerably aid the final assessment.

The relationship of specific types of environment to behaviour patterns is unknown (c.f. Barker, 1968). Experience suggests that children, even those from very poor homes, respond favourably to civilised surroundings which are comfortable and aesthetically pleasing though not so 'posh' as to frighten and alienate those who come from predominantly working-class homes. The need for durability of fabric and finish is a crucial aspect in the design of the environment to prevent rapid and accelerating deterioration of otherwise acceptable surroundings (Advisory Council on Child Care, 1970; DHSS, 1971).

The extent and diversity of material resources provided depends on the level at which the assessment is to be carried out. The creation of a 'normal' caring environment demands that children should have access to appropriate playthings and recreational equipment.

Materials for assessment depend on the particular source of information being tapped. Tests, questionnaires, simulators and measuring instruments may be provided to make particular forms of assessment possible. Depending on the complexity of the organisation, facilities may also be required for storage and retrieval of information.

Aspects of Security

Secure accommodation is required for curbing the movement of those children who either present unacceptable risk to the public or who, by persistent absconding, make assessment difficult. Such provision raises complex issues which are discussed at length elsewhere (Howard League, 1977; Hoghughi, 1978c; Millham *et al,* 1978).

Strictly in terms of assessment, however, security raises particular problems. It may either arouse or dampen anxieties in the child which would affect his behaviour in unpredictable ways. He may, for example, bend all his efforts on escaping from the facility. In the course of this he may engage in generalised or specific aggressive and destructive behaviour which may lead the staff to believe he is always like this and describe him in these terms, without realising the situational specificity of the behaviour.

Staff also have particular and shifting priorities in relation to the assessment and management of children in security. These affect their views of children as sources of risk which may create and spread a halo effect on their interpretation of the child's attributes. A child who presents risks of persistent absconding or other disruptive acts is likely to be described in generally more adverse terms.

More specifically, the inevitably structured environment of a secure setting restricts the range of stimuli to which a child can respond. Most children behave in a less disordered fashion (that is, relative to the 'outside world') under secure conditions. This makes it difficult for the staff to evaluate the full range and depth of their problems. It, therefore, becomes necessary to take special care to ensure that the child has the opportunity to respond to a wide array of stimuli, stressful or otherwise. The greater the similarity of the behaviours, the more valid the conclusions are likely to be about the stability of the child's attributes.

Human Resources

These encompass not only the specific assessment staff but also all other persons who are required to care for and help provide information on the child and his problems. As has already been indicated, adults are a critical component of the behavioural environment of the child, and the assessment staff members are crucial in determining his behaviour in the assessment agency and making decisions about him. Their diversity and ability to take on different roles in relation to the child will be an important source of information about the child's response to different behavioural environments.

Qualities of Staff

This ability in turn depends on the staff's basic human characteristics. The demands made on these are probably no greater in an assessment setting than they are in any other agency that deals with problem children. The necessary attributes include intelligence, sensitivity, personal warmth, maturity, stability, tolerance and a thick skin. They are discussed at length elsewhere (Hoghughi, 1978c). The technical demands of assessment specially emphasise the need for intelligence and sensitivity. The requirement to communicate the results of assessment calls, additionally, for articulateness and literacy.

One thing that an assessment setting does not need is 'relationships' in the emotional sense used in dynamic psychology and social work (e.g. BASW, 1977). The necessary components of trust, affection, dependence and predictable reciprocity do not have the chance to become established in the short period of acquaintance of the subject and the assessor. Nor is there any reason to suppose that if the assessment period were lengthened it would enable the development of a relationship which may make assessment 'better'. The give and take of any relationship brings a new dimension to the interactive behaviours involved which further complicates an already complex situation. This is one reason why special caution should be exercised in interpreting the evidence of those who do have a relationship with the child, such as parents, neighbours and others. Additionally, in an assessment facility which is intended to have only temporary contact with the child, the necessary severance of ties due to the child's discharge may create additional difficulties for an already problematic child.

It is also morally questionable to establish a relationship *in order* to get information out of the child. In practice, children react positively to the open and honest statement that they are being assessed as an aid to resolving their problems. Such openness seems better than leaving the purpose of assessment either hidden or to the child's imagination. Given a caring attitude to the children, it is surprising how much open frankness they can tolerate.

None of this is intended to imply that it is not crucially important to establish a caring and settled environment for the children in which the difficulties of interaction with a new group of adults do not exacerbate their anxieties and other problems. The development of some sort of relationship with the child is in any case inevitable. The difficulties arise mainly when the assessment agency sees it as an essential part of its task to establish relationships with the children and seeks to arrive at its assessment *through* such relationships.

Specialist Staff

Specialists are the most scarce resource in the total process of assessment. It is important to know how best to make use of them, and depends to a large extent on the particular agency and even more centrally on the competence and personal characteristics of the specialists. Particular individuals may have skills which considerably transcend their specialism. In view of this, it is not particularly helpful to define the contribution that each speciality can make; additionally, the geographical distribution and availability of specialists to individual assessment agencies renders this into a somewhat academic exercise. Nevertheless, to provide some guide as to which specialists can be of help in the determination of particular attributes, we have given in Part 2 broad indications for their deployment in each problem area.

Considerations of Care

Useful assessment information cannot be provided adequately or in an ethically acceptable manner if the child's primary care requirements are not met. These care requirements encompass *physical care*: adequate feeding, clothing, sleeping and shelter; *emotional care*: support to achieve a reasonably stable frame of mind and some degree of happiness; and *social care*: protection and encouragement as an aid to acceptability and satisfaction in interaction with peers. Standards of care vary from agency to agency but there is some consensus about acceptable minima which should guarantee an adequate level of care.

An additional aim of providing care is to bring about a level of behavioural and psychological stability against which the child's behavioural baseline may be established. A child who is abnormally upset is likely to behave in an abnormal fashion. Any information gained about his behaviour in such circumstances is likely to be only of benefit in indicating how he behaves when he is upset and would be of little value in predicting his behaviour under other conditions. Also, a child whose behaviour is unstable due to environmental conditions is likely to create major problems for the organisation and create difficulties for the assessment of other children.

This is particularly true of those children whose problems are so great that they have to be removed from home and placed in some form of residential provision, be it a hospital, a remand centre, or an assessment facility. The removal from home and the anxiety of separation from a familiar environment as well as the need to adjust to the new and potentially threatening setting are likely to induce panicky responses and other forms of transient disorder.

Although these may be of value in providing unusual information about a child, they are also likely to increase the error in evaluating the child's predominant response pattern and his behaviour other than under those specific circumstances. In view of this, the priority task of any assessment facility should be to stabilise the child and familiarise him with the new environment until he has acquired what appears to be a basic stability and confidence to cope before the proper programme of assessment gets underway. With some children this task may be so difficult and protracted as to take several months. With the majority, however, this is achieved in a matter of hours or days if the environment is caring and competent enough to ensure that the child is welcomed and minimally stressed in his new setting. The length of time each child takes to settle down is a valuable guide to his adaptive ability, given that staff efforts to this end are relatively constant.

Who Does the Assessment?

As has already been indicated there are several sources of assessment information. Under normal circumstances this information is provided by individuals who follow particular objectives and adopt different viewpoints. There is, therefore, no good reason to believe that the focus of these differently orientated persons on the same child will produce an integrated view of his problems. The use of the same language, and identical words such as 'aggressive' or 'withdrawn', does not necessarily imply that connotations of those words are understood uniformly and hence likely to lead to similar actions. In any case, because such assessment by individuals is frequently done in isolation and in the absence of comprehensive briefing by and consultation among those individuals, there is much duplication and wasted effort in the assessment of children.

In the case of children with a wide range of problems, this approach is likely to be of little use as it fragments the child and does not provide a coherent focus for action. The person to bring the various strands of assessment together and draw out their treatment implications requires such high levels of understanding, knowledge and integrative skills that he is not likely to be in overabundant supply.

Because of this, it is preferable to refer the more problematic children for assessment to integrated teams who are capable of providing coherent information at different levels of expertise. These teams, by virtue of learning through working together, are likely to have acquired a basic understanding of each other's language and areas of concern. By concentrating together on a child they are more likely to provide a more integrated view of his problems than isolated individuals. They are also normally organised in a manner that specifies how the information provided by each of them is to be integrated into the whole and who is to draw together into a coherent pattern of problems the different strands of assessment.

Such a pattern is likely to be of considerably more use than discrete bits of information. Teams, by virtue of belonging to the same organisation, can potentially provide a more rapid and efficient service because they can short-cut the necessity of transmitting the information from one place to another and bringing together, if necessary, the various persons to share in the discussion and the decision making. The organisation of an assessment team is subject to the same constraints and possibilities as any other organisation and does not necessarily imply that the team is residentially based.

Where to Assess?

The initial reason for assessment is that the child is presenting a problem which is deemed to be sufficiently serious to warrant intervention. Depending on the risk factors involved, consideration is given to whether the child's environment should be changed for purposes of assessment. The vast majority of children who present problems are assessed by specialists of various sorts while they continue to live at home. Visits to the child guidance clinic or the psychiatrist or visits by a health visitor or a school psychologist take place while the child's normal routine is continued. This happens usually when the problem presented by the child, such as difficulties in reading or sleeping or onset of offending, are so mild as not to present 'major' risk either to the child or to his surroundings. Any such risk is weighed against the disadvantages of removing the child from home, such as intolerable stress to the parents or the child, or subsequent difficulties of re-integration into his normal setting.

Costs and Benefits

In any intervention in a child's life, a price has to be paid which includes not only the expenditure of scarce human and material resources but also potential damage to the child and/or his environment and the risks involved in either taking or failing to take a particular course of action. Taking an action presumes that the beneficial outcome makes the price worthwhile. All practitioners have some intuitive grasp of contending pressures in their work with children and their actions follow, even if confusedly, from their evaluations of the reasons for and against alternatives. In practice, referral for assessment is determined by a worker's access to facilities and by the severity of the risk presented to or by the child.

Access to a facility depends on the worker's knowledge of that facility, what it can and cannot do, and how far it is likely to help the particular child. It is also related to the facility's geographical distance and its acceptability to the agency in terms of cost, orientation, past performance and other aspects. Other considerations relative are waiting lists, attitude to the referral agent and *his* needs and any other matters which affect the approach to or avoidance of that facility.

Official agencies, such as Social Services Departments and workers within them have, if they are knowledgeable, a notion of a hierarchy of assessment facilities which are relevant to the seriousness of the problems of a particular case. These notions are often inexplicit and vague, more so in the case of those social workers who have a minority of children on their caseloads and who need to use assessment facilities only on rare occasions. The knowledge of facilities is more often passed by word of mouth and agency attitudes than by hard and valid information (Hoghughi, 1979a).

Evaluation of *risk* arises from the worker's perception of the condition of the child. In this sense, some form of 'pre-assessment', however vague and intuitive, is an inevitable and logically necessary aspect of any form of social intervention of which referral for assessment is one example.

The risks presented to or by the children arise from the six grounds laid down in the 1969 Children and Young Persons Act and related circumstances which warrant the issue of a Care Order. Each of these six grounds – hindrance of physical and psychological development; ill treatment; truancy; exposure to moral danger; being beyond control; and offending – judged against their extent, intensity, urgency and duration, enable the social worker to come to a decision as to 'how bad' the problem is. This then leads to a judgment of how the problem is likely to develop and with what consequences to the child, the community, the official agency and the worker.

These elements interact in every form of deliberate intervention in the lives of children. The perception of a child as a 'problem child' or 'child with problems' implies that some action should be taken. This judgment, based on some form of 'pre-assessment' by the referral agent, begins to foreclose the alternatives.

The above elements interact to produce a balance of reasons for and against a course of action. Such actions are of an ascending order of 'seriousness' in response to what the referral agent sees as the problem. The more serious the condition, the more serious the action taken. A child who is periodically absent from school may provoke the Head Teacher to contact the parents, one who is more persistently absent may warrant the intervention of an Education Welfare Officer or a Child Guidance Clinic and the most persistent truant is likely to be taken to court and removed from home.

But such decision making is rarely carried out in an explicit, logical manner. Because of its ambiguities and frequent miscalculations, it results in much avoidable damage to and deterioration of children's condition. This is partly determined by a current 'minimalist' ethos of social agencies. This ethos revolves around a set of beliefs and feelings that any person presenting problems should be subjected to minimal intervention, on grounds of both ethics and cost. This applies as much to assessment as to other forms of intervention. This is understandable and socially approved. However, the fact that so many children's problems go from bad to worse suggests that the 'minimal intervention' in the form of both assessment and treatment has been inadequate (Hoghughi 1978b).

Generally the decision to seek assessment (as opposed to the many other things assessment facilities do) will be based on the referral agent's realisation that he does not know enough about the child, systematically or in sufficient depth, to be able to decide on and take the appropriate action. At this stage, the referral agent must decide what is the most important manifest problem of the child. Is it a physical, family or behavioural problem that needs attention?

On this basis, he can then make a primary reference to an appropriate agency, such as the family doctor for physical; Child Guidance Clinic for a cognitive problem; the social services department for family and social problems. Each agency can be asked to assess its own speciality problem and thereby contribute to a collective picture that may also reveal difficulties in the other areas.

However, in practice, organising such a sequence of reports is very time consuming, inefficient, cumbersome and devoid of much utility. The reports present discrete and even incompatible pictures of the child – like the elephant described by six blind men – which do not help the referral agent to formulate what he should do to alleviate the problems.

For these reasons, specialists and others are increasingly organised in teams which provide central, reasonably efficient and coherent facilities for the assessment of children. Usually all the referral agent has to do is to refer the child and help provide background information. The assessment facility then undertakes the other tasks, including the calling of the assessment meeting or case conference at which the child is discussed and appropriate courses of action determined.

Such organisations range from child and adolescent units, both general medical and psychiatric, Child Guidance Clinics, day centres in social services departments, through the full range of residential provision from the local 'O & A' Centres to specialised regional facilities. A recent report on children with special educational needs (The Warnock Report, 1978) takes cognisance of the need to relate the complexity of children's problems to ever higher levels of team-based, assessment expertise.

Day or Residential?

When the risks are judged to be high, workers almost invariably opt for residential rather than day assessment. The crisis orientation of social workers, their heavy caseloads, the unremitting pressure on them to act and the probable social and professional consequences of not having acted well and in advance, impels them to try to remove the child from home not only as a way of reducing risk to the child but also as one of ensuring that the particular worker can share that risk with others and seek expert information of a kind that he may not himself possess. This need to take out 'insurance policies' is heightened and becoming more explicit as a result of a number of notorious recent cases (e.g. Shearer, 1979).

The social worker's task is, therefore, one of achieving the 'best fit' between the child and the appropriate level and venue of assessment in terms of a particularly desired outcome. Against this background and with a clear appreciation of its shortcomings, a tentative list of classes of reasons for and against referral for residential assessment is presented below.

FOR RESIDENTIAL

The Child

1. Are his problems not likely to improve if he stays at home (or normal setting)?
2. Are his problems likely to get worse?
3. Is he likely to be at risk from his family and/or others?
4. Are his problems such that an available day agency such as outpatient hospital service, child or adolescent psychiatric unit, Child Guidance Clinic, school psychological service, social services day assessment centre or peripatetic teams cannot cope? Have you checked?
5. Are these agencies not interested or available in the time or manner required?
6. Is there a particular assessment agency with other facilities/attributes which would benefit the child?

The Community

1. Is the community likely to be (feel it is) at risk from the child if he remains at home?
2. Is the community likely to be concerned that the child has not been removed for assessment?

The Organisation

1. Is your organisation likely to be criticised if the child stays at home?
2. Is it the organisation's policy that certain children should be residentially assessed?
3. Does this child fall into that category?
4. Does the organisation only take certain actions when a residential assessment has been carried out?

The Referral Agent

1. Are you likely to be censured or otherwise at risk if you do not seek residential assessment?
2. Do you need a certain type of assessment that you know/believe you can get from a particular agency which is residential?

Affirmative answers to any of the above may indicate the need for residential assessment. The more the number of affirmatives, the stronger the indication.

AGAINST RESIDENTIAL

The Child

1. Are the child's problems likely to get worse if he is removed from home (or natural setting)?
2. Which problem is most likely to deteriorate?
3. Are there likely to be serious consequences for his ties and support systems – such as the family?
4. Is he likely to suffer from particular problems if he is removed to a specific assessment agency?
5. Is he likely to be stigmatised or emerge with more problems than he went in?
6. Is the removal likely to have adverse consequences for his resettlement at home (or normal setting)?

The Organisation

1. Is the assessment too expensive in time and money and in terms of its probable outcome?
2. Is the assessment likely to be unhelpful in determining what you should do with this child and others like him?

The Referral Agent

1. Are you likely to be censured or otherwise at risk if you place this child away for assessment?
2. Are you likely to end up as a result of such assessment with having to do more than you can or want to do with the child?

Affirmative answers to one or more of the above questions would contra-indicate placement in a residential setting. It should, however, be borne in mind that such referrals are made frequently for other reasons than strictly assessment.

It is at present difficult to formulate and solve such equations of contending factors but it is possible to make reasonably informed guesses about them which can in due course be tightened up to form the basis of research and provide empirical guidelines for future action. As is observed throughout this book, we strongly believe that intervention in the lives of children is capable of systematic approach and evaluation. It does not have to remain in the present morass of partial knowledge and mystical belief which places powerless problem children at the mercy of inconstant feelings of those who deal with them.

Information from referral agencies is of varying quality reflecting the standards of that agency and, that information provided may not be of the level expected or usable by the assessment facility. In view of this it may be necessary to provide a basic checklist of information to be obtained at the time of contact with the referral agency. This information would cover demographic particulars of the child such as age, sex, address, his current state, reasons for referral, the source of referral and such background or supportive information as may be deemed necessary.

Information from proximal sources can range over all those agencies and sources which have had contact with the child. The most important of these are the parents, school and any other specialised agencies which have been involved with the child. Depending on the quality of contact between the assessment agency and these sources, information of varying length and depth may be sought. There are numerous questionnaires for completion by parents, school and others, developed for a variety of purposes. Reproduced below are two such questionnaires.

School Questionnaire

Name: *Home Address:*

Present Age: *Date of Admission to your school:*

---

1. Attendance
Termly attendance figures during past year

Nature and extent of truancy since child's admission:

Other information, e.g. special arrangements to ensure attendance, degree of success, etc.

2. Appearance
Please comment on the child's state of dress, personal hygiene and habits when attending school:

3. Relationship with other children
Please mention choice of friends, degree of acceptance, problems of bullying, and any other social difficulties:

4. Relationship with staff
Please comment on his manner, response to different personalities, and any general problems:

5. Acceptance of control and rules
Please indicate attitude towards adult management, effective forms of control, and the nature of approaches made by staff:

6. Critical incidents since the child's admission
Please include the date and all relevant detail of circumstances. Continue overleaf if necessary:

7. Strengths and weaknesses in different areas of the curriculum
Please be specific about curriculum content and the child's level of performance:

Note: We would be pleased to receive and retain any samples of work that you might consider to be of interest.

8. Results of attainment tests
Please include name of test and date of administration:

9. Special teaching provision
Please note the date, duration, nature and extent of any special educational help provided for the child within the school:

10. External referral
Please record any referral to Child Guidance Clinic, Schools, Psychological Service or other agency, noting date and name of agency:

11. Interests and skills
Please give any information regarding the child's known interests, leisure pursuits, aspirations, and sporting skills:

12. Parental interest and support

13. Any other comments

Signed................................

Date .... Position ....

Parental Questionnaire

(a) Natural Parents:

	Full Name	Age	Occupation	Address	State whether married separated or divorced
Father					
Mother					

(b) Brothers and sisters still living:

Full Name	Date of Birth	Address if different from above	Occupation or School	Married Yes/No	Number of children

(c) Other adults who may live, or have lived in the home since the child was born:

Full Name	In the home		Relationship to Child
	From	Until	

(d) Please give details of members of the close family, including grandparents, who have died since the child was born:

Name	Relationship to Child	Date of Death	Age of Death	Reason for Death

(e) If any members of the family suffer or have suffered any of the following, please state who:

Tuberculosis (T.B.)		Fits	
Diabetes		Other serious illness	
Rheumatic Fever			
Mental Illness		Serious injury	

Name and address of Family Doctor

Dr. ____________________

(f) Previous addresses where your child has lived:

Address	Lived there		Lived with	Reason for change
	From	Until		

(g) Has your child suffered from any of the following:			
Whooping Cough		Bronchitis	
Measles		Eczema	
Scarlet Fever		Diabetes	
Mumps		Fits	
German Measles		Bedwetting	
Chickenpox		Poor eyesight	
Asthma		Serious ear trouble	

(h) Has your child been protected against the following:	
Diphtheria	
Smallpox	
Whooping Cough	
Measles	
Tetanus	
Polio	

(i) Please give below details of any injury or operation your child has received, including lengths of stay in hospital, and the child's age at the time:

(j) Child's Development - Before school age:

Place of Birth		Birth Weight	lb. oz.
Were there any difficulties of birth?			
Was the child slow/average/quick to walk?			
Was the child slow/average/quick to talk?			
Please mention any problems the child had before going to school:			

(k) Schools your child has attended:

Name of School	Attended		Did (s)he truant?	Did (s)he like this school?
	From	Until		

(l) Ages 5 - 11 years

Please mention here any problems the child had between the ages of 5 and 11: his behaviour, his moods, his worries, his difficulties, the way he gets on with people and so on:

(m) Ages 11 onwards

Please mention here any problems the child has had since the age of eleven: his behaviour, how he spent his time, who he mixed with, his moods and so on:

It has been found from experience that more detailed information cannot be and is not routinely provided by parents and schools though it is possible to use more detailed questionnaires regarding specific behaviours. Almost invariably, questionnaire information has to be augmented by face-to-face interviews.

In obtaining information from both referral and proximal sources it is necessary to have the type of professional relationship with them that guarantees willingness not only to provide information but also to ensure that it is accurate and usable. This is a particularly sensitive area in the case of problem children with whom some degree of mismanagement by the agency providing the information may be implicit. At the present time, few agencies are obliged to provide information and even when they do so there are no standards to which they have to conform in terms of comprehensiveness or accuracy of information. It is, therefore, crucial to ensure that the relationship of the assessment agency with these sources of information is such that there is no worry about misuse of information either against the interests of the child or those who have provided it.

This is also related to the possibly careless dissemination of information which undermines the confidential nature of much of the relationship between the source of information and the child and his parents. The need to develop a positive professional relationship between the assessment agency and source of information is emphasised by the fact that there is now a vast preoccupation with giving and obtaining reports. This creates an air of uninterested routine about much reporting and resistance to produce anything but the minimally acceptable. The involvement of the sources of information with the final decision making about the child and their knowledge that the information they have provided is important in such decision making may help foster and maintain their interested participation.

Specialists are familiar with the need to provide reports on their specialised investigations. By virtue of their work, however, they are likely to write reports which, although satisfying their own criteria, may not be of much use to non-specialists or for incorporation in an integrated report on the child. This may be either because of the use of specialised vocabulary or of the statement of conclusion whose premises are not made explicit. As any report is only as good as the use that may be made of it, it is important that specialists should write their reports in such a manner that they may be used by a wide variety of non-specialists concerned with the child's assessment.

Presentation of Information

Information can be conveyed with varying degrees of efficiency and accuracy which ranges from one extreme of ambiguity to another of exactness. The medium through which information is presented can also vary from words to visual materials such as graphs, curves and tracings, auditory and visual recordings to numerical data. Specialists use a variety of forms of presentation of data which can nevertheless be translated into words. Ultimately the two most commonly used information media are words and numbers, though numbers must in the end be related to words. All assessment reports can, therefore, be presented in one form or other or both.

Words are the normal medium of social communication. They vary in complexity, exactness and nuance. As such they can communicate not only factual information but also considerable emotional and social overtones regarding the state of the child and his impact on the speaker/writer. But these virtues also constitute the major shortcomings of verbal communication. Even common words such as 'disordered', 'anxious' and 'withdrawn' have different meanings to different individuals and professional groups. Words are difficult to store and because of the diversity of their meanings they are difficult to use as sources of information for research purposes, unless the key words are used according to a glossary.

But whatever the difficulties, it is not possible to dispense with words. Numbers, as the only other alternative, are inappropriate for communicating information about problem children. They are, however, particularly useful for codifying assessment information for purposes of subsequent research.

In this book all problems, their attributes and related behaviours, are coded in sets of two-digit numbers. This will not only provide an easy method of identifying and specifying problems but also provides an aid to cross indexing and reference to appropriate treatments which may be similarly coded. We have found that this enormously facilitates and focuses communication among people concerned both with pinpointing children's problems and subsequent research.

Assessment Meetings

The whole process of assessment is intended to describe the child's problems as a prelude to alleviating them. In order to arrive at this stage, assessment data are evaluated, placed in a coherent structure and used as a basis for decision making. Where separate reports are obtained from a variety of agencies, the task of integrating and making sense of the reports falls upon whoever has been responsible for initiating the search for information. Difficulties inherent in this approach have already been outlined. In social services particularly, there are currently no established methods of comprehensively evaluating information from discrete sources and unifying it in a manner which points to treatment plans. It is, therefore, particularly difficult for a person in this capacity to bring the reports together, sort out the essential from the less so, reconcile different points of view and translate the problems and the recommendations into an action programme and give individual components their order of priority and then refer to the necessary treatment agencies.

Contrary to prevailing attitudes, assessment of an even moderately problematic child seems too complex to be carried out by an individual person, be he a psychiatrist, a psychologist or a social worker. It is, therefore, preferable to present the assessment information in a group setting with an explicit decision-making pattern, mode of presentation of information, and recording of decisions. An assessment meeting, appropriately chaired, which brings together the persons most knowledgeable about and involved with the child, is a reasonable medium for processing the assessment information.

There is some controversy about whether children and their parents should participate in assessment meetings. The uncertainties have centred on whether sharing in the information and decision making is a 'natural right' and how this should be reconciled with notions of confidentiality and the legal responsibilities of agencies such as social services departments. The issues are too complex to be elaborated here and relate, in any case, to all forms of social control rather than just assessment. The subject of children's rights (e.g. Mercer, 1975; Rosenheim, 1976; Hoghughi, 1978c; 1979b; Harris and Hyland, 1979) is too recent to have become an established part of jurisprudence. Any arguments would, therefore, be strictly tentative.

It may, therefore, be more useful to adopt a pragmatic approach to this issue. If the participation of the child and his parents in the assessment meeting is likely to enhance either the process or its outcome, or conversely, if there are no 'good and urgent' reasons why the parents should not participate, then they should be asked to do so. Such participation is likely to enhance their understanding of the problem, the reasons for a particular course of action and thereby help the treatment process. This should, however, be set against possible costs of a less efficient and satisfactory assessment meeting, if it inhibits free and open communication among its members.

Whether the assessment report is prepared in an integral form by an assessment team or prepared separately from a variety of sources, varied experience suggests that it may be best if individual participants in the meeting present report in the following order: the child's particulars and reason for referral; family and social background; current status of the child including results of observations; medical, physical and educational assessment and psychological/psychiatric state. The person chairing the meeting would then summarise the problems and cross check his summary for comprehensiveness and accuracy with the rest of the group. Problems can be enumerated in the order presented in this book, at a level of specificity felt to be desirable for the users of the assessment report. The Chairman would then proceed to make treatment recommendations which directly correspond to the problems highlighted. These stages would also be discussed with group members to ensure consensus.

Having summarised the problems and specified the treatment recommendations, it then becomes necessary to consider where best, and by whom, individual components or the total treatment programme may be carried out, over what sort of time span, with what kinds of resources and expected outcome, and the method of monitoring which will be employed throughout the process. The determination of the venue of treatment can range from the general, such as the child's home, 'an ESN school', to the naming of a specific agency or person who may undertake the treatment of the problem. The meeting will be concluded by recommending when the child's case should be reviewed.

Such a structure of the meeting recognises the need for intensive and free interchange between members of the group in order to provide and communicate accurate information. However, it also recognises that an assessment meeting is a meeting with a purpose which can be fulfilled with varying degrees of efficiency. There is sometimes a tendency on the part of the participants at assessment meetings to use the venue as a platform for ventilation of feelings about the child and other matters which may be of dubious relevance to either the identification of the child's problems or the determination of methods of alleviating them. Thus, a high degree of structure in such meetings is desirable, conducive to concentrated and efficient processing of information and reducing of error related to the personal feelings of participants. Information may not be accurate in the first place but there is little sense in increasing its inaccuracy by allowing it to become confused with people's feelings unless those very feelings are part of the problems.

Skills of Chairman

The chairman of the meeting is the most significant determinant of the quality of the end product of assessment – the summary of problems, treatment recommendations and identification of appropriate treatment agency. However good the assessment information, it would be wasted if it cannot be adequately, accurately and efficiently transmitted to its users. Anyone entrusted with this task must, therefore, possess the necessary qualities to ensure that the task is adequately achieved. The following attributes appear central to this task.

Considerable knowledge of the structure of assessment and its sources of information are required. It is not necessary for the chairman to know the child, because all the relevant information is presented at the meeting and in the reports. Indeed, there may be some merit in the chairman not knowing the child so as to be able to arrive at an impartial synthesis of information.

He must have sufficient technical knowledge to be able to question the content and quality of the reports presented including, where appropriate, those from specialists.

He should be sufficiently sensitive and sympathetic to detect overtones and draw out double meanings and misgivings that participants may hesitate to express. At the same time he must be sufficiently firm to resist attempts by anyone to swamp and sway the meeting with his own idiosyncratic view of the child and what should be done with him.

He should have considerable analytical ability to be able to discern from the mass of information the most important elements and to synthesise them in a pattern of problems which is comprehensive, relevant and makes sense to the participants. For this reason, he must also be literate and articulate.

He should have knowledge of treatment approaches and facilities and be sufficiently authoritative and persuasive as to arrive at a consensus about what should be done with the child.

He must, besides, have those elusive qualities of a good chairman who induces in his meeting the feeling that a satisfactory job has been done. Many of these qualities are personal and inborn but they can be enhanced by training, experience, recording techniques and decision making aids. To this end, summary sheets of the information presented, checklists of problems and treatment are of considerable help.

Monitoring Assessment

Sensible comments about a child can only be made to the extent in which his similarity to or difference from a reference population can be determined. For this reason it is necessary to establish baselines about critical attributes of children in general and about the particular population which is the concern of the assessment agency. For example, in order to know whether the child is undersize and underweight, it is necessary to have general norms about the size and the weight of children in different age groups. The same criteria apply to other aspects of physical and intellectual functioning, though less readily to other problem areas such as family structure, social relationships, social behaviour and personal circumstances. Information about criteria of adequate functioning in physical and cognitive areas is generally available.

Information regarding population norms in the other problem areas, such as family, social relationships, behaviour and personal conditions (other than in relation to specific test norms) is not readily available. Nor is it easy to see what might be accepted as the 'norm' in these areas. It is, therefore, necessary to establish specific agency baselines (averages, percentages, distributions) against which the state of a child may be evaluated. The lack of such baselines is a major reason for the deficiency of much assessment. For this reason it is important to record and store assessment information for subsequent retrieval and monitoring on all children referred. The extent and the detail of information collected varies according to the resources and requirements of the agency (e.g. Hoghughi and Porteous, 1976). It is necessary to have, even at a basic level, enough solid comparative information in order to differentiate one child from others. This requirement becomes crucial in the case of the seriously disordered, who by virtue of their dramatic behaviour, create a 'halo effect' which renders them liable to blanket, frequently damning judgments. In reality, they may be no different from most other children in critical respects.

Depending on the type and quality of assessment information available, many methods of storage can be used. In addition to such demographic information it is worthwhile to collect data about the disposal of the children and their subsequent histories. This becomes an essential prerequisite for the development of empirical assessment and treatment systems.

Research and Training in Assessment

The comments so far have shown the considerable ambiguity that surrounds every aspect of assessment, its use and organisation. Bearing in mind the extensive investment of human and material resources in assessment facilities of one sort or another, both day and residential, the importance which is attached to it and the price paid by society and children to achieve assessment which may or may not be of use, it is surprising that no attempt has been made either to systematise the process or to subject it to empirical research. We regard this as a matter of the utmost importance and urgency and one which is likely to pay early dividends by ensuring a better service.

Any survey of assessment services for children shows that considerable uncertainty surrounds the following topics on which research should concentrate:

- The process of referral: who is referred, for what kind of assessment, on what grounds, to what sort of facility;
- What determines the form of assessment, the main sources of information utilised, the sequence of processes and their relation to outcome;
- The reliability and validity of individual elements and whole processes of assessment in relation to particular groups as well as relevance and utility of different assessment reports;
- The effects of context – structure, physical security, different

sizes and mixtures of peer and adult groups and professional orientations on children's behaviour;

- Who uses assessment reports, for what purpose and with what results;
- Do different assessment processes lead to different outcomes and forms of treatment? Are types of assessment *reports* differentially related to processes and forms of treatment?

Every stage of the assessment process from 'pre-assessment' and referral to the final writing and utilisation of assessment reports suggested by the above questions requires training. Such training should be aimed not only at higher levels of expertise in managing, caring and assessing but also at rational evidence-based decision making in assessment and the monitoring of its outcome. Every practitioner should be taught to do *some* critical analysis of his own assessment activities, because no researcher, however acute, will know the details of the processes involved to be able to research and validate them.

There is already some fragmented training in assessment. Medicine's focus of activity is diagnosis and treatment and assessment is therefore the core of training of its practitioners. Both teachers and psychologists acquire assessment skills as part of further, specialised training.

Social work, on the other hand, pays hardly any attention at all to either the issues or practice of assessment. And yet, paradoxically, it is the social workers, both field and residential, who are likely to be lumbered with the most complex, disordered children in need of assessment. Even setting this aside, none of the above professions are trained to carry out team assessment which is increasingly recognised as the more beneficial.

Part of the difficulty lies in the absence so far of a unifying assessment orientation which would make such training possible. The Problem Profile Approach as presented here, can provide such a unified basis for training, particularly of teams which are required to carry out integrated assessment of the child. Without training, no disciplined approach to assessment can be adopted. Without such discipline, assessment of problem children will remain an unfamiliar terrain from which some children will be guided on to a safe path, others will emerge bruised, and yet others irrevocably lost.

Selected Reading

Cone, J. D. & Hawkins, R. P. *Behavioral Assessment,* New York: Brunner Mazel, 1977.

Haynes, S. N. *Principles of Behavioral Assessment,* New York: Gardner Press Inc., 1978.

Hersen, M. & Bellack, A. S. *Behavioral Assessment*, Oxford: Pergamon Press, 1976.

Hobbs, N. *The Futures of Children,* San Francisco: Jossey Bass, 1975a.

Hoghughi, M. S. *Troubled and Troublesome – Coping with Severely Disordered Children*, London: Burnett Books in association with André Deutsch, 1978b.

Horrocks, J. E. *Assessment of Behavior*, Columbus, Ohio: C. E. Merrill Books, 1964.

McReynolds, P. *Advances in Psychological Assessment,* San Francisco: Jossey Bass, 1975.

MIND *Assessment of Children and Their Families*, London: National Association for Mental Health, 1975.

Mischel, W. *Personality & Assessment,* London: John Wiley, 1968.

Mittler, P. (ed). *The Psychological Assessment of Mental and Physical Handicaps,* London: Methuen, 1970.

Reinach, E., Lovelock, R., Roberts, G. *First Year at Fairfield Lodge*, Portsmouth: Hampshire Social Services Dept., 1976.

Rutter, M. *Helping Troubled Children*, London: Penguin Books, 1975.

Social Work Service *Use and Development of Observation and Assessment Centres for Children,* London: DHSS, 1977.

Part II: Practice

5/How to Use this Book

THE PREVIOUS CHAPTERS have attempted to set out some of the main issues in the practice of assessment. The second part of the book is concerned with elaborating the Problem Profile Approach (PPA) and with ways of obtaining answers to questions about aspects of children's problems. The purpose of this chapter is to provide some guidelines on how this second part may best be used.

THE MASTER CODE

This is the name given to an orderly compendium of children's problems presented in a manner to enable easy reference. The Master Code is divided into the six problem areas of physical, intellectual/educational, home and family, social skills, antisocial behaviour and personal. Within each problem area, the 'attributes' relating to distinctive, unacceptable conditions are enumerated. Within each attribute the behaviours which, for the purposes of the PPA, are subsumed under it, are laid out. There are, therefore, three levels of analysis: (1) the problem area, (2) the attribute and (3) behaviour. Each is given a number so as to enable quick coded references and facilitate storage and retrieval in data storage systems.

The table of contents and the book index indicate where a particular problem has been discussed and enable quick reference for this book. If a problem is not cited it may be that in the authors' judgment it has not been sufficiently widespread or serious as to merit inclusion, or alternatively, it is entered under a different name. One of the major difficulties in the assessment of children is that because of the involvement and diversity of many professional groups, there is a huge, sprawling, overlapping and diffuse terminology which does not command universal acceptability. Therefore, a major aim of this book is to attempt to enumerate and specify some of the more critical terms used in the assessment of children so as to enable more productive communication among those concerned with helping them.

We have, throughout, used common English words. Although we have tried to avoid inferential or diagnostic terms, regrettably and in the interests of communication, we have succeeded only partially. We have continued to use certain diagnostic words such as psychotic or neutoric, because there are no satisfactory or widely current alternative words available. In our usage, these are essentially 'communication bridges' and carry no diagnostic significance. Attention should be directed to the behaviours associated with them.

Neither the attributes nor their associated behaviours are ranked in order of importance. Rather they are set out in an order which appeared to us, subjectively, to make good sense. The attributes are, simply, clusters of behaviours. Although these clusters emerge in practice and have some support in linguistic usage and research, they have not been statistically derived. Such a refinement, though not necessary, is possible but must await considerably greater rigour in descriptive assessment of children's problems.

By the same token, the Master Code is not exhaustive. Practitioners with particular interests can add further attributes and behaviours to each of the six problem areas and, cumulatively, create a more comprehensive Master Code.

Layout of the Chapters

Each of the six problem areas is tackled in a separate chapter. Each chapter starts with a brief introduction to the problem area, its significance, and any particular points that should be noted in its assessment. The attributes falling within each problem area are then dealt with in the order set out in the Master Code (see next section). The behaviours associated with each attribute are placed at the beginning of each section so that it is possible to see at a glance whether the behaviour of concern is subsumed under that attribute. The attribute is then introduced and attention is drawn to any particular matters of note.

As was pointed out in Chapter 3, there are three major sources of information – questions, observations and tests. The assessment of each attribute is laid out accordingly.

Questions relate to the information which can be elicited by either perusing available documentation or by asking questions directly of all referral, proximal and specialist sources. As with the rest of this book, these questions are not standardised or exhaustive. Depending on the user and his particular focus of interest, additional or alternative questions may be asked. The questions and observations are not set out for specialists but rather any intelligent person who is attempting to discover and describe the child's problems. Each question can also be reworded to suit the linguistic competence of the source of information.

Observations are essentially a medium through which certain questions are answered. Therefore, many of the questions form points of reference for making appropriate observations. There is, therefore, some overlap between questions and observations. In a limited number of cases the questions and observations relating to particular behaviours have been separated out. For the sake of economy, elsewhere, they have been presented in blocks.

It should be evident to the user which questions or observations relate to particular behaviours. However, because behaviours subsumed under separate attributes have a considerable degree of overlap and may be described and interpreted together, we would advise that the whole attribute is assessed rather than particular behaviours within it.

Depending on the child, it may also be necessary to examine wider aspects of the same attribute in more than one problem area. For example, 'speech' appears under both 'physical' and 'cognitive' problems. Although seen from different viewpoints, it may be worthwhile to ask both sets of questions and the relevant observations in assessing a speech-disordered child.

The assessment of each attribute concludes with an Action Guide. These are diverse, aimed initially at limiting the impact of the problem and intended to point to where the assessment agent may seek further appropriate help. They are not exhaustive and are not treatment prescriptions. They may, however, help focus the assessor's attention on particular areas of difficulty which warrant intervention if deemed to be sufficiently serious.

With minor exceptions throughout this chapter, the child has been referred to in the masculine gender. This is not due to any preference for the male sex and does not imply that they are the most troublesome, but rather for the sake of brevity and in order to avoid the irritating 'he or she' phrase. Also for the sake of brevity, we have refrained from repeating that appropriate tests are not available in every case where this appears to be so. Certain tests and measures may only be available to and used by accredited specialists. These are referred to as 'restricted'. Information about them may be obtained from textbooks and other specialist sources.

The PPA is a descriptive rather than a diagnostic or explanatory system. In order to provide a comprehensive profile of the child's problems, it is necessary to evaluate him in each of the six problem areas against the parameters of extent, intensity, duration and urgency. In setting out the questions and observations we have refrained wherever possible from addressing ourselves to these particular parameters because we believe that the assessment agents should do so in every case. It would be tedious to print the same questions over and over again in relation to each problem behaviour.

It may, therefore, be worthwhile to set them out here. For every problem, the following questions should be asked:

Extent: How widely pervasive is this problem?
Intensity: How severe or deep-seated is this problem? A rating of 0–4 with 0 for non-existent to 4 for severe may be attempted.
Duration: How long has this problem been present? Since birth, for . . . years . . . months . . . weeks?
How urgently should this problem be dealt with? Immediately, soon, fairly soon, in due course?

The comprehensive assessment of the child is complicated by the methodological necessity of eliminating certain types of problems in order to pinpoint others. This is particularly true in those areas where an attempt is made to understand the *source* of the child's difficulty as well as describing his current problem. As an example, it may be necessary to eliminate the possibility of visual defect in a child before it is concluded that he cannot read, although the latter statement is functionally and logically different from the former.

This leads to another crucially important notion. Every form of measurement (an assessment involves many forms of measurement) carries different types and amounts of error. Degree of error can only be established by careful experimental and statistical evaluation. What cannot be ruled out logically is that some form of error will be made. Accordingly, with this approach as with any other, there are certain children *with* problems who are likely to be missed out, when evaluated even by the most exhaustive methods. Conversely, there are some children who are likely to be regarded as having problems which they do not. To reduce these errors, it is necessary to answer as many of the questions and make as many observations as possible, supported by test data, if appropriate.

Notes on Behavioural Assessment

Ordinary language has to be used to describe children. Descriptive adjectives are common currency even of specialists and are likely, therefore, to be used as pervasive descriptions of the child's behaviour. This is likely to create generalised perceptions of the child so that he may be regarded as 'aggressive', 'unstable' or 'anxious'. These judgments are questionable because the behaviour which underlay the original description was limited to a particular time and place and could not be used as a general description of the child. The description may indeed lead to the treatment of a child in a way which would provoke the particular behaviour and thus become a self-fulfilling prophecy. For this reason, and particularly in those areas where the description contains a larger element of judgment and interpretation than factual description, it is necessary to pinpoint in what settings the child's problems arise. It may, therefore, be helpful to answer the following questions in relation to any behaviour which is thought to be problematic. Where appropriate, these have been incorporated into the particular form and content of questions and observations but they should be borne in mind as general guidelines.

- Are there any groups or types of people in whose presence this behaviour is more or less marked than usual?
- Are there any situations in which this problem is more or less marked than usual?
- Has this always been the case? If not, when was it first noticed?
- How do people (adults and children) usually react to this?
- What impression does this give of the child's emotions and reactions?
- Has any attempt been made to change this problem?

For all problems the following format may help clarify the information obtained and ensure that relevant data are collected:

Example

Problem:	Stands too close
Who finds it problematic:	Women
When:	Most obvious when men are absent
Consequences:	Seems rude and threatening; women avoid being alone with him
Previous History:	Has always done it, not recognised as a problem until he reached puberty
Specific Details:	Stands so close as actually touching until women step back and push him away; thought to be sexual in intent.

THE MASTER CODE

01 *Physical Problems*

01 Brain Damage
01 impairment of memory
02 motor incoordination
03 overactivity
04 impulsivity
05 emotional instability

02 Motor Disorders
01 tics, twitches
02 bizarre postures
03 poor fine coordination
04 poor gross coordination

03 Epilepsy
01 Grand Mal seizures
02 Petit Mal seizures
03 minor fits

04 Psychoses
01 impairment of cognitive functioning
02 language disorder
03 delusions
04 hallucinations
05 mood swings
06 social withdrawal
07 attention interference
08 loss of pleasure
09 lack of insight
10 loss of personal identity
11 ideas of reference

05 Physical Condition
01 poor physical condition
02 poor personal hygiene
03 emaciation
04 infections related to hygiene
05 frequent minor ailments
06 obesity

06 Eyesight
01 defective vision
02 colour deficiency
03 squint

07 Hearing
01 permanent hearing loss
02 temporary hearing loss

08 Speech
01 stammer
02 lisp
03 other articulatory defect
04 aphasia

09 Genito-urinary
01 nocturnal enuresis
02 diurnal enuresis
03 defects of genital organs

10 Venereal Disease
01 gonorrhoea
02 syphilis
03 non-specific urethritis
04 other specified disease

11 Menstrual Disorders
01 menstrual pain
02 cessation of periods
03 irregular periods

12 Defaecation
01 nocturnal encopresis
02 diurnal encopresis
03 retention of faeces

13 Psychosomatic Disorders
01 bronchial asthma
02 overbreathing
03 alopecia
04 eczema
05 nettle rash or hives
06 psoriasis
07 anorexia nervosa

14 Dietetic
01 diabetes mellitus
02 undereating
03 overeating
04 food fads

15 Drug Use
01 medical drug abuse
02 non-medical drug abuse
03 abuse of alcohol
04 excessive smoking
05 solvent abuse

02 *Intellectual and Educational Problems*

01 Social Adaptation
01 little knowledge of outside world
02 limited self-help skills
03 limited survival skills
04 lacks pertinent personal information
05 cannot tell time
06 cannot handle money
07 over dependent on others' guidance

02 Intelligence
01 severely limited intelligence
02 limited intelligence
03 superior intelligence
04 verbal skills deficit
05 practical skills deficit
06 functioning well below potential

03 Distractibility
01 easily distracted from tasks
02 poor span of attention

04 Memory
01 short term memory deficit
02 long term memory deficit
03 auditory memory deficit
04 visual memory deficit

05 Speech
01 idiosyncratic speech
02 confused

06 Reading
01 cannot read
02 severely retarded in reading
03 poor comprehension of written material
04 inadequate vocabulary
05 poor word building skills

07 Spelling
01 severely retarded in spelling
02 retarded phonic skills
03 reverses letters/words

08 Written Communication
01 illegible handwriting
02 poor written expression
03 punctuation problem
04 distorted grammar

09 Mathematics
01 severely retarded in mathematics
02 cannot count
03 cannot measure

10 Negative Attitude to School
01 embarrassed by poor work skills
02 disinterested
03 expects to fail
04 avoids school

03 *Home and Family Problems*

01 No Home Base
01 No parents* or whereabouts unknown
02 no relative willing to accommodate
03 parents homeless/scheduled accommodation
04 parent(s) unwilling/unable to accommodate

*Where appropriate, items apply to 'parent substitutes' such as grandparents, aunts, cohabitees and others.

02 Locality
01 slum clearance
02 poor amenities
03 delinquent area
04 culture contrary to family's

03 Status in Neighbourhood
01 stigmatised
02 ostracised
03 victimised
04 violent conflict with community

04 Material Deprivation
01 substandard house
02 overcrowded
03 outside w.c. and/or no hot water
04 gas and/or electricity cut off
05 parents on Social Security
06 insufficient food/clothing
07 lack of personal possessions

05 Child's Status
01 illegitimate
02 adopted
03 fostered
04 doesn't know parents

06 Parents Apart
01 one parent dead
02 single parent family
03 divorced
04 separated
05 living apart
06 child unsure which to live with

07 Family Instability
01 parental separations
02 short term cohabitation
03 promiscuous parent(s)
04 other disturbing person in house

08 Adverse Parental Factors
01 physical ailment/defect
02 mental disorder
03 alcoholic/heavy drinker
04 gambler
05 offender
06 violent/cruel
07 rigid/authoritarian
08 anti-authority
09 employment
10 prostitution
11 attempted suicide

09 Parental Inadequacy
01 physical
02 intellectual
03 coping with outsiders
04 coping with each other
05 coping with housekeeping
06 coping with children

10 Family Conflict
01 marital disharmony
02 verbal abuse
03 physical aggression
04 parental conflict with children
05 children's conflict with each other

11 Family Involvement
01 parental over protection
02 parent ⟷ child indifference
03 parent ⟷ child rejection
04 siblings ⟷ child indifference/rejection

⟷ suggests that either parent(s) or the child can show this characteristic to the other

12 Affectional Bonds
01 parents ⟷ child overdependent
02 parent(s) intolerant
03 parent ⟷ child hostile

13 Parental Guidance
01 denies the need
02 inadequate
03 inconsistent
04 deviant

14 Parental Control
01 inadequate
02 inconsistent
03 harsh
04 through 'bribes'
05 through collusion against other parent
06 through collusion against outside authority

15 Child Abuse
01 pawn between parents
02 emotional blackmail
03 scapegoating
04 physical
05 sexual

16 Adverse Sibling Factors
01 physical defect
02 mental disorder
03 alcoholic/heavy drinker
04 prostitution
05 in care
06 offender
07 DC/borstal/prison
08 residential establishment

17 Deviant Identification
01 with parent(s)
02 with siblings
03 attitude and behaviour to self
04 attitude and behaviour to others

18 Child's Attitude to Home
01 runs away
02 wanders away
03 steals from
04 stays out late
05 destructive/violent

04 *Social Skills Problems*

01 Presentation
01 dirty, odorous
02 odd body movement or posture
03 odd facial features
04 odd speech rate/volume
05 poor eating habits

02 Basic Interaction Difficulties

01 odd visual contact
02 misuse of facial expression
03 inappropriate use of gesture
04 stands too close/too far
05 touches people inappropriately

03 Conversation Skills

01 makes noises while others speak
02 interrupts
03 persistent, inane questioning
04 lies
05 constantly complains

04 Social Discomfort

01 shy, uneasy
02 easily embarrassed
03 avoids social contact
04 shows anxiety in interaction
05 inept attempts to make friends

05 Unpopularity

01 ignored by others
02 disliked by others
03 bullied by others
04 scapegoated
05 taunted by others
06 has no friends
07 friendships short lived

06 Attitude to Children

01 unattached
02 manipulatory
03 domineering
04 antagonistic
05 submissive
06 over dependent

07 Attitude to Adults

01 untrusting
02 defiant
03 hostile
04 over familiar
05 over dependent

08 Sensitivity

01 under sensitive to cues
02 misinterprets cues
03 ignores cues
04 does not alter behaviour to fit social environment

09 Sympathy

01 does not offer to help
02 shows no interest in others
03 does not say nice things to or about others
04 unsupportive when others are troubled
05 does not show appreciation
06 does not share things
07 does not concede
08 does not co-operate
09 does not show affection

10 Specific Situational Problems
01 being served in shops or cafés
02 speaking on a telephone
03 making dates with the opposite sex
04 talking to the opposite sex
05 visiting friends or being visited at home
06 interviews
07 skills for getting a job

05 *Anti-Social Behaviour*

01 Disruptiveness
01 stirs up trouble; disturbs others
02 allegations
03 temper tantrums
04 runs around
05 makes odd/inappropriate noises

02 Truancy
01 does not attend school – occasional
02 does not attend school – persistent
03 school refusal

03 Absconding
01 runs away from staff
02 plans and executes attacks on property to escape
03 hangs round doors and attempts to squeeze out
04 encourages others to abscond
05 runs away from home and other placements

04 Self-Destructiveness
01 takes overdoses or poisons
02 self inflicted wounds
03 attempts to obtain offensive materials
04 tattoos
05 serious suicide attempts

05 Verbal Aggression
01 criticises
02 antagonises
03 threatens
04 swears
05 gestures/snarls
06 screams abuse

06 Physical Aggression
01 nips
02 hits/punches
03 kicks
04 spits
05 bites
06 throws objects as missiles
07 physically assaults
08 head butts
09 bullies
10 violent to animals
11 injures others deliberately

07 Uncommon Sexual Interests

01 engages in transvestism
02 engages in fetishism
03 engages in exhibitionism
04 engages in homosexuality

08 Sexual Misbehaviour

01 attempts to masturbate others without consent
02 attempts to persuade others to engage in sexual activity
03 talks a lot about it
04 over-indulgence in sexual contact
05 no control of sexual urges
06 soliciting

09 Sexual Offences

01 indecent exposure
02 sexual assault on younger person
03 sexual assault on others of same sex
04 sexual assault on others of opposite sex
05 sexual assault on older person
06 rape

10 Property Offences

01 aiding and abetting
02 theft
03 motor theft
04 burglary
05 robbery
06 robbery with violence
07 destroys property
08 damages property

11 Arson

01 lights fires
02 assembles and sets bombs
03 attempts to obtain flammable materials

12 Management

01 defies staff
02 tests out limits
03 forces confrontation
04 unreasonably seeks attention
05 demands counselling/medication/services for no good reason
06 provokes frequent conflicts
07 wears out staff

06 *Personal Problems*

01 Extraversion

01 seeks company to excess
02 constantly seeks excitement
03 talkative to excess
04 tells all to others
05 seeks group recognition to excess
06 over exuberant
07 dependent on others for stimulation

02 Introversion

01 avoids groups
02 prefers quiet routine
03 secretive
04 loner
05 introspective
06 inexpressive (keeps himself to himself)
07 actions/thoughts directed inward
08 prefers own company

03 Egocentricity

01 uses others for own ends
02 never helps others
03 selfish
04 greedy, over demanding
05 envious
06 interested primarily in self
07 indifferent to others
08 no genuine interest in feelings and welfare of others
09 seeks to achieve personal sense of superiority

04 Immaturity and Precocity

01 engages in behaviour appropriate to younger child
02 engages in behaviour appropriate to older child
03 prefers company of others mostly older or younger than self

05 Frustration Tolerance

01 lacks patience
02 cannot tolerate delay of gratification
03 shows tantrums/aggression if does not get own way immediately
04 easily disappointed
05 easily disheartened
06 easily gives up on tasks

06 Personality Disorders

01 extreme egocentricity
02 extreme coldness
03 calculating
04 no remorse or guilt
05 does not learn from mistakes
06 lacks feeling for others
07 high need for excitement and variety
08 cannot defer gratification
09 lacks inhibitions
10 hostile
11 cheats, lies, steals
12 views others as enemies

07 Impulsivity

01 acts without thought, volition or deliberation
02 does not control self
03 restless
04 easily bored
05 no resistance to temptation
06 immediate reaction to stimulus

08 Emotional Lability
01 cries/laughs easily
02 gets over excited
03 sulky, petulant
04 over reacts to stress
05 has pronounced mood swings
06 superficial, shallow emotions
07 bland, never shows emotion
08 emotionally cold
09 fearful, scared

09 Depression
01 excessively and continually unhappy
02 self deprecation
03 appetite loss
04 sleep disturbance
05 preoccupation with self
06 persistent lethargy and apathy
07 unusual pallor
08 poor muscular tone
09 gross under activity
10 guilt feelings
11 suicidal ideas
12 self pity
13 weeping with little or no provocation
14 lack of attention to others

10 Anxiety
01 tense, unable to relax
02 restless
03 over active
04 apprehensive
05 indecisive
06 needs constant reassurance
07 irritable, jumpy
08 tics and tremors
09 feelings of impending disaster
10 sleep disturbance
11 palpitations or pallor
12 excessive perspiration
13 nausea
14 constipation or bedwetting
15 seems impervious to stress

11 Obsessive-compulsive Neurosis
01 rigid conformist
02 strictly conventional
03 orderly
04 insists on perfection
05 scrupulous
06 intolerant
07 inflexible
08 does same things over and over again
09 over preoccupied with daily routine
10 unspontaneous
11 uncreative
12 self righteous
13 complains of persistent, irrational thoughts, impulses and actions

12 Phobic Reaction
01 fear of animal
02 fear of situation
03 fear of person
04 fear of place
05 fear of object

13 Hypochondriasis

01 exaggerated concern with one's physical and/or mental health
02 over sensitive and over responsive to the normal fluctuations of health
03 uses extreme measures to safeguard health
04 frequently complains of minor ailments
05 numerous visits to sickbay/surgery with spurious complaints

14 Hysteria

01 loss or disorder of sensory functions
02 loss or disorder of motor functions
03 loss of voice
04 sleepwalking
05 loss of memory
06 disorders of eating
07 disorders of excretion

15 Self-concept

01 does not agree with how others see him
02 unrealistic
03 inflated
04 fluid
05 confused
06 self reproaching
07 negative

16 Moral Development

01 cannot correctly label right and wrong
02 only distinguishes acts on fear of external punishment
03 minimal concern for the impact his behaviour has on others
04 ignores rules/obligations
05 identifies with, and emulates delinquent standards
06 anti-authority attitudes and proclivities
07 no guilt or shame

6 / Assessment of Physical Problems

THE PHYSICAL AREA contains a wide range of problems resulting from physical disorders or deficits. These problems may have their causes in genetic or hereditary factors, difficulties during pregnancy, the birth process itself or as a result of accidents and illnesses during life. The area represents problems concerning the whole body or any of its organs or subsystems. It is thus a wide one covering diseases such as diabetes and epilepsy, congenital or acquired conditions producing or leading to, for example, visual, hearing or speech abnormalities, 'psychosomatic' disorders such as alopecia, asthma and skin rashes and some areas of psychoses, for example, withdrawal and poor contact with reality as well as other disorders such as enuresis, encopresis and anorexia.

Because the human organism is integral, physical problems may lead to difficulties in other areas. Speech, hearing or visual defects can result in intellectual backwardness, learning difficulties as well as social and personality problems. As an example, a severe hearing deficit could impair the appropriate learning of language and speech, retard conceptual development and reading ability, lead to social embarrassment and withdrawal and result in the development of a paranoid and prickly personality.

We will not, however, be concerned with the vast array of possible medical problems from which children suffer. We will not, for instance, catalogue and describe those purely medical problems such as appendicitis and pneumonia which are appropriately and effectively dealt with by medical practitioners and whose assessment and treatment causes no confusion or difficulty.

A number of physical problems, however, do not have such a clear-cut medical basis or associated procedures. Frequently, those concerned with a child's overall assessment may not be aware of a physical problem, know how to formulate it, or when to refer the child for further specialist assessment. There are also problems with a known medical basis such as brain damage, which have a direct impact on the wider problems of the child and for the diagnosis of which a medical specialist may need additional information from the assessment agency. For these reasons, we present in this book a framework for the minimal assessment of those physical problems which are usually presented by children in any assessment setting and of which the staff should be aware.

Although a strict categorisation is not possible, physical problems can be placed into three rough groups. Problems occurring in the various body systems or organs, problems where physical abnormality is not apparent within the organ or system which manifests the problem; problems where no obvious deficit or abnormality is demonstrable within the body or its organs or subsystems.

---

01 Brain Damage

01 impairment of memory
02 motor incoordination
03 overactivity
04 impulsivity
05 emotional instability

The brain is the central and most important organ of the body. What happens in the brain determines the functioning and coordination of almost everything else in the body. For this reason, a number of researchers have attributed the wider problems of children, including their anti-social behaviour, to various forms of brain dysfunction, even though research results have rarely supported the theories. There is, however, general consensus about the importance of a healthy brain as a necessary but not sufficient prerequisite of normal functioning in every other area of living.

The brain may be adversely affected by injuries such as oxygen deficiency (such as birth asphyxia), mechanical trauma (difficulties during birth), headblows or penetrating injuries. Brain injuries may affect directly the emotional stability of the child as well as his motor and sensory functions. In addition, a direct result of brain dysfunction, such as overactivity, may lead to other secondary problems such as difficulties of social learning and behaviour. The groups of signs which may describe the child with brain damage includes overactivity, motor incoordination, distractibility, impulsiveness and perceptual disorders. The term 'minimal brain dysfunction' is preferable to brain damage when describing this group. The group of signs described generally may occur in children whose intelligence is about average or above average. The characteristics mentioned are most common in brain damaged children but they may also occur as isolated problems in otherwise normal children and in disordered children free of brain damage.

Assessment

Questions
Were there any birth difficulties?
Is there any evidence that oxygen deficiency may have occurred during birth?
Was he a blue baby?
Did the child require mechanical assistance during birth?
Has the child ever had a head injury?
Has the child ever been poisoned?
Has the child ever had a serious illness or one which involved the brain?

Observations
Is the child overactive or clumsy?
Is motor incoordination or distractibility evident?
Is the child impulsive?
Does the child have difficulty in seeing or hearing?
Has the child demonstrated any specific learning difficulties?
Does the child's mood change quickly and with little provocation?
Are the mood expressions extreme?

Tests Restricted.

Action Guide If brain dysfunction is suspected, refer to the G.P., psychiatrist or psychologist who will advise whether further specialist help or examination is necessary.

---

02 Motor Disorders

01 tics, twitches
02 bizarre postures
03 poor fine coordination
04 poor gross coordination

Motor disturbances are varied and occur commonly with mental disorders or are present on their own. These disturbances may include the psychomotor slowing down as in depression, rapid, exaggerated movements in manic states, restless and repetitive movements in agitated depression, limited repetitive movements as encountered in tics, tremors and habit spasms. Bizarre postures, stiffness and oddness of bearing, grimacing, mannerisms of gesture, twitchings and rituals and sudden impulsive actions are indicators of possible psychoses such as schizophrenia.

Poor coordination in the form of clumsiness, coarse and fine tremors, may be organic, psychiatric, or the side effects of drug treatment.

Repetitive, involuntary jerky movements of the body are quite common in childhood and usually take the form of blinking or sideways movements of the head. Tics are usually mild and generally disappear if ignored. However, tics accompanied by emotional disturbance of those which persist may require attention.

Assessment

Questions
Do parents and others report tics and twitches?
Do they or others complain of clumsiness or the fact that he has accidents, etc.?
Do they say he cannot do things with his hands expected of his age?
Is the child aware of these problems? How does he react to and explain them?

Observations
Does the child show any abnormality of movement?
Is this because he moves too much, too little or what he does is odd?
Does he seem to be able to coordinate his movements?
Is he more gawky or clumsy than other children of his age or state?
Does he bump into things, drop objects or show difficulty in playing games?
Is he on any medication which has such a side effect?
How frequently do these problems occur?
What are the child's reactions to them?

Tests Restricted.

Action Guide If motor disorder is present, refer to the G.P., psychiatrist or psychologist who will advise whether further specialist help is necessary.

---

03 Epilepsy

01 Grand Mal seizures
02 Petit Mal seizures
03 minor fits

Epilepsy covers a wide variety of paroxysmal behaviours, generally accompanied by loss or alteration of consciousness associated with brain dysfunction characterised by abnormal EEG patterns of brain activity. It is not in itself a disease, as its features, course and prognosis depend upon the conditions underlying it. Underlying conditions may include brain damage or tumours, metabolic disorders, infections and toxic conditions.

In a Grand Mal seizure, the person falls to the ground unconscious, making no attempt to save himself. He becomes rigid with hands clenched and feet extended and often with eyes rotated to one side. His chest is fixed and breathing is difficult and he becomes blue. After a few seconds, he passes into a second stage when he begins to twitch, the face, the eyes and limbs all involved; he may bite his tongue or pass urine and froth at the mouth. The second stage may last for a few minutes when the shaking stops, leaving the person in a coma. He may then sleep for a while or return to consciousness a little confused and complaining of a headache.

Petit Mal seizures generally begin during childhood and only rarely start after puberty. They are characterised by a sudden, transitory loss of consciousness. This lasts for about five to ten seconds and may be accompanied by small muscular twitches about the face and in the upper limbs. There is no warning and the fit may pass unnoticed by those around, for the subject does not fall and resumes whatever activity he is engaged in, possibly after shaking his head as though to reorientate himself. Some variation occurs in the length of time or the frequency of the attacks. When the attacks last longer than five or ten seconds, complex motor activities may be noticed, such as lip smacking or chewing. At other times, the only clear-cut abnormality is in the EEG recordings, the subject showing no outward evidence of alteration in consciousness.

Minor seizures include those where complete or partial loss of consciousness is not accompanied by convulsions and many other varieties whose differentiation is a complex, specialist task.

Assessment

Questions

Is there any previous history of seizures, faints or unaccountable falling?
Is there any history of head injury?
Is there any particular activity or behaviour associated with the seizure?
Does the child say he notices anything before the seizure, such as flashes of light or odd sensations?
Is the child under medical surveillance for seizures and is he receiving medication?

Observations

Does the child make any noise or cry just prior to the onset of the seizure?
Does he lose consciousness and fall?

Does he show rigidity of muscles (hands clenched, feet extended)?
Does he show any twitching or convulsions? Does he bite his tongue or froth at the mouth?
Does he wet or mess himself?
Are you sure he is not conning?

Tests Tests will usually be arranged by the doctor through the specialist and an electroencephalograph examination usually forms part of the examination.

Action Guide Refer to G.P., who will seek specialist help and provide appropriate treatment.

---

04 Psychoses

01 impairment of cognitive functioning
02 language disorder
03 delusions
04 hallucinations
05 mood swings
06 social withdrawal
07 attention interference
08 loss of pleasure
09 lack of insight
10 loss of personal identity
11 ideas of reference

Psychoses are forms of disordered behaviour which generally cannot be understood as an extension or exaggeration of ordinary experience. Psychoses can conveniently be divided into two groups, functional and organic. Functional psychoses are those in which an organic pathology is not shown. They comprise schizophrenia, including paranoid states, depression and mania.

Organic psychoses are those which are a primary result of disturbance of brain function, for instance following disease, poisoning, accidents, degeneration or deficiency. Frequently, in organic psychoses there will be some impairment of memory, orientation, intellectual functioning and judgment with shallow, changeable emotion.

The functional psychoses (schizophrenia and manic depressive psychosis) occur only very rarely before puberty. With the onset of adolescence, the psychoses are more frequently manifested and by late adolescence, the peak age for the presentation of schizophrenic symptoms has been reached. Characteristic of psychoses are loss of contact with reality, delusions, hallucinations, social withdrawal, bizarre language, poor insight and loss of identity. These and other symptoms may exist separately or coexist to varying degrees.

There is considerable controversy regarding the status of psychoses. Whatever theoretical view is adopted, it is evident that the behaviours associated with this category are the most seriously inimical to social functioning. We have included it in the area of physical problems not because we have a particular theoretical orientation but because, so far at least, the only accepted and generally available remedies for psychotic behaviour are varieties of psychotropic medication.

The criteria by which psychoses are recognised in childhood are necessarily different from those in adult life. It is not generally possible in the young child to decide whether there is reduced contact with reality or whether insight is lacking. Conventionally, the term is used to refer to the types of conditions in infancy in which the child fails to develop or loses the capacity for normal social functioning. A child who shows clear evidence of deterioration (as opposed to failure to progress) may possibly be suffering from brain disease. In such circumstances, medical referral should be made without delay.

Psychotic states can vary between social withdrawal and difficulty in experiencing feelings of pleasure to gross disturbance in psychological functioning resulting in an inability to meet the ordinary demands of life. Frequently, a progressive rise in frequency and intensity in problems may occur.

Questions and observations, where appropriate, will be outlined after each behaviour has been described. There are numerous tests of psychosis, but these are of use only to researchers and specialists. They will not, therefore, be enumerated.

Impairment of cognitive functioning

Irrational thought and shift from abstract thinking may occur. The child may give irrelevant answers to questions, repeat fixed words or phrases or drift away from the subject under discussion. His thinking may also be dominated by fears, wishes and fantasies.

Assessment

Questions
Is the child exhibiting vagueness in speech? Does his speech convey a lack of information?
Does his speech lack coherence and display a paucity of ideas?
Do others say this of him?

Questions to the child
Do you feel as though thoughts have been put into your head from outside?
Are you able to think clearly or is there any interference with your thoughts?
Do your thoughts get mixed up and sluggish?

Do people read your mind?
Are you aware of anything like telepathy going on?

Language Disorder

Language disorder is an indication of underlying thought disorder. In psychotics, talk may be either reduced or continuous and difficult to interrupt. Speech may show strangeness of manner and content. One theme or phrase may be used continuously and out of context and questions or final words of the interviewer may be repeated. The manner of speech may be affected, stilted and new words made up by the subject.

Assessment

Questions
Is the child's speech reduced or absent as compared with previous patterns of speech?
Is the child's speech continuous? Is it difficult to break into conversation?
Is his speech inappropriate?
Does he use one theme or phrase continuously and out of context?
Has the child shown a propensity to repeat questions or final words of the questioner?
Has the child shown a tendency to make up new words?

Delusions

Delusions are false beliefs which are unaffected by a reasonable demonstration of their untruth or improbability and are out of keeping with the culture and educational background of the child. Delusions vary in content and duration. The content often reflects the person's moods. In systematised delusions, the connection may be reasonable and logical if the original assumption is granted, for example, if a child believes his thoughts are being read he may believe a nearby piece of equipment, such as the telephone, is the means of doing this. In the case of religious delusions, allowance must be made for normal children from strong religious backgrounds.

Assessment

Questions
Does the child hold odd or distorted beliefs? If so, what?
Are they systematic or disjointed?
Are they unusual for a child of his age, background and ability?

Questions to the child

Do you feel particularly close to God? Does He communicate with you? How?

Can you communicate with others without actually speaking?

How do you explain what is happening?

Are there any things like radio waves, laser beams, transmitters affecting you?

Do you feel that some power or force other than yourself is able to control you? What?

Do you think that some people are saying things about you behind your back?

Are people following you about?

Do you ever see anything in the papers or TV that has a special meaning for you?

Do you think someone is helping you or protecting you?

Do you have any special qualities or powers?

Are you important or are you related to someone very important?

Is anything wrong with your mind or body?

Hallucinations

Hallucinations are false perceptions having no public stimuli. The most common occur in mental illness as 'voices' and 'visions' and are most frequently encountered in schizophrenia. The hallucinations may be attributed to an internal or external cause and the subject usually has a strong conviction of their reality. Hallucinations can involve one or more of the senses – sight, touch, smell, taste or hearing.

Mood or behaviour may be observably affected by hallucinations, especially auditory, and the subject may act aggressively or impulsively in response to auditory commands or abusive comment.

Hallucinations may be experienced by normal people, particularly when dropping off to sleep or between sleeping and waking. Hallucinations occur in mental illness, brain disorders and in some systemic illnesses. Occasionally, highly detailed and organised hallucinations occur in hysteria.

Assessment

Questions

Does the child ever behave as if he is hearing or seeing something which others do not?

Are these associated with going to sleep or waking?

Do they occur at other special times and places?

Are you satisfied that the child does not have a straightforward visual or auditory problem?

Are you satisfied that the child is not conning you?

Questions to the child
Do you ever hear noises or voices that you can't explain?
Do you ever hear noises like talking, murmuring or music?
Do the voices threaten you or say bad things to you?
Have you had visions or seen things that other people couldn't see?
Do you see these things with your eyes or in your mind?
Were you sleeping or fully awake at the time?
What time of the day did it occur?
How would you explain what you saw?

Mood Swings

Mood refers to the feelings of the person, particularly feelings which are experienced internally. Mood is commonly referred to as 'affect'. Occasional mood swings from euphoria and well-being to being fed up and miserable are seen in normal people and exaggerated in the neurotic. Fluctuation of feelings between severe depression and mania occur in psychotic depression.

Assessment

Questions
Are the mood swings extreme and beyond what can be considered normal?
Are the feelings experienced in the absence of any apparent causes?

Questions to the child
Do you feel reasonable or have you been depressed or miserable recently?
Have you felt that life wasn't worth living?
Have you felt especially cheerful and enthusiastic without any particular reason recently?

Observations
Does the child appear inactive or withdrawn?
How does he respond to stimulation?
Does he participate in games or other activities?
Is his face blank? Or gloomy?
Does he behave in an exaggerated or reckless fashion?
Does he babble and go from one topic or activity to another?
Is he easily irritated?

Social Withdrawal

Social withdrawal in psychosis includes a generalised loss of interest in the environment and a reduction in response to external stimuli, particularly in emotional responses. There tends to be a loss of interest and natural affection for relatives and friends and the subject may react to important and dramatic events with indifference. He may also show an unusual preoccupation with himself.

The subject is apathetic to external activities and a lack of drive and initiative is generally evident. The extreme form of withdrawal is stupor. He will lack spontaneity in thought and action but is aware of external events. Generally, consciousness is clear and memory is unaffected. There is a withdrawal from interpersonal relationships, a retreat into inner life and reduced contact with reality.

In children, social withdrawal may result from fear, faulty learning or poor social skills, rather than psychoses. Introverted adolescents tend to avoid group settings and their preferred self-isolation could be viewed as a normal variation of personality. Psychotic social withdrawal tends to be severe and usually associated with some of the other behaviours in this category.

Assessment

Questions
Has the child demonstrated a loss of interest in external matters recently?
Has he shown a reduction in his emotional responses?
Has he shown an unreasonable lack of affection for family and friends?
Is he unusually preoccupied with himself?
Is he apathetic?
Does the child possess poorly developed social skills?
Has the child shown a deterioration in his social involvement?

Observations The above questions form the basis of observation of socially withdrawn behaviour.

Attention Interference

In psychotics, attention interference will generally be manifested by an impaired capacity for concentrating and focussing attention on a specific topic. There will be an inability to exclude irrelevant material.

Assessment

Questions
Has the child shown a marked loss of concentration and attention recently?
Does he show difficulty in directing his attention to a particular topic?

Does he tend to include unnecessary and irrelevant material in his speech?

Loss of Pleasure

This feature refers to the impaired ability of the child to experience or integrate feelings of pleasure. Experiences previously enjoyed no longer give pleasure or appeal to him.

Assessment

Questions to the child
Is there anything that you like doing at present?
Is there something that you used to get pleasure from but don't any longer?
Can you tell me something that amuses you?
If someone told a funny joke do you think you would laugh easily?
Do you consider that you are a serious person?

Observations The above questions form the basis of observations made of the child's behaviour under a variety of circumstances.

Lack of Insight

Insight refers to a person's understanding of himself and his problems. 'Normal' people vary quite considerably in this respect. Lack of insight occurs in psychotic states such as delusional episodes, hallucinations and disturbances of mood and thought and consists of an inability to realise, or tendency to deny, that one's behaviour is abnormal. In delusions, hallucinations and severe disturbance of mood and thought, the loss of insight is clear. With improvement or partial delusional states, some insight may be present.

Assessment

Questions
Does the child express doubt about his beliefs and perceptions?
Does he talk to others about what he feels and why?
If others talk to him about his state, does he seem to understand?

Questions to the child
Even when you feel convinced of what you are hearing and/or seeing, do you ever think at the back of your mind that you may just be imagining things?
When you are not actually feeling depressed, do you think that you understand why you feel unhappy at times?
What do you think about the way you feel?

Loss of Personal Identity

Loss of personal identity refers to a confusion and blurring of boundaries between self and the external world and also a belief that others can invade and control one's inner life.

Assessment

Questions to the child

Do you feel that some power or force other than yourself is able to control you?
Does this force or power make you do things against your will?
What are the sorts of things it makes you do?
What sorts of things can it not make you do?
Do you think other people are like you in this respect or different?
Do you ever think you might be dissolved into someone else or just disappear?

Ideas of Reference

Essentially, ideas of reference consist of correct perceptions but misinterpretations of statements or events through self-consciousness, guilt or suspicion. Other people's opinions, comments or gestures are inappropriately applied to oneself as disapproving, demeaning or persecutory. For example, a TV or radio report concerning a criminal might be interpreted by the child as an accusation against him.

Assessment

Questions

Does the child have a 'big chip' on his shoulder?
Does he ever unreasonably accuse others of acts against him?
Does he pick out particular people or is he indiscriminate?
Is he generally very suspicious?

Questions to the child

Do you think people are saying things about you behind your back?
Do you ever see anything on TV or in the newspapers that is meant for you?
Do you think that things are specially arranged to harm you? What?
Do you think that certain people are disapproving of you? Who and why?
Are some people making accusations against you?
Do you think anybody is trying to get you? Who?

Action Guide If you are fairly sure that there is something wrong in one or more of the above areas, refer the child to psychiatrist for evaluation and treatment.

---

05 Physical Condition

01 poor physical condition
02 poor personal hygiene
03 emaciation
04 infections related to hygiene
05 frequent minor ailments
06 obesity

Bodily health is difficult to define and the concept of an 'average healthy' boy or girl proves mythical and elusive. Physical condition is determined by a number of factors such as weight, height and progress in development. A wide variation exists in the weights and heights of healthy children. There are many reasons why a child may be too short or tall, too fat or too thin. A common and natural cause of shortness is heredity. Small parents are likely to have small children.

Growth may be retarded by poor nutrition or physical ailments. Occasionally, it is necessary to use drugs or other treatments which may have an adverse effect on growth. Some children's heights and weights are below the normal range because they are developing more slowly than is usual. They will eventually reach normal proportions when adults but they will take longer to do this.

If children are very tall, this is most commonly due to inheritance, although there are certain rare diseases which cause excessive growth. Many children who are very tall are simply early maturers who as adults will be within the normal range of stature.

When children are too fat, the cause is almost always over-eating. Obesity in children as a result of disease is very rare. Poor physical condition through under-nutrition and inappropriate diet may lead to frequent ailments and infections and if prolonged will produce emaciation. Poor physical hygiene under these circumstances will contribute to the risk of infections and ailments.

Assessment

Questions

Does the child's weight and height fall within the normal range?

In unusually tall, short, thin or stockily built children, is the body build similar to that of the parents?

Does the child have a normal appetite and is his diet normal?

Did the child pass through his developmental milestones early, normally or late?

Observations In obese children, close observation will determine realistic assessment of calorie intake.

In apparently undernourished children, observation can establish that the food offered at mealtimes and at other times is actually eaten and not secreted or spat out.

Action Guide If the child's physical condition is abnormal and worrying, refer to the G.P. who will evaluate the condition and prescribe the necessary treatment.

AVERAGE HEIGHTS AND WEIGHTS

Children from birth to eighteen years

Boys			Age (years)	Girls		
Height (ins)	*Weight* Kg	lbs		*Height* (ins)	*Weight* Kg	lbs
20	3·4	7½	Birth	19½	3·2	7¼
29½	9·9	22	1	29	9·5	21
34	12·2	27	2	34	11·7	26
37	14·0	31	3	36	13·1	29
39	15·4	34	4	40	15·8	35
42	17·6	39	5	43	18·5	41
44	19·9	44	6	45	20·4	45
46	21·7	48	7	47	22·6	50
48	24·0	53	8	49	24·9	55
50	27·6	61	9	51	27·6	61
52	30·3	67	10	53	30·8	68
55	33·1	73	11	55	33·5	74
56	34·9	77	12	57	37·1	82
58	38·5	85	13	60	43·9	97
62	43·9	97	14	62	45·8	101
64	50·8	112	15	63	50·8	112
67	56·6	125	16	63½	53·0	117
68	59·8	132	17	63¾	54·4	120
69	67·1	148	18	64	54·8	121

The above figures are only a guide and it should be realised that for each age group there may be variations. The normal range of variations is 3 inches above and below the figures given for 2 year olds and as much as 7 inches for the 12 year olds.

Weight may vary by 2 Kg (4 lbs) at two years and 12·5 Kg (28 lbs) at 12 years. Provided that the child who is above average weight is also above average height, there is no cause for anxiety.

---

06 Eyesight

01 defective vision
02 colour deficiency
03 squint

Human beings rely more on their sight for social living than on any other of their senses. In the case of children, sight is even more crucial because they are still, intellectually and socially, in their formative years.

Visual defects are usually related to long or short sight, asymmetry in the curvature of the cornea (astigmatism), failure to control the movement of the eye (squint) and disturbances of colour vision where a particular or whole spectrum of colour may not be perceived by the individual.

Most visual defects are quite common, to the extent that in mild cases many people are not even aware of them. Most are also easy to correct, particularly if they are detected early.

Assessment

Questions
Do parents or others report visual difficulties?
Does the child himself?
Has he ever been referred to an optician or ophthalmic surgeon?

Observations Does the child have difficulty in focussing on near or distant objects?
Does the child screw up his eyes when trying to focus on words or objects?
Does he confuse similar objects of different colours?

Tests General screening tests may be carried out by asking the subject to read standard typewritten material or words from a newspaper. The child's reading level should be ascertained and words or appropriate symbols used in the tests.

Other generally available tests include Snellen's Test Chart, Near Vision Test Card, Ishihara Test for Colour Blindness, Farnsworth Dichotomous Test for Colour Blindness and the Martin Lantern.

Action Guide If you suspect a visual defect, refer the child to ophthalmic surgeon through the G.P.

---

07 Hearing

01 permanent hearing loss 02 temporary hearing loss

A child with a hearing defect is at a major disadvantage in normal social transactions. Additionally, he is likely to suffer educationally unless special measures are taken to counteract his deficiency. He may be accused of insolence or disregarding instructions when he simply may be hard of hearing.

Forms of deafness are commonly classified according to the site of the pathological condition believed to cause the deafness. The three major types of deafness are called conductive deafness, sensory deafness and nerve deafness. Each type of deafness is evaluated in terms of severity (total or partial) and duration (temporary or permanent).

Assessment

Questions
Do parents or others report that he does not seem to hear?
Does the subject present any speech or language difficulties?

Observations
Does the child behave as if he does not hear well?
Does he turn his head to one side when listening?
Does he still seem to be hard of hearing when you quietly talk to him about something nice?

Tests Tests of hearing and auditory discrimination are available to appropriately trained professionals, such as nurses, psychologists, audiometricians and ENT consultants.

Rough testing may be carried out as a screening test. Hold a watch close to each ear in turn. A subject with normal hearing should be able to hear the tick of the watch when there is no background noise. The examiner should check that the watch tick is audible by holding it to his own ears first. Faint whispers should be audible at ten feet. Prepare a list of words. Whisper to both ears first, then to each ear separately by asking the subject to put a finger in the opposite ear.

Action Guide If you suspect a hearing deficiency, refer to the G.P. and School Health Service Officer who will arrange appropriate assessment and treatment.

08 Speech

01 stammer
02 lisp
03 other articulatory defect
04 aphasia

Speech disorders seldom arise from any single cause. Speech development is complicated and a number of systems are involved in its production. A defect at any part of a long and complex chain can produce a speech disorder, and defects may be present at any site from the speech centre to the vocal apparatus itself. Hearing defects may be overlooked and can produce speech delay or other problems. Emotional disturbance may both cause and result from speech disorders.

Common speech disorders are stammer, stutter and lisp as well as a variety of articulatory defects. Basically, stammering consists of difficulty in commencing or completing words and is characterised by abrupt interruption of the flow of speech or by the repetition of sounds or syllables. Stuttering is the condition in which the even flow of speech is interrupted by hesitations and repetition of particular words. Both stammering and stuttering occur in normal people from time to time, particularly under stress.

Articulatory defects are more frequently caused by difficulties in coordinating the complicated movements of the tongue, on which clear speech depends.

Lisp usually refers to the substitution of 'th' for 's' or 'w' for 'r' sounds, 'yeth' for 'yes' and 'wubbish' for 'rubbish'. Sometimes articulatory defects sound so like the correct sound, like 'f' for 'th' as in 'fumb' for 'thumb', that there is no difficulty in understanding.

Aphasia literally means the loss of speech but it is also used in a wider sense to refer to whole or partial loss of expression or comprehension in speech, writing or gesture. Reference here is made only to impairment of production of spoken language. Aphasia may be suspected when spontaneous or elicited speech is inappropriate or disjointed or ungrammatical when taking into account the intellectual, educational and social background of the subject. Allowance should be made for local dialect and verbal responses.

Assessment

Questions

Does the child stammer or stutter? If yes, under particular conditions or generally?
Is there any obvious association between these and fatigue or distress?
Does any member of the child's family lisp or show other speech disorders?
Does his difficulty improve when he is speaking slowly with only one person, or singing?

Is spontaneous speech inappropriate?
Is his speech ungrammatical?
Does the child convey a sense of confusion by his speech?
Has the child ever been referred to a speech therapist?

Observations The above questions form the basis of observations when disordered speech occurs.

Tests (Tape recorder or video). Children can be asked to read a written text or recite something from memory, such as: What is your full name? What is your full address? Tell me three things you did today. Tell me more about it. Count to 21. Recite the alphabet.

Detailed evaluation may be carried out by various specialists using other tests.

Action Guide If the speech disorder is mild and not distressing to the child, reassure him and encourage others to tolerate it. Otherwise, refer to a speech therapist through the G.P. or school health service.

The following is a useful timetable. The child should be referred to a speech therapist at: two years old if not talking; three years old if saying no more than single words or is unintelligible to the family; four years old if unintelligible to strangers or is stammering frequently; six years old if speech draws attention to itself.

---

09 Genito-urinary Disorders

01 nocturnal enuresis
02 diurnal enuresis
03 defects of genital organs

Bedwetting is a common problem among children. In most children, bladder control is achieved by about the age of two but in a small proportion, bedwetting continues for some considerable time. It is more common among boys than girls.

Physical abnormality is a rare cause of enuresis. Often enuresis runs in families and genetic factors may be involved in a number of cases. In others, enuresis may be associated with delayed maturity or with inappropriate toilet training. A large proportion of enuretics have emotional or behaviour difficulties, though it is not certain whether this is the cause or the effect of just one adverse factor among many others they suffer from.

Involuntary urination during the day (diurnal enuresis) is much less common than nocturnal enuresis and, when it occurs, is usually associated with nocturnal enuresis. Bladder control during waking hours is achieved before control while asleep. Occasional involuntary urination during the day following the development of primary control may be associated with serious stress or upset. Continuing diurnal enuresis without development of primary control may indicate physical abnormality. Excessive urination may be associated with certain diseases or physical conditions such as diabetes and infections of the bladder and urinary tract.

Abnormalities of the bladder, urethra and genitalia are usually the result of defects related to intra-uterine development. Some of these defects may predispose to infection or enuresis.

Assessment

Questions
Was the child toilet trained by about the age of two years?
If not, when was adequate bladder control achieved?
Is the present problem a continuation of wetting since infancy or of recent origin?
Has the child's enuresis given cause for concern before?
Have there been any previous attempts at treatment?
If yes, with what results?
Does the child wet himself only in bed or also out of it?
Is wetting associated with particular states such as stress due to change of circumstances or illness?
Is the child obviously distressed by the wetting?
Has he done anything to control it or asked for help?

Observations The above questions would form the basis of establishing the frequency and circumstances under which bedwetting occurs.

Action Guide Reduce the child's embarrassment and anxiety. Refer to the G.P. to rule out physical abnormalities. Ask a psychologist from a hospital or child guidance clinic to help you design an appropriate training or treatment programme.

---

10 Veneral Disease

01 gonorrhoea
02 syphilis
03 non-specific urethritis
04 other specified disease

Veneral diseases are infectious diseases that are seldom transmitted other than by sexual contact. The common veneral diseases are gonorrhoea, syphilis and non-specific urethritis. These diseases are only mentioned in this book because there is a suggestion that greater sexual freedom among adolescents has brought with it a greater risk of exposure to such diseases. Their assessment is only warranted if a child is known to have had sexual contact with a person who may have been infected. Routine screening of adolescents can only be justified if the particular population is known to be at risk and the possibility of its transmission outweighs considerations of embarrassment and privacy.

Other diseases, not necessarily acquired by sexual intercourse, include Reiter's disease, genital warts, scabies, balanitis and genital herpes.

Assessment

If the child is suspected of infection through sexual contact, experiences pain in passing urine, observes discharges or other abnormalities in the genital area, he should be referred to the G.P. or a special clinic to carry out the necessary investigation.

Action Guide Refer for medical attention without delay.

---

11 Menstrual Disorders

01 menstrual pain
02 cessation of periods
03 irregular periods

Most girls cope reasonably well with their menstruation, its uncomfortable corollaries, and whatever else menstruation itself may signify. It is, however, known that the menstrual cycle is particularly sensitive and vulnerable to any upsets which a girl may experience. For this reason, problem girls seem to have rather more menstrual complaints than others, though the exact nature of the association is not known.

The most common menstrual disorders are excessive pain associated with periods (dysmenorrhoea), cessation of periods (amenorrhoea) and irregular periods. Menstrual pain is particularly debilitating and affects many girls from their first period, or soon after, well into adolescence. Cessation of periods does not cause any concern apart from its usual association with pregnancy. Irregular periods may signify either a hormonal imbalance or undue susceptibility to stress.

Assessment

Questions

Has the girl begun to menstruate?
Is the onset of periods associated with pain and obvious discomfort?
Has this always been a problem?
If the periods have stopped, is pregnancy suspected?
Have there been previous stoppages?
Is the stoppage or irregularity associated with any obvious changes in circumstances or stress?

Does the girl complain of her condition?
How does she show the distress?
What help does she seek?

Action Guide Seek medical help to reduce pain and evaluate need for referral to gynaecologist.

---

12 Defaecation
01 nocturnal encopresis
02 diurnal encopresis
03 retention of faeces

Encopresis or faecal soiling is much less common than enuresis. It is a major source of discomfort to the child and of distress and anger to those who have to deal with him. It is more common in boys than girls. Soiling during the day is more common than at night and encopresis is generally more associated with psychiatric and psychological disturbances than enuresis. In some cases, its origin may lie in physical disorders.

Three types of encopresis may be roughly recognised. First, there is in the younger child a failure to gain control over his bowels. The soiling is frequently associated with urination and faeces are passed wherever the child is at the time he needs to defaecate. A second type is where there is blockage of the bowel by hard faeces and secondary overflow with loose motions. Thirdly, encopresis may take place in a child who has gained control of defaecation but then starts soiling as part of a wider range of disordered behaviours.

Assessment

Questions
Had the child previously developed control of defaecation?
Has there been a continuous history since childhood or is the encopresis episodic?
Is the failure of bowel control associated with urination?
Does he have any control over defaecation? Is he able to delay defaecation for any length of time after he feels the need to defaecate?
Do the episodes occur randomly or is there a pattern?
Are the episodes associated with any obvious events or upset?
Is the child very upset at his state?
Has there been any previous attempts at treatment? If yes, with what results?

Action Guide Reduce stress as much as possible. Refer to doctor to exclude disease or physical cause then refer to clinical psychologist to draw up a treatment programme.

---

13 Psychosomatic disorders

01 bronchial asthma
02 overbreathing
03 alopecia
04 eczema
05 nettle rash or hives
06 psoriasis
07 anorexia nervosa

Psychosomatic disorders are those in which psychological distress is believed to cause physical ailments. They are included here because the problem, regardless of its origin, is a physical one. The list of disorders subsumed under this heading at some time or other is very long and of dubious utility. We have included here only a short list of those disorders which are most commonly encountered in problem children and which cannot be directly attributed to physical causes.

These disorders include bronchial asthma and other respiratory difficulties, certain skin conditions such as eczema, and the major eating disorder of loss of appetite.

Emotional factors have an effect on the respiratory system, notably in bronchial asthma and overbreathing (hyperventilation). Asthma is characterised by episodes of wheezing. Emotional factors play a part in precipitating this condition. Hyperventilation consists of either an increase in breathing rate with frequent sighing, or in its severe form, rapid, shallow breathing which may lead to light-headedness and dizziness. Loss of hair (alopecia), eczema, nettle rash (urticaria) and psoriasis are all skin disorders in which emotional factors and stress appear to play a considerable part in perpetuating the conditions. Alopecia is a sudden, patchy loss of hair without obvious physical cause. Chronic eczema is a persistent, patchy, mild, itchy inflammation of the skin. Nettle rash or hives (urticaria) is an eruption of weals on the skin which are red, itchy and clearly demarcated. Psoriasis is a disorder manifested by red blotches covered with silvery scales, occurring most often on the scalp, back and arms.

Anorexia nervosa is a disorder which characteristically occurs in young women or girls. The basic feature in all cases is a fear of regaining normal weight accompanied by restriction of food intake. The onset of this disorder is apparently associated with some emotional conflict, commonly sexual conflict about accepting the female role. Other conflicts may involve the parents, especially the mother. Occasionally, the dietetic restriction starts because the girl considers herself too fat or has been teased about her weight. There is often confusion and discomfort about body image.

Assessment

Questions

Are the disorders very obvious?
Are they of recent origin and, if so, associated with any obvious events or sources of stress?
Has the child received treatment for any of the conditions?
Does the child use overbreathing or asthmatic attack as a means of getting out of difficulty?
Has the child been discovered in an asthmatic attack even when no obvious gains were to be made?
Is the girl's refusal to eat adequately quiet or public and blatant?
Does it apply to all foods or to some only?
Does it occur only in some environments or everywhere?
Is it associated with any obvious upset and does it improve from time to time? If yes, under what circumstances?
Has any treatment been attempted and with what results?
Do you believe the eating problem is a manipulatory ploy?
Why? What end do you think it serves?

Observations The observational frame would consist of the above questions, watched for frequency and intensity.

Action Guide Alleviate any obvious stress to the child. Refer to the G.P. for skin disorders and alleviation of physical aspects of asthma. If asthma does not respond and anorexia becomes a matter of serious concern, remove child to a setting where the necessary treatment skills are available.

---

14 Dietetic

01 diabetes mellitus
02 undereating
03 overeating
04 food fads

Most children present some dietary problems in the course of their growth. Apart from diabetes, most grow out of the problem, but some continue until dietary problems become either focal or add to the burden of others. Diabetes is a group of physical disorders characterised by thirst, with associated drinking of excessive amounts of fluids and consequent frequency of urination, overeating and loss of weight. If the disease process continues for any length of time before treatment, the weight loss may be considerable and signs of emaciation begin to show. Both excessive and insufficient intakes of carbohydrates and unusual rates of physical activity can lead to a coma in which the child can die unless either food is taken or insulin given.

Children use up a tremendous amount of energy which needs replacing through food. The rate of taking and using up energy varies considerably and, therefore, some children may be thought to be overeating. The term should only be used when a child overeats abnormally and when his weight gain is above the expected limits. Some instances of overeating are thought to be responses to anxiety, while other cases may reflect a habit acquired in early childhood.

Undereating is uncommon because the body requires far fewer calories than it is usually given. Some children may refuse to eat or lose their appetites when distressed. Food fads are widespread and only become a problem when they begin to exclude common foods or what may be available. Children usually grow out of their fads and most will eat any food when hungry enough.

Assessment

Observations

Is the child drinking excessive amounts of fluids?
Is he passing urine frequently and/or in unusually large amounts?
Does his breath or urine smell sweet?
Is he eating excessive amounts of food?
Is he losing weight?
Does the child eat much more than expected for a child of his age and level of activity?
Does the child dispose of his food onto others' plates or otherwise conceal his reduced eating?
Does he do this to draw attention or is it done unobtrusively?
Is he losing weight below acceptable limits?
Can the fads be easily accommodated?

Action Guide Refer suspected diabetic to the G.P. immediately. Allay any obvious distress to the child. Regulate the environment to reduce overeating. In the more serious disorders, seek medical/psychological help towards treatment.

---

15 Drug Use

01 medical drug abuse
02 non-medical drug abuse
03 abuse of alcohol
04 excessive smoking
05 solvent abuse

To the general public a drug is a medicine or a substance used in the treatment of a disease. However, a more complete definition of a drug is any substance, other than food, which alters physical or psychological functioning. Some medical drugs are mild and harmless, others are dangerous if not taken as prescribed. The use of certain dangerous drugs is controlled by law.

In recent years, there has been considerable public alarm at media accounts of drug taking by youngsters. While there seemed to be an upsurge in some forms of drug abuse, the upsurge seems to have abated with the switch of public attention to other problems presented by youngsters. Nevertheless, there is understandable concern at the risk presented to children as a result of drug taking which may escalate on to other pursuits more harmful to the child and society.

With the repeated use of any mood-modifying or behaviour-changing (psychotropic) drug, an individual may develop dependence. The drug assumes an (increasingly) important role in his subjective life, whether his body requires increasing doses of the drug or not. This applies equally to medical drugs, non-medical drugs, alcohol, nicotine and solvents such as petrol.

In considering drug abuse and dependence, three classes of drugs can be identified: firstly, depressant drugs including narcotic pain killers (analgesics), tranquillisers, barbiturates and non-barbiturate sedatives; secondly, stimulant drugs (amphetamines); and thirdly, hallucinogenic drugs (LSD and mescaline). Cannabis may be included in the last group.

The use of excessive amounts of psychotropic drugs will generally lead to clearly defined and observable side effects. Lethargy and apathy will follow high doses of narcotics, hypnotics, sedatives and tranquillisers. Euphoria, restlessness and expansive mood may follow the use of stimulant drugs. Hallucinogenic drugs may produce odd behaviour depending on the hallucinated state. Alcohol induces merriment, courage and disinhibition, which may precipitate further unacceptable acts. The effect of nicotine addiction is more dramatic and long term but less visible. For most youngsters, solvent abuse is a passing phase but may develop into dependence which could result in serious physical and psychological deterioration.

Assessment

Questions

Are any members of the family, including the child, on medication for a mental state?

Is the child suspected of having taken drugs prescribed for others?

How did the suspicion arise?

Has the child ever been suspected by police or others that he may have associated with drug takers?

Is there any evidence that he may have taken non-medical drugs?

Does any member of the family drink excessively?

Has the child been suspected of drinking by parents, teachers or others?
On the basis of what evidence?
Do the parents sanction smoking by the child?
Has he been suspected of smoking by parents or others?
Is there any evidence of craving for cigarettes? Long standing or of recent origin?
Have the parents, police or teachers suspected glue or other solvent sniffing?
If yes, for how long and on what evidence?
Has the child ever been referred because of drug abuse problems?

Observations
Do random checks of the child's hiding places reveal any drugs or materials indicative of drug abuse?
Does the child become restless in a cyclical fashion and appear to return to a state of tranquillity after an absence?
Have other reasonable alternative explanations been ruled out?
Does the child show any evidence of undue lethargy and apathy after absences?
Does the child ever have an unusual breath smell?
Do his eyes water, or his skin seem irritated?
Does he have any abrasions or needle marks on the forearm or inside of elbow?
Can he adequately account for the use of his income?
Does his breath smell of alcohol?
Does he cadge or procure cigarettes and cigarette ends?
Does he become agitated if deprived of cigarettes?
How would he react to a solvent container 'accidentally' left around?
Does the fact that he may be observed make any difference?

Action Guide Seek specialist assessment and treatment through the G.P., local police, Synanon or other relevant agency. Curb exposure to the drug – usually by removing the child to a more regulated environment. Beware of withdrawal reactions.

Selected Reading

Brain, Lord *Speech Disorders,* London: Butterworths, 1961.
Bruch, H. *Eating Disorders*, London: Routledge, Kegan Paul, 1973.
Geschwind, N. *Selected Papers on Language and the Brain,* Boston: Reidel, 1976.
Gulick, W. L. *Hearing, Physiology and Psychology*, London: Oxford University Press, 1971.
Heaton, J. M. *The Eye. Phenomenology and Psychology of Function and Disorder*, London: Tavistock Publications Ltd., 1968.

Herbert, M. *Problems of Childhood,* London: Pan Books Ltd., 1975.
Hofman, F. G. *A Handbook in Drug and Alcohol Abuse*, London: Oxford University Press, 1975.
Hutt, C. *Males and Females*, Harmondsworth: Penguin Education, 1972.
Lachman, S. J. *Psychosomatic Disorders: A Behavioral Interpretation*, New York: John Wiley and Sons, 1972.
Lezak, M. D. *Neuropsychological Assessment*, New York: Oxford University Press, 1976.
Mittler, P. (Ed). *The Psychological Assessment of Mental and Physical Handicaps*, London: Methuen and Co., 1970.
Munro, A. & McCulloch, W. *Psychiatry for Social Workers*, Oxford: Pergamon Press, 1969.
Osgood, C. E. and Miron, M. S. *Approaches to the Study of Aphasia*, Illinois: University of Illinois Press, 1963.
Renfrew, C. E. *Speech Disorders in Children*, Oxford: Pergamon Press, 1972.
Rutter, M., Graham, P. & Yule, W. *A Neuropsychiatric Study in Childhood*, London: Spastics International Medical Publications, in assoc. with Heinemann Medical Books, 1970.
Rutter, M. *Helping Troubled Children*, Harmondsworth: Penguin Education, 1975.
Rutter, M. & Hersov, L. *Child Psychiatry*, Oxford: Blackwell Scientific Publications, 1977.
Savage, R. B. *Psychometric Assessment of the Individual Child*, Harmondsworth: Penguin Books, 1968.
Wing, J. K., Cooper, J. E. & Sartorius, N. *The Measurement and Classification of Psychiatric Symptoms*, Cambridge: Cambridge University Press, 1974.
Wingate, P. *The Penguin Medical Encyclopaedia*, Harmondsworth: Penguin Books, 1976.
The Diagram Group *Man's Body. An Owner's Manual*, New York: Paddington Press, 1976.

7 / Intellectual and Educational Problems

AN INDIVIDUAL'S COGNITIVE ABILITIES are a key to how he functions in almost every area. Any deficiencies are, therefore, important not only as problems in their own right but also in generating others. Thus, for example, an individual of very low intellectual competence would have difficulty in acquiring the self-help skills necessary for survival, likely to be a major source of stress to his family, and incapable of forming social relationships. He may also present and be subjected to major social risk because of his inability to predict the consequences of his behaviour.

Psychologists' view of what constitutes intelligence has become increasingly complex and cautious. It is now widely accepted that, other than for narrow academic purposes, it is not very sensible to talk of a person's intelligence or intellectual potential in disregard of his other attributes. This is because what a person can do with his potential depends on his personality, his interests and the social demands made on him. For this reason, it is becoming much less common to ask 'What is this child's IQ' and expect a sensible answer.

Alongside the theoretical changes in the concept of intelligence, its measurement has also become increasingly sophisticated and subject to reservations and qualifications. Tests of intelligence elicit only samples of children's intellectual competence and tend to emphasise certain cultural preoccupations. As such they are not wholly 'fair' to children from subcultures where the values may be different.

Many intelligence tests in common use today still test acquired or learned knowledge in addition to skills of a more innate variety. What a child has learned may well be a good guide to his present functional level, but not necessarily an indication of his potential capacity for learning. Children from home environments which are intellectually deprived or unstimulating frequently have marked deficits in areas such as 'general knowledge', yet they are able to perform relatively much better at more abstract practical tasks. They obtain low scores on verbal intelligence tests, yet may do reasonably well at more practical, non-verbal items. Caution must, therefore, be exercised in the interpretation of test results.

There is considerable controversy about the origins of intelligence. It is the traditional battlefield of the contending nature-nurture armies and has of recent years acquired an extra dimension of political significance. Arguments on both sides are complex and incapable of being wholly settled by research evidence. A balanced view holds that people are born with a given intellectual capacity or potential, but for this potential to be realised, they need a great deal of stimulation and a wide range of opportunities for learning.

An intellectually limited child may, therefore, have a poor endowment. Alternatively, he may have been brought up in an intellectually unstimulating environment. In either case, it is worthwhile to attempt improving his intellectual skills, though in both cases there will be limits to how much can be achieved. The question is how soon those limits will be reached – and that can only be answered by trying.

Deficits in verbal skills may result from a lack of stimulation already referred to, but when this explanation is ruled out, other causes of a more specific nature, such as a poor auditory memory, should be investigated in depth. Children who find specific difficulty with certain practical tasks should also be the subject of more detailed investigation, where such areas as visual memory and specific perceptual abilities are evaluated. Detailed findings are only useful insofar as they may lead on to treatment recommendations, and lengthy reports full of impressive findings rich in psychological jargon are often of little practical value.

A distinction should be drawn between 'backwardness' and 'retardation'. The concept of 'backwardness' relates to children of limited ability who, primarily for this reason, are poor at basic attainments. 'Retardation', on the other hand, relates to children who are not deficient in intellectual potential but who have fallen behind significantly in basic attainment. The use of attainment tests yielding standardised scores enables a direct comparison to be made between intelligence and attainments, in a way that is not readily possible with tests yielding age equivalents.

Many of children's intellectual and educational problems are connected with unrewarding school experiences. Which is the 'cause' and which the 'effect' is an unresolvable question. It is clear, however, that many of these problems would be tolerated and alleviated in a stimulating school environment which is concerned with the total social competence of the child. Teachers are, therefore, in the best position not only to assess but also to alleviate the problem. However, because of the specialised nature of much of the (more advanced) assessment, close liaison with psychological facilities has been emphasised in this chapter. Our checklists provide the grounds on which the teacher can legitimately seek help from those scarce facilities as well as help determine what help they may be able to give themselves.

To this end, the teacher and assessor may be tempted by the plethora of tests and measures available in this area. Because the best tests, particularly of general ability, are restricted, much caution should be exercised in basing important decisions on test results.

---

01 Social Adaptation

01 little knowledge of outside world
02 limited self-help skills
03 limited survival skills
04 lacks pertinent personal information
05 cannot tell time
06 cannot handle money
07 over dependent on others' guidance

Most children acquire basic adaptive skills in the course of growing up in a normal social setting. Some, however, because of severely limited intelligence and/or sociocultural deprivation, find it difficult to cope with even minimal social demands so that in an increasingly complex society they become subject to risk.

What is regarded as 'basic social competence' obviously depends on the child's social context. Such social requirements vary considerably both between and within societies. But given such variability, it is still possible and sensible to talk about what skills are necessary for the child's survival in a society. These are numerous. Only those which fundamentally relate to the intellectual competence of the child are included here. Indeed, it may be argued that the most important aspect of intelligence is the degree to which it contributes to such *basic* social adaptation. Everything else is the gilding of the lily.

Because of the involvement of psychologists and educators with mentally handicapped people over a long period, useful and comprehensive measures have been developed for quantifying children's adaptive difficulties. Because of their wide availability, relatively less emphasis will be placed on questions and observations which are better covered by the available batteries.

Assessment

Questions

Does the child have any general knowledge of the world around him?
Does the child have a basic fund of knowledge, such as coinage, hours/minutes of time, the calendar, immediate neighbourhood (one mile radius), general locality (up to, say, five miles)?
Is the child able to look after his own basic everyday needs, such as going to the toilet, washing, dressing and eating?
Has the child developed competence in freedom of movement?
Does he venture a reasonable distance from home without becoming lost?
Can he make and receive telephone calls, including the use of a public call box?
Can he catch buses and find his own way to places outside the immediate locality?
Can he do simple shopping?
Does the child know his own name and date of birth/age?
Does he know his address, and how to locate it?
Is the child able to tell the time quickly and accurately?
If not, is it because of a lack of experience?
Can the child handle money quickly and accurately?
Can he tender the correct amounts of money?
Can he give correct amounts of change?
Does he rely on others either to help with everything or to do things for him?
Have you ruled out the possibility that he may have been denied the necessary learning experience or may have other (physical and social) difficulties which prevent him from acquiring the above skills?

Observations These would seek corroboration of the answers to questions in either real life or simulated conditions.

Tests There is a wide array of tests and measures concerned with the evaluation of basic social competence. Some are either restricted or part of wider batteries. Of the commonly available ones, the following are useful, particularly with the younger and more profoundly handicapped children. The 'Progress Assessment Charts' by H. C. Gunzburg (National Association of Mental Health); 'The Manchester Scales of Social Adaptation' by E. A. Lunzer (National Foundation for Educational Research); 'Steps to Self-Sufficiency' by J. R. Burland (Chelfham Mill School); 'Vineland Social Maturity Scale' by E. A. Doll (National Foundation for Educational Research).

Action Guide Institute a systematic and comprehensive programme of basic skills training, tailor-made to remedy the individual's specific shortcomings. Monitor progress using one of the tools available and referred to in this section.

---

02 Intelligence

01 severely limited intelligence
02 limited intelligence
03 superior intelligence
04 verbal skills deficit
05 practical skills deficit
06 functioning well below potential (under-achieving)

As a general factor, intelligence is regarded as having two main components – verbal and practical. The traditional expression of intelligence in terms of an 'IQ' can thus be misleading because it disguises variations not only between these two components but also their constituent elements and from one situation to another. Furthermore, most people tend to regard intelligence as a 'thing' of which a person has 'more' or 'less' and the IQ as denoting this quantity rather than an arbitrary statistic with many sources of error.

Apart from general interest in children's characteristics of which intelligence is one, attention may also be drawn to possible difficulties they have in this area. They may be generally retarded in coping with the tasks their peers happily tackle, they may seem slow and may do things which an 'intelligent' child would not do.

Most people evaluate one another's 'intelligence' in the course of everyday living as part of their normal social interaction, though this is not how they would construe it. With children, the assessment of intelligence needs to be particularly careful and cautious as any negative findings may have particularly far reaching and damaging consequences.

The brief guidance given in the present context is simply intended to alert the assessor to the possibility of difficulties in this area which would lead to the conclusion that the child *seems* to have a difficulty which warrants future evaluation.

There are several general tests of ability available which can be administered by persons other than psychologists. These include both verbal and non-verbal reasoning tests and can be found under those headings in the current NFER Educational (open) Tests Catalogue. Other publishers also provide numerous versions of this type of test.

Severely limited intelligence

Children of severely limited intelligence present so many difficulties from infancy onwards that they are usually detected, assessed, and appropriately dealt with at an early age.

Questions
Do the parents say that the child was slow at walking, talking and toilet training?
Are there reports from health visitors and others that the child was generally retarded?

Observations
Is there evidence of physical retardation?
Are the child's motor skills retarded?
Does the child seem to have difficulty in achieving even ordinary tasks?
Can he speak in a moderately intelligible and cogent manner?

Tests The Manchester Scales of Social Adaptation (E. A. Lunzer, NFER, Level P Test).
The Progress Assessment Charts (H. C. Gunzburg, NAMH).

Both of these tests provide a good picture of all round development in cases where intelligence is thought to be seriously deficient. These tests also provide a checklist of the child's skills and abilities in different areas and – especially the PAC – are, therefore, valuable in formulating treatment plans. The MSSA provides normative data which enables the extent of retardation to be estimated with some accuracy.

Limited intelligence

This term is used to describe children who are of well below average intelligence, such that they require special educational provision. They are sometimes referred to as 'slow learners', ESN (M) (educationally subnormal (mild)) or ESN (educationally subnormal).

Because such children's learning difficulties are less prominent than those of the children in the group with severely limited ability, it is more probable that difficulties become evident at a later stage in their lives. Some, indeed, especially those whose social skills are reasonably well developed, escape notice until perhaps secondary school, by which time it is usually too late to provide the specialist help which is necessary if these children are to develop their full potential.

Questions
Do the parents say that the child was slow at walking, talking and toilet training?

Are there any school reports of general retardation?
Do the parents and others say child seemed to be having difficulty in coping with new situations, compared with other children?
Has the child been described as a 'slow learner' or 'ESN'?

Observations
Are the rest of the family reasonably bright or do they also appear slow?
Among other children, does the child stand out as particularly dull?
Do the other children treat him as if he were dull?
Can he play ordinary games with reasonable competence?
Does everything have to be explained to him more than once even when he is cooperative?

Tests Restricted. If the answers to the above questions suggest limited intelligence, referral to an educational psychologist for assessment is imperative.

Superior intelligence

This may at first not appear to be a legitimate problem, but it may result in under-achievement and incompatibility with or even rejection by the peer group.

Very intelligent children sometimes pass unnoticed in a class group, in cases where they are content to drift along with the crowd, not achieving their potential. Since such children do not present management problems, they are rarely referred for further investigation. If, however, they are to reach their potential, they will require intellectual stimulation and a more demanding scholastic and social programme.

Questions
Do reports suggest that the child has shown signs of brightness?
What sort of signs?
Do the school reports speak of above-average attainments?
Does the child say he finds no difficulty in carrying out fairly demanding tasks?
Is the family likely to recognise and foster the child's brightness?

Observations
Is the child particularly competent in such areas as problem solving or verbal reasoning?
Is he often the first to produce a correct answer to a question?
Does he stand out from the group in a range of demanding activities?
Do other children treat him as someone brighter? Are they themselves reasonably bright?

Tests Initial confirmation of a high ability level is yielded by objective tests such as the Moray House Tests (Hodder & Stoughton) which are available to teachers.

A more detailed psychological assessment of the child is likely to establish the level of the child's intellectual superiority, how the problem may have arisen in relation to it and how it may be resolved.

Verbal skills deficit

Most people, in ordinary encounters, tend to judge each other's intelligence more by what they say than by what they do. Some children are deficient in verbal skills and are treated as if they were generally of dull ability. It may be worthwhile even in ordinary, as opposed to specialist assessment situations, to look at verbal and practical aspects of intelligence separately.

Questions
Are there school or other reports regarding the child's poor verbal ability?
Does he come from a verbally unstimulating environment where high level verbal skills are not emphasised?
Does he say he has difficulty in expressing himself?

Observations
Does the child have difficulty in verbal reasoning or expression?
Any more than other children?
Are you sure he is not just being uncommunicative?
Are his vocabulary and reasoning powers restricted?
Does he ever get flustered with his attempts at communication?

Tests Word comprehension tests, of which there are many available, for example, the GAP test (Heinemann 1970), may be used to determine the level of comprehension.

Vocabulary definition tests may be devised by taking any dictionary and selecting words of successively increasing difficulty.

Practical skills deficit

'Practical' skills can be regarded as those having to do with action or practice rather than thought or reasoning. A relative deficit in practical abilities is less common than shortcomings in verbal skills, but its deficiency is viewed with more concern. This is because, while verbal difficulties are usually associated with unstimulating environments and poor schooling, practical deficits may denote fundamental perceptual difficulties. It is, therefore, particularly important to be alert to this aspect of the child's functioning so as to detect it at an early date and refer for specialist evaluation prior to undertaking whatever remediation may be deemed necessary.

Questions
Is the child said to have had motor difficulties during early life?
Do reports speak of clumsiness, accident proneness, coordination difficulties and the like?
Are there reports of difficulties in doing practical tasks?
Does the child say he has trouble doing things with his hands?

Observations
Does the child have any noticeable gross motor difficulties?
Does he have difficulty in doing tasks which require relatively fine finger work?
Does he show any frustration with such work?
How does he manage to do a reasonably easy jigsaw puzzle or other tasks that his age mates do fairly easily?
Does he have difficulty even when in a tranquil, cooperative mood?

Tests Fine hand control can be tested with mazes, copying, colouring and tracing exercises. Task-specific practical tests can be easily devised: sorting objects into types, screwing nuts onto bolts, threading needles and similar tasks. Standardised tests such as the Benton Revised Visual Retention Test (NFER) and Bender Gestalt Test (NFER) are more specific but require specialised skill in administration and interpretation.

Under-achieving

A child's performance level in basic attainments may belie his true ability, yet in the classroom situation teachers may consider a child to be 'dull' on the basis of poor attainments. Although such under-achievement may be regarded as the cultural heritage of many, particularly working class, children, it is not inevitable. It may, therefore, merit evaluation and if the motivational obstacles can be overcome, remediation.

Questions
Do school reports suggest under-achievement?
Do parents complain (if they are concerned about the child's education) that he is not doing as well at school as he should?
Does he go around with a group to whom school is important?

Does he express disinterest or dislike of school?
Does he say he could do better if he tried or wanted to? Can he give any evidence? Can anyone else?

Observations
Are there occasional sparks of intellect above the child's assumed ability level?
Is the child poorly motivated/lethargic in the classroom learning situation?
Is the child performing poorly in all subjects or only in certain areas?
Can the child's poor performance be accounted for by variables, such as poor attitude towards the teacher?
Is the child's whole attitude towards school poor, and does his family take little interest in his progress there?
Does he truant or try to miss out on schooling whenever he can?

There are no satisfactory tests of under achievement as this can only be established by comparison of results on standardised tests of intelligence and those of attainments.

Action Guide As the child's intelligence and any deficits within it have a fundamental impact on the rest of his (problem solving) behaviour, it is imperative to refer the child for specialist cognitive assessment before conclusions are drawn and remedial action is begun.

---

03 Distractibility
01 easily distracted from tasks   02 poor span of attention

Attention and concentration are necessary to any form of purposive learning. The more complex the learning task, the higher will be the attention required. Concentration is related to interest and motivation and has, therefore, to be achieved through the process of socialisation. A child may have failed to learn to concentrate and this will in turn militate against his cognitive learning as well as become a source of distraction to other children in a group learning situation.

Children who are habitually incapable of concentrating and attending may manifest this problem either because they have a physical disorder, or they have failed to learn to concentrate through poor schooling and deficient socialisation, or may be subject to transient stresses, or there are things and events more worthy of their immediate attention.

Assessment

Questions

Is the child easily distracted from tasks – more so than other children?
Is this as true at home as well as in a formal setting?
How much does this apply to both group and one-to-one situations?
Does he say there are things on which he can concentrate?
Does he lose concentration and interest after only a short while?
Does he lose concentration even when there are no significant distractions?
Do his friends say he is scatterbrained?

Observations The above questions would form a framework for observing the child's distractibility. Additionally, it should be noted whether, given the same conditions, the child is more easily distracted than others; when distracted, it is more difficult to get him to concentrate again; his span of attention is greater for some tasks and under some conditions than others.

Tests Although no standardised test specifically measures this problem, it is a key variable affecting performance in many cognitive tests, particularly the timed items.

Action Guide Rule out possible physical causes, particularly if the problem is long standing. Otherwise refer to psychologist for advice on approaches to developing 'on target' behaviour.

---

04 Memory

01 short term memory deficit
02 long term memory deficit
03 auditory memory deficit
04 visual memory deficit

Memory is an essential component of all social and intellectual behaviour. A child with a memory disorder has difficulty in drawing upon past experience to cope with new situations, so his learning is seriously impeded.

Like many other attributes, the strength of memory is one of degree. On the whole, the more intelligent children have better memories, though children with poor memories are not necessarily unintelligent. They may have a specific disorder of memory related to one of the senses such as vision or hearing, over the short or the long term. Although such a deficit will undoubtedly impair certain aspects of intellectual functioning, it need not create a general impairment and may indeed be compensated for by developments in other areas.

Memory, and its various manifestations, have received a good deal of attention from psychologists. There are many good tests of memory available but most require specialised training to administer and are, therefore, restricted. In the present context, emphasis is placed on certain easily accessible clues which may indicate the need for more specialised assessment.

Assessment

Questions
Does the child find difficulty in following instructions, especially when these relate to a sequence of actions?
Can the child remember small lists of items?
Can he remember a sequence of digits, and up to what length?
Are there variations in the child's apparent capacity to memorise?
Is the child said to be 'absent minded'?
Does he seem to forget past events easily?
Are instructions of a long term nature forgotten?
Are all past events forgotten, or are some remembered quite clearly?
Does the child seem unable to remember spoken instructions, yet can cope with written ones?
Does he find difficulty in memorising rhythms and tunes?
Can he repeat words of several syllables accurately, when these are presented in spoken form?
Can the child remember numbers given orally, such as telephone numbers?
Does the child confuse or forget symbols such as geometric shapes and mathematical signs?
Does he seem to forget pictorial material quickly?
Can the child remember spoken instructions much better than printed ones?

Observations These would relate to getting answers to the same type of questions as posed above in real life. Specially devised situations and games such as 'Kim's game', where the child is asked to recount the names of objects seen on a tray for a limited period, may also be useful.

Tests Restricted.

Action Guide If there is a serious and glaring memory deficit, refer to a psychologist for closer evaluation and possible treatment.

05 Speech

01 idiosyncratic speech (makes up own words)
02 confused

Since speech is a major component of a person's social functioning, speech difficulties are relatively uncommon. If they are present, they are usually associated with other serious disorders. Here only two of the commoner forms of speech disorders are included (see also Speech Psychoses in previous chapter).

Assessment

Questions
Are there previous reports of idiosyncratic or confused speech? Are these independent of other reports concerning the child's poor scholastic performance?
Have his speech oddities attracted particular attention by teachers?
Has any attempt been made to correct them? With what results?
Does the child give any evidence of being aware of or affected by his idiosyncratic or confused speech?

Observations
Does the child make up his own words?
Does he commonly mispronounce words?
Is there any evidence of general confusion or disorder of thought?
Is this type of speech peculiarity or confusion a generalised occurrence, or is it specific to certain situations?
Does he have periods when his speech is lucid and normal?
If it is situation-specific, is it a response to stress?
Could he speak properly if encouraged to do so?
Do other children comment on his funny or peculiar speech?
Does his idiosyncratic speech make any special sense? What?

Action Guide Refer to a clinical or educational psychologist for specialist assessment and appropriate treatment.

---

06 Reading

01 cannot read
02 severely retarded in reading
03 poor comprehension of written material
04 inadequate vocabulary
05 poor word-building skills

Reading is the most fundamental of cognitive achievements. In a developed, achievement-orientated society, it has assumed a disproportionate importance. The fact that someone can read fluently does not guarantee status and riches, but the inability to read is likely to prove a powerful impediment to these ends.

Reading is also a most complex cognitive task involving, as it does, general intellectual competence, perceptual acuity and coordination, memory, expressive ability, concentration, motivation, cultural and familial support. It is because of such complexity of factors that so many children suffer from inadequate reading skills.

Reading difficulties range from total inability to read to mild retardation. The difficulties may be due to any one or combination of the above factors. As befits the subject, the assessment of reading difficulties is the most advanced and complex in the fields of educational psychology and special education. Because of this, it is best to refer the child to an educational psychologist or specialist teacher for special assessment. The present brief guide is an aid to determining whether the child has a problem that warrants such a referral.

Assessment

Because of the levels of problems subsumed under reading difficulties, the assessment of each particular difficulty will be separately described.

CANNOT READ

Questions

Are there reports suggesting that the child cannot read or has reading difficulties?
Has the child received remedial help, and, if so, what type, for how long, and with what results?
How does he explain his difficulty to read? How do others?
What do the school reports say about his reading?

Observations

Does the child avoid situations where reading skills are required?
Does he ask others openly or in a roundabout fashion to read to him?
Can he recognise letters and how many?
Can he copy letters and words?
Can he visually and orally distinguish between similar letters. e.g. b, d; p, q; n, u?
Can he read simple words?

Tests Tests of copying, letter recognition, and visual and aural discrimination are all included in Daniels and Diack's 'Standard Reading

Tests', which is a useful diagnostic aid for teachers and others. It enables an evaluation of what 'pre-reading' skills the child may have failed to develop.

READING RETARDATION

Questions
Do your sources of information suggest that the child has difficulty in reading?
Is there a school report to this effect?
Has severe reading retardation been hinted at or diagnosed?
Have the sources of difficulty been identified?
Has there been any specialist remedial teaching?

Observations
Can the child read simple material?
Can he read words of more than two syllables?
Does he attempt to read on his own?
Can you coax him to read?
How does he respond?
Does he appear to mind that he has a reading difficulty?

Tests Any one of the many reading tests available from educational suppliers, such as the Revised Burt/Vernon or the Neale Analysis of Reading Ability (NFER) may be used to determine the level of mechanical reading difficulty. Tests such as the Wide Range Achievement Test (NFER) are useful in providing a 'standard score' for reading which enables comparison with similar scores on tests of general ability.

INADEQUATE VOCABULARY

Questions
Is the child from the sort of impoverished background which you would expect would give him a poor vocabulary?
Are there comments from teachers and others about his poor vocabulary?
Is his vocabulary inadequate for his probable needs?

Observations
Does the child stumble over many words while reading aloud?
Does he ask often what a word is?
Are these words simple and common or complex and unusual?
Does he slide over a word he does not know or substitute another word for it?

Tests Any standard readily available reading test, such as the Revised Burt/Vernon (NFER), or simply a newspaper passage or page of a simple dictionary (such as Thorndike's Junior Illustrated Dictionary) may serve as a standard vocabulary test for the purpose of an unspecialised assessment.

POOR COMPREHENSION

Questions
Are there any previous (school) reports suggesting that the child's comprehension of written material is poor?
Does the child say anything about his difficulty to understand?
Does he express concern?
Have there been any attempts to remedy the problem and with what results?

Observations
Does the child talk about anything he has read?
Does he scowl, look puzzled or show other signs of incomprehension when presented with material that he can read?
How does he respond if you ask him to read a passage and tell you about it?

Tests 'Cloze' procedures where the child has to supply the right missing word in a passage are frequently employed. Such procedures can be adapted to a wide range of abilities. However, their standardisation, as those of multiple choice tests, requires high levels of skills and their interpretation also demands much care. In view of this, it may be best at this level of assessment to simply ask the children to read passages and paraphrase them. This would provide an adequate measure of whether the child's comprehension is seriously deficient.

POOR WORD-BUILDING SKILLS

Questions
Are there reports of any specific reading disorders such as 'dyslexia' in the child's school reports?
Has the child been subjected to psychological examination to determine learning disorders?
Does the child appear motivated and intelligent enough to read, has had the opportunity to learn, but still cannot read?

Observations
Does the child spend time struggling to read written material?

Does the child seem to guess at words from the first letter and bluff his way through?
Can he break a word down into its component syllables?
Does he recognise common words by their shape (i.e. 'look and say') or can he build them up phonically?
Does he fail equally with those 'regular' words which conform to phonic rules and the 'irregular' ones which do not follow a systematic rule?

Tests Common reading tests will provide an indication of the child's word building abilities, if the type and frequency of error is noted. One useful approach is to ask the child to build up words 'out loud' syllable by syllable. This will indicate whether the child understands how words are constructed and where syllables begin and end, and provide both an assessment and a baseline for subsequent remedial work.

Action Guide Refer for specialist assessment of reading skills by an educational psychologist or specialist teacher before commencing remedial work.

---

07 Spelling

01 severely retarded in spelling
02 retarded phonic skills
03 reverses letters/words

This skill used to be accorded much greater importance in the past than it is now. Not only were teachers better spellers themselves, but they also insisted on correct spelling by their pupils. Nowadays many otherwise well-educated and literate people make spelling mistakes without much opprobrium. This is because correct spelling has become non-essential for the communication of written material – as is evident from the reading of any daily paper.

Spelling difficulties in children result primarily from inadequate emphasis on correct spelling during early schooling. But because spelling is a complex cognitive and perceptual task any important disorders in the mechanics or processes of visual and auditory perception and memory, phonic and auditory skills would affect the eventual level of spelling.

Assessment

Questions
Do school reports say anything about poor spelling and difficulty with written work?
Has he received remedial help for spelling and with what results?

Has such help been confined to spelling or has it involved other basic attainments?
Does the problem prevent effective written communication?
Has he reversed letters and words ever since he started school?

Observations
Can he spell simple words? Up to what length?
Is there difficulty with all words or only the less common, 'irregular' words?
Do his errors bear any resemblance to the original word or are they bizarre?
Does he use a phonic approach even when the spelling is incorrect?
Does the child reverse letters occasionally or regularly? Which letters?
Are whole words reversed and how often?
Does the child sometimes produce 'mirror writing' where whole sentences are reversed?
Are you satisfied he is not playing or being inventive?

Tests There are spelling tests available such as the Wide Range Achievement Test (NFER) which provide reasonable bases for assessment of spelling ability. Augmented by passages of a child's normal writing, they provide a basis not only for more specialised assessment but also for subsequent remediation.

Action Guide If spelling is intolerably bad, refer for assessment by educational psychologist or specialist teacher before commencing remedial programme.

---

08 Written Communication

01 illegible handwriting
02 poor written expression
03 punctuation problem
04 distorted grammar

Children's writing difficulties do not give rise to the same concern as do their problems in other scholastic areas. This is partly because few children need to engage in much writing other than at school. Even then, such difficulties as erroneous punctuation and grammar and poor handwriting are regarded as so common and culturally determined that correcting them usually comes low on the teacher's list of priorities, particularly in secondary school.

Writing difficulties are usually found in a wider context of other educational difficulties such as reading and spelling. In their more serious forms they may be associated with general intellectual or perceptual problems.

Assessment

Questions

Has the child been taught handwriting in a systematic way?
Are there previous reports of difficulties in writing?
Is the child aware of and admit to having writing difficulties?
Does he understand what various punctuation marks are for?
Is he aware of his incorrect or idiosyncratic grammar?

Observations

Does his handwriting vary according to his mood and interest in the subject matter?
Is his handwriting consistently illegible?
Is he left handed or ambidextrous?
Is there any hand tremor apparent?
Is his writing meaningless or of unclear meaning?
Does his expressiveness vary according to subject matter?
How does he respond when you ask him to write about a favourite subject?
Is his writing completely lacking in punctuation or is the punctuation wrong?
Is his writing so grammatically incorrect that it cannot be understood at all or only with great difficulty?

Tests There are no relevant tests but writing can usefully be evaluated under different conditions: in normal class exercises; where children are asked to make a special effort with writing; and where attention is focussed upon the above aspects of writing and marks are given for it.

Action Guide Rule out the possibility of other disorders. If seriously problematic, refer for sustained remedial work on the relevant aspect of writing difficulty.

---

09 Mathematics

01 severely retarded in mathematics
02 cannot count
03 cannot measure

Traditionally there seems to have been more emphasis on reading than on numeracy, and there is some evidence that standards of numeracy have declined. And yet, on the other hand, employers in an increasingly technological society are demanding better standards of basic numeracy.

One particular characteristic of arithmetic is the cumulative nature of the subject matter. New information is frequently dependent upon previously learned matter, more so than in either reading or spelling. Children who have not mastered the basic skills are, therefore, unlikely to make progress in more advanced areas of number work. Some children at the secondary level of education are unsure of their arithmetical tables and do not possess any alternative conceptual framework to substitute for them, and as a result progress in the subject is often halted.

Assessment

Questions
Are there reports of mathematical difficulties from school or other sources?
Has he received remedial or other help with number work and with what results?
Is the child aware of and report difficulties with number work?

Observations
Can the child perform any or all of the four basic processes of addition, subtraction, multiplication and division?
Does he find specific difficulties in any particular area?
Has the child received remedial help, and what type?
How does he respond to playing card games which involve recognition of numbers and counting?
Is he able to count aloud? Can he count money?
Is he able to measure length, volume and weight?
Can he tell the time?

Tests Any standardised test of mathematical attainments will provide appropriate evidence of child's ability (e.g. Vernon Graded Arithmetic-Mathematics Test, Hodder & Stoughton). In addition, there are now checklists of mathematical skills available (e.g. 'Yardsticks', Thomas Nelson) which are designed to point out those processes that have been mastered.

Action Guide Refer to a specialist teacher who, after further assessment (if necessary), will undertake remedial teaching.

---

10 Negative Attitude to School

01 embarrassed by poor work skills
02 disinterested
03 expects to fail
04 avoids school

Irrespective of a child's ability, he will not do well at school if he is not interested in schoolwork or finds school and matters associated with it stressful. These may result from the absence of motivation for schoolwork or counter-attractions.

The issue of attitudes has in the past often been played down or even overlooked and although truancy has always been highlighted, many children opt out of school by passively withdrawing in the classroom. They are often overlooked, especially if they do not actually present management problems within the school. Truancy is often only an overt and extreme form of disinterest in or antipathy to school.

Thus, negative attitudes to school are manifested in a wider range of behaviours, only some of which have been included here. These attitudes reflect and in turn generate negative experiences at school. A child who stands out or is ridiculed for his scholastic incompetence is likely to avoid school; one whose parents undervalue schooling will not see much reason for persisting with difficult cognitive tasks; one who expects to fail will avoid the test and one who becomes part of a delinquent group is likely to find other activities more exciting and worth pursuing than persevering with frequently boring school work.

'School phobia' is a contentious topic and one which has come to be used dubiously in all sorts of situations where there is no intense, irrational, debilitating fear of school, although undoubtedly some children suffer from this condition. Because the diagnosis is frequently based on an inadequate examination of alternative explanations, we prefer to use the more descriptive term 'school avoidance' or school refusal. Any phobias or intense anxieties will fall under the appropriate headings in Personal Problems and will be dealt with there.

Assessment

Questions

Do teachers and others comment on his poor work skills?
Has his inadequacy been made public by teachers or parents and with what results?
Does he say that he is embarrassed or worried about poor scholastic skills?
Have the parents shown much interest in his school career?
Are they likely to devalue the school to their child?
Has the child's attendance at school been spasmodic without other good reason?
Do school reports suggest general disinterest or only disinterest in certain subjects?
Are there school or other reports suggesting that the child expects to fail, and, therefore, refuses to try or avoids school?
Are these expectations realistic? For what reasons?
Is the child said to dislike or fear school?

Are there any obvious reasons for this problem?
Have other members of the family experienced similar problems?
What is the school's view of this problem?
Has the child been referred to an Education Welfare Officer or been taken to court for persistent truancy? With what results?
Has he been referred to the Child Guidance Clinic or other specialists for his avoidance of school? What have they said about his problem?
Is the problem so severe that it has been described as 'school refusal' or 'school phobia'?
What are his feelings about school and how does he express them?

Observations
Does the child try to 'cover up' for his poor work skills by bluffing or opting out?
Does he fail to finish his work or hand it in in a manner others are not likely to notice?
Is he a passive observer rather than active participant in the classroom?
Does he grumble or more actively reject school work?
Are special efforts by teachers likely to produce a more interested response?
Is he more interested in some teachers' subjects than others?
Does the child behave as if whatever he does he is likely to fail?
Does he give up easily in resignation or defiance?
Does he say anything to the effect?
Does the child actively resist going to school?
Does he become tearful, sick or aggressive if his school attendance is enforced?
Is there anxiety, tension or severe unhappiness apparent when he is at school?
Does he stay away from school at the slightest reason such as being 'unwell' or problems at home?
How does he respond to attempts to make him more interested or welcome in school?
Do sanctions or threats make any difference to his reaction?

Action Guide See what can be done to get the school and the parents to make it more worthwhile for the child to like the school and schoolwork. If there is severe avoidance associated with distress, refer to the Child Guidance Clinic for treatment.

Selected Reading

Blackham, G. J. & Silberman, A. *Modification of Child and Adolescent Behavior*, 2nd edition, Belmont, California: Wadsworth Publishing Co., 1975.

Block, N. and Dworkin, G. (Eds). *The I.Q. Controversy: Critical Readings*, London: Quartet Books, 1977.

Burland, J. R. *et al. Steps to Self Sufficiency*: Chelfham Mill School, Barnstaple: Viaduct Publications, 1977.

Chazan, M., Moore, T., Williams, P. and Wright, J. *The Practice of Educational Psychology*, Harlow: Longmans, 1974.

Child, D., *Psychology and the Teacher*, London: Holt, Rinehart and Winston, 1973.

Daniels, J. C. & Diack, H. *The Standard Reading Tests*, London: Chatto and Windus, 1972.

Garrison, K. C. & Magoon, R. A. *Educational Psychology: An Integration of Psychology and Educational Practices*, Columbus, Ohio: Merrill, 1972.

Gunzburg, H. C. *Progress Assessment Charts and Manual*, Birmingham: SEFA Publications, 1975.

Hunter, I. M. L. *Memory*, Harmondsworth: Penguin Books, 1964.

Johnson, D. J. & Myklebust, H. R. *Learning Disabilities: Educational Principles and Practices*, New York: Grune & Stratton, 1967.

Lunzer, E. A. *Manchester Scales of Social Adaptation* (*Manual*), Windsor: NFER, 1966.

Mittler, P. J. (Ed). *The Psychological Assessment of Mental and Physical Handicaps*, London: Methuen and Co., 1970.

National Foundation for Educational Research (NFER), Test Dept., Darville House, 2 Oxford Road East, Windsor. All types of tests – educational and psychological.

Thorndike, E. L. *The Thorndike Junior Illustrated Dictionary*, London: University of London Press, 1947.

8/Home and Family Problems

FAMILY is the central institution of all human societies. It is the chief medium through which the socialisation of children is achieved. In the assessment of children's problems, the family background is almost the first area to be looked at and evaluated. It is by now part of folklore of Western society that most children's problems emanate from difficult home circumstances. This is largely supported by research findings which show that practically every aspect of children's problems is to varying degrees associated with difficulties within the family unit.

From an assessment point of view, family problems present the most complex and heterogeneous area. To start with, a family is an integrated functioning entity with a complex network of communications, affection, roles and power relationships. These factors and others associated with them are logically different from each other, and diverse and manifested in a multiplicity of variants. It is not always possible to adequately differentiate whether family problems cause children's difficulties or are themselves reflections of difficulties presented by a particular child. Additionally, family influences merge with those of the wider society and it is, therefore, difficult to disentangle them. For this reason, it may be best to adopt a pragmatic approach and simply group together all those factors which are generally associated with adverse family circumstances whether they directly affect the child or not. This is indeed the basis for official intervention of social agencies in children's lives whether the adverse family circumstances can be proved to be directly affecting the child's development or not.

Family disorders can emanate from the failure of the family to fulfil its basic functions of providing for the physical, social and emotional needs of its members. Other orientations to the family as a system of roles, network of relationships or medium for psychological and social development, would similarly suggest other forms of dysfunction which may be regarded as worthy of assessment. Failure in any of these areas can be regarded as a passive contributor to the potentially disorderly development of the child.

The problems of the family range from its physical state, such as the physical and structural quality of the home and the neighbourhood, through the relationships between the parents and their children, to aspects of emotional care, methods of control and qualities for modelling presented to the child. Within this wide range only some of these problems are directly concerned with what a child *does*. The problems presented to and by the child's home include the impact of the community, the interaction between the community and the family, the relationship between the parents, interaction between parents and children and interrelationships of the children with one another.

These items are qualitatively different from those in other problem areas in the sense that some of them, such as problems with the community, may have no direct impact on the child but because of their wider effects are potential sources of adversity which should be considered in any comprehensive assessment of the child and his difficulties.

The assessment of family problems primarily involves the compilation of a factual catalogue of apparent and reported difficulties, a history of significant events within the family which are thought to have impinged on the child, and the making of inferences and judgments based on questions asked of the family and observations made of the behaviour of its members. Testing is largely inappropriate other than in determining the particular characteristics of one member of the family.

The family is the most close knit and intimate unit of social interaction coming under the scrutiny of social agencies. It is the most difficult to penetrate and evaluate not only because of the intensity of its interrelationships but also because each community and subcultural setting manifests its influence on the family in different ways. It is not, therefore, always possible to be even moderately sure that what may be regarded as generally deviant and unacceptable in the wider society is necessarily so in one particular family's case in relation to their subculture or that it is having an adverse effect on the child. While it is possible to say that a family is problematic or is having an adverse influence on the child, it may not always be possible to be specific about the sources of difficulty. Equally, while some assessment agents are particularly insightful about family problems and can evaluate its difficulties comprehensively, others' evaluations are deficient and their judgments should not be treated as sacrosanct. These reservations are necessary as a corrective to the frequently glib and patronising judgments made about family dynamics. This caution is particularly important in dealing with families in trouble, who are powerless and incapable of countering negative value judgments passed on them. This is an area which is more susceptible to idiosyncratic judgments and the use of socially and ethically evaluative terms than any other.

Therefore, one major concern in this book is to provide a possible checklist of problems and elaborate those where wider assessment is relevant. The scheme adopted in this chapter is one of pragmatic grouping of adversities presented to or by the child within his home ranging from the wider community to interactions with siblings. Although the term 'behaviour' in the third level of analysis is semantically inappropriate as a designation of social factors, it has nevertheless been retained for the sake of continuity with other chapters. Similarly, the usual format of the other chapters has been maintained in order to facilitate reference.

---

01 No Home Base

01 no parents or whereabouts unknown
02 no relative willing to accommodate
03 parents homeless/scheduled accommodation
04 parents unwilling/unable to accommodate

A child's home is the arena in which his basic requirements for survival and growth are met. The home provides the major source of perceptual stability in a child's life from which the first elements of his identity begin to emerge. This does not appear to be any less important in adolescence than in childhood. Additionally, the absence of a constant home base indicates the possibility of other major adversities in the home which require special compensatory measures.

Assessment

Questions

Has the child been in care because he has no parents?
If he has parents, how long have they been away and untraceable?

Have attempts been made to trace them?
Have any agencies attempted to find if child has relatives?
Have they been asked or encouraged to have the child?
Are the parents homeless? Why?
Are they in scheduled accommodation?
If yes, for how long?
Are parents unwilling to have the child?
Is this recent or long standing?
Is the refusal because of the child or changes in their own circumstances?
Are there any periods of circumstances in which they may be prepared to have the child?
Do you believe the situation is likely to change for better or worse and why?

Action Guide If the child is homeless, an alternative home should be found through adoption, fostering or a residential facility.

---

02 Locality

01 slum clearance	03 delinquent area
02 poor amenities	04 culture contrary to family's

From the moment the child ventures outside his own home he comes under direct and indirect influence of his wider social surroundings and the people who inhabit them. There is considerable research to show that particular parts of cities and regions are associated with greater incidence of individual problems. The extent of social and educational provision within an area not only reflects its deficiencies but also the unwillingness of both the inhabitants and administrators to make the necessary provision.

Assessment

Questions
Is the area designated for slum clearance?
Are the authorities not making adequate social and educational provisions for this reason?
Do the police and social services say the area is one of high delinquency?
Do the parents accept their child's behaviour and contacts with his peers as normal?
Do they regard the lawbreaking by other youngsters to be expected?
Do they see themselves out of place in the locality?
Is this because they are better or worse than the rest?
Is this with good reason?

Observations
Is the area derelict and run down?
Is the dereliction so pervasive that the family is sucked into it?
Is there much sign of vandalism?
Is the family distinctively different from other residents in the locality?
Is this difference based on origin, colour, religious pursuits or concern with themselves and the children?

Action Guide If the particular locality is severely inimical to the interests of the family and the child, effort should be made to get them moved to another locality.

---

03 Status in Neighbourhood

01 stigmatised
02 ostracised
03 victimised
04 violent conflict with community

Depending on the size, homogeneity and stability of a neighbourhood, one family may be more or less prominent. Prominence of a family arises either from the attribution of positive qualities such as wealth, size of house, status of the parents, or negative factors such as poverty, mental and physical illness, or other dramatic visible differences between the family and the rest of the community.

Both positive and negative factors can lead to conflict between the family and the wider social setting and the stigmatisation of the family by the rest of the locality.

Stigmatisation results from the attribution of particularly adverse factors to the family which create social distance and conflict between the family and others. The stigma can relate to the history of the family, the state of their home and current financial status, particular characteristics of parents, or the behaviour of the child.

The stigmatisation can create social isolation and ostracism of the family and, in more extreme circumstances, their victimisation by the rest of the neighbourhood. Ostracism is manifested through attenuated or severed social contacts between the family and outsiders and their isolation from each other. Victimisation is shown in negative acts such as deliberate damage to the fabric of the house or exclusion of the family from the use of amenities or deliberate picking on by a variety of people. Violent conflict takes the form of fights and destruction emanating either from members of the community or the family with one another.

Assessment

Questions
Do the family or any of its members have a reputation for any particularly bad characteristics? According to whom?
Is this belief about the family or its members widely shared by the community or only restricted to a small number?
How far are the family shunned by the rest of the community, particularly neighbours?
How ready are the other members of the community to talk about and justify their ostracism?
Do you believe that the family or any of its members are being victimised by a smaller or wider range of other community members?
Are the family aware of this?
How do they react to it?
Is the victimisation justified on the basis of established facts or is the family being unjustifiably scapegoated?
How extensive is the conflict between family members and others?
Are they general or only occur under specific circumstances?
Are they serious and likely to deteriorate?

Observations It is unlikely that specific situations can be created in which this attribute can be seen to operate. Observations can be made in chance encounters between members of the family and others such as community agencies or neighbours.

Action Guide If the status of the family in the neighbourhood is so bad as to cause concern about the child's development, consider taking specific measures to improve it (very difficult), attempt to rehouse the family in another area, or in the most serious cases, remove the child.

---

04 Material Deprivation

01 substandard house
02 overcrowded
03 outside w.c. and/or no hot water
04 gas and/or electricity cut off
05 parents on social security benefits
06 insufficient food/clothing
07 lack of personal possessions

There is by now considerable literature on the effects of poverty on social and psychological development of children. Poverty and its consequent material deprivation are a matter of degree within and between subcultures, are perceived with various degrees of resignation by those affected and have, in turn, variable effects on people according to the presence or absence of other adversities.

It is, however, generally accepted that poverty is associated with numerous social hardships and that it is itself the direct cause of problems such as poor physical health, intellectual development, low achievement, considerable family conflict, high levels of delinquency, and generally depressed and negative self-concepts. In materialistic societies where physical amenities are taken as indicators of social and psychological wellbeing, the absence of adequate physical provision creates tensions which have potentially severe consequences for the child and his family.

Assessment

Questions
Is the home structurally and decoratively in poor repair?
Are there more than one and one-half persons per room?
Does the home lack an inside w.c. and hot water?
Are gas and electricity not readily available?
Are parents in receipt of social security or other special benefits? As much as they are entitled to?
Do any members of the family complain of lack of adequate food and clothing?
Would you judge the amount of food and clothing available as adequate and reasonable?
Do members of the family, particularly the child, have personal possessions?
Are family members, particularly the child, concerned with the lack of personal possessions?
Is there adequate space for privacy in the home?
Is this family worse off than the rest of the locality in any of the above respects?
Has it done anything to upgrade itself?
Are the parents and children aware of their status?
How do they feel about it?

Action Guide If the family are materially deprived, get help from social services, social security department, or other sources of finance. Make family aware of its welfare rights and how it may obtain them.

---

05 Child's Status

01 illegitimate
02 adopted
03 fostered
04 doesn't know parents

The normal status of a child in Western society is that he is born after the parents' marriage and continues to live with them. However, there appears to be an increasing trend towards birth of children outside wedlock as well as a tendency to find alternative homes for those children who come from particularly adverse family circumstances. It is recognised that the child derives his major identity from parents and that illegitimate birth still carries adverse social and psychological consequences.

Assessment

The answers to the first three items are based on factual information and can be established from inspection of appropriate documents. The child's knowledge of his parents can be established by asking him the appropriate questions. Care should be taken to ascertain whether the child has already been asked that question and how he has reacted to it. The effect of further questioning on the child should be considered before further questions are asked.

Action Guide Little can be done about the child's history. Consider when and how it is necessary to tell him about his parentage.

---

06 Parents Apart

01 one parent dead
02 single parent family
03 divorced
04 separated
05 living apart
06 child unsure which parent to live with

In most societies there is considerable delineation of parental roles with which each parent undertakes a set of overlapping but specific functions in relation to the child. Thus, both parents are regarded as necessary for the child's normal social and psychological development. The increasing attention to fragmented and one-parent families has brought to light the many adversities they suffer as a direct result of their state.

The causes and consequences of parental separation are diverse and complex. It is, however, important to ascertain the state of the family as an aid to evaluating its wider consequences.

All the elements in this area can be established by asking specific questions or through inspection of documents and other social enquiry methods. All but the last are a matter of fact and can be stated as such. It may be also worthwhile to state the causes of the separation, if known, its duration, and its impact on the remaining parent and the child.

When parents are alive and both retain something of a positive relationship with and responsibility towards the child, he may be unsure which one to live with. This is presumably because the positive and negative characteristics of the parents or their wider circumstances are in a state of balance at any given time. This creates anxiety, conflict of loyalties and a good deal of uncertainty in the wider functioning of the child, particularly as it may become difficult for the child to derive the full benefit of modelling from one particular parent.

Assessment

Questions to the child
You are living with this parent. Why?
What would make you change your mind to live with the other parent?
Do you worry about your parents being apart?
Would you like them to be together again?
Both parents and other siblings or relations can be asked the same question about the child.

Observations If the opportunity arises to see the child with both parents, his distance from each parent, who he sits with or stands closer to and how he behaves towards them may be useful signs of his particular state.

Tests The Family Relations Indicator, Children's Apperception Test or other similar tests which provide information about parent-child relationships can be used to throw light on the child's level of certainty regarding his current state when parents are living apart.

Action Guide Consider bringing family together, changing child's place of residence, or reconciling him to his present state.

---

07 Family Instability

01 parental separations
02 short-term cohabitation
03 promiscuous parent
04 other disturbing person in house

It is generally believed that for a family to fulfil its function in providing care and support for a child it must be relatively stable in the composition of its members and their interrelationships. It is, therefore, necessary to look at the stability of the family with a view to ascertaining whether it is likely to have adverse consequences for the child. The depth and extent of family instability and its specific consequences for a particular child are a matter of individual detailed determination in specialist contexts. The fact of family instability, however, can be fairly accurately established.

Assessment

Questions

Have the parents ever been separated and for how long?
Has the parent with whom the child has been living ever brought in another person to live with him/her in the house? For how long?
Has either parent had extramarital affairs?
Are these affairs known to the other parent and to the children?
Have the partners in the affairs been brought into the home?
Have these affairs been a source of conflict between the parents and/or them and the children?
Are there any other persons in the house who aggravate the child?
What form of aggravation does this take and how deeply does it affect the family and the child?

Observations As well as asking the above questions, parents can be observed in their own home when the cohabitee or other persons are present.

Tests An open-ended test such as Repertory Grid can be used to evaluate the effect of a loose family structure on the child's life, particularly the impact of cohabitee or others.

Action Guide Little can be done apart from removing the child in case of obvious damage.

---

08 Adverse Parental Factors

01 physical ailment/defect
02 mental disorder
03 alcoholic/heavy drinker
04 gambler
05 offender
06 violent/cruel
07 rigid/authoritarian
08 anti-authority
09 employment
10 prostitution
11 attempted suicide

Parents are persons with particular characteristics in their own right, over and above their qualities as parents. But their personal characteristics fundamentally affect the kind of parenting they can provide for the child. A parent's difficulties affect the impact he makes on his family though the quality of that impact is also dependent on the balance of other positive and negative influences in the home. In the evaluation of family problems, considerable weight should, therefore, be given to evaluating adverse parental factors and, where possible, determine their impact on the wider family and the child.

As has already been indicated, evaluation of family problems is primarily conducted through asking questions both of family members and agencies who are concerned with the family and inspection of documents. Testing is inappropriate unless the particular characteristics of a family member, such as mental illness, are being determined, in which case that would fall under one of the other problem areas with its own specific assessment techniques. In view of the diversity of items under this heading, individual problems are separately considered.

Assessment

PHYSICAL AILMENT/DEFECT

Questions
What ailment or defect does parent suffer from, if any?
How debilitating is it to the parent?
How adversely does it affect the child and other family members?

Observations
What are the perceptible effects of parent's ailment or defect on other members of the family or the child?

MENTAL DISORDER

Questions
What form of disorder is the parent suffering from?
Who says so?
How insightful is the parent about the disorder?
How well controlled is the disorder?
What is its impact on the family and the child?

Observations The above questions form the basic observational frame in which the manifestations of the mental disorder and its effect on the child and the family can be gauged.

ALCOHOLIC/HEAVY DRINKER

Questions
Has either parent been diagnosed as an alcholic? By whom?
Has either parent received treatment for alcoholism?
Is the parent regarded as a heavy drinker, by himself, members of the family, or others?
Has the parent been charged with behaviour under the influence of alcohol, lost a job, or suffered other adversities related to alcohol usage?

Is the family's financial condition seriously affected by parent's alcohol usage?
Has the drinking parent sought help from Alcoholics Anonymous or other agencies?

Observations The parent's frequency of drinking, state at the time of interview, his eagerness to get a drink by offering the interviewer one or by terminating the interview in order to go to the pub, can all be noted. The parent's treatment of their children when under the influence of alcohol can be observed.

GAMBLER

Questions
Is either parent known to gamble?
Is this associated with the more common horse racing and football pools' gambling or the visiting of gambling clubs and meetings?
Has the gambling caused serious disruption and conflict in the family?
Are there any offences associated with gambling?
Has the parent sought help for gambling?

OFFENDER

Questions
Has either parent a history of offences?
Are these offences against person or property?
How recent are they in origin?
What were the consequences of offending?
Is the parent currently on a charge, on probation, or in custody?

VIOLENT/CRUEL

Questions
The other parent, children and others can be asked whether either mother or father resort to physical aggression and under what circumstances.
Do they physically hurt their victims by drawing blood and leaving marks?
Do they use any implements?
Do they have a favourite victim or is their violence indiscriminate?
Do they physically or verbally hurt 'for its own sake' rather than when in a temper or as a means of achieving another end?
Does this hurting go on even after the victim has submitted?
Are they cruel generally or do they have a favourite victim?
Is parental violence shown inside or outside the home?

Observations There are no very good criteria regarding what constitutes violence. It is a matter of the interaction and intents of the 'violent' person and the perceptions of his victim. It should be evaluated in terms of its range, intensity and whether it is expressive, or instrumental, as a means of achieving another end. Parental violence can be observed when it is happening and in terms of its visible results, such as bruises or the terrified reaction of the child to the parent's presence or other acts which may presage violence. Particular caution should be exercised in (a) interpreting a parent's forceful acts as 'violent' and (b) not being aware of the subtler forms of cruelty and violence by either parent. A socially responsible person is unlikely to be present at the time of parental violence and be in a position to 'observe' the violence.

Tests There are a number of tests of aggressiveness available but it is unlikely that they would be used in evaluating parental violence.

RIGID/AUTHORITARIAN

Parental rigidity can be evaluated in terms of their unswerving and inflexible adherence to moral and religious codes, their close-mindedness, their inability to accept the legitimacy of behaviours which diverge from their own, under a variety of circumstances. Particularly skilful interviewing is required over a wide range of social and moral topics to elicit an accurate idea of rigidity. Additionally, however, the other parent and the child can be asked such questions as:

Do you find him a hard person?
Can you get him to change his mind?
Does he always strictly stick to what he says?

Authoritarianism is often associated with social and moral rigidity but in addition connotes a black and white idea of morality, considerable concern with power, punitiveness and tendency to interpret personal and social acts in terms of power struggles and obeisance to superior power and contempt for the less powerful. Subtle and wide ranging questions tailored to the particular situation are required to elicit evidence of parental authoritarianism.

Observations will be limited to the form and content of parental response to general conversation and interviewing.

There are very good tests of moral and social rigidity and authoritarianism available. However, it is most unlikely that such tests can be given to parents unless they themselves become subjects of intensive assessment.

ANTI-AUTHORITY

Questions to the parent

What do you think of the police, magistrates, social workers and others?
Do you find them helpful or not?
Have they been any use to you in the past?
Do you think they are against you?
If you were in trouble would you ask them for help?
The other parent and the child can be asked to project what the parent's feeling may be to particular authority figures.

Observations

Are the parent's statements derogatory to authority figures?
Are they general or specific?
Does he give any particular reasons for his attitude?
Is the parent willing to help social agencies with the management of the child?
Does the parent lie to social agencies? Is there any apparent reason for this?
Does the parent refuse to meet or to carry out requests made by social agencies?
Does the parent talk about social agencies in a derogatory manner in front of the child?
Does he try to turn him against them?

Tests As with previous sections, particularly good instruments for testing attitudes to authority are available but these are likely to be found unacceptable as means of ascertaining parental attitudes under normal circumstances.

EMPLOYMENT

Parental employment is the normal source of family income. Any major problems of employment are likely to result in family poverty and major tensions.

Questions

Do either or both parents have jobs?
Does the father have a history of stable employment?
Is he described as a good worker?
If there is unstable employment, is this because of general unemployment problems or is he particularly susceptible to losing his job?
Does he get much satisfaction out of his job?
Is his job a major source of stress?
Does he, by virtue of his job, have to be away from the family for long periods?
Has this raised any problems?

Do his job problems spill over onto his family?
How do the family members, including the child, see his employment?
Are there any problems associated with mother's employment?

PROSTITUTION

There are diverse views among theorists and practitioners about the significance for children of parental prostitution. Some regard it as a pathological reaction and others as a form of earning a livelihood which is no more damaging than many others. Regardless of these views, however, no statutory agency can knowingly condone parental (almost always mother's) prostitution and has to consider it as an adverse factor in evaluating the child's family conditions.

Questions
Is the parent suspected of prostitution?
What is the evidence?
Does she have a police record for soliciting and 'immoral earnings'?
Does anybody else in the locality talk of her as a prostitute?
Is this an occupation or just a part-time activity?
Is the activity carried out in the family home or elsewhere?
Are the other parent and children aware of it?
How do the rest of the family react to it?
Is the activity conducted explicitly for money or for other reasons?
Is she open about her activities or are they denied?

ATTEMPTED SUICIDE

Attempted suicide appears to be associated with serious personal pathology or social and familial disorder. The reasons for it and its manifestations are as diverse as the people who attempt it. Its effects on the family are usually cataclysmic, generating intense anxieties and maladaptive patterns of coping with them, particularly among the children. It is this latter factor which frequently warrants close scrutiny of the child when a parent has attempted suicide.

Questions
Has either parent attempted suicide?
How and with what immediate effect on the family?
How recent was the attempt?
How serious was it?
Has there been more than one attempt?
Did it require hospital treatment?
Did the child witness it?

What reason does the parent give for it?
What reason do other family members?
Has the parent received psychiatric or other help for it?
Have there been long term consequences?
Does the parent still threaten it?

Action Guide Any one of the above problems may have a catastrophic effect on the child. Depending on the severity of either one or more, the parent or the child may have to be removed from the home or intensive effort be made to reduce the impact of the problem on the child.

---

09 Parental Inadequacy

01 physical
02 intellectual
03 coping with outsiders
04 coping with each other
05 coping with housekeeping
06 coping with children

The quality of parents' adaptation to the normal stresses of living and bringing up children is determined by their ability to cope in a variety of circumstances. This is important to evaluate, not only in relation to their own stability but also in terms of the sorts of models they present for their children's social learning. An inadequate parent is more likely to produce a child who not only suffers because of parental inadequacy but one who may become inadequate due to lack of countervailing models. Parental inadequacy can arise from any of the factors mentioned in the previous attributes. How far these factors restrict the ability of parents to cope with outsiders, with each other, with housekeeping and with their children, can be established through asking the relevant questions.

Assessment

Questions
These can be asked of either parent or children or others who have occasion to know of parents' difficulty to cope in a variety of areas.

Are there things parents cannot do because of physical infirmity or deficiency?
Are they said to be dull or slow and at a loss how to manage their lives because of this?
Is there any evidence for this?
Do they find it difficult to deal with demands made on them by official agencies and others?
Is there anyone in particular? Under what circumstances?

Do the parents have trouble in coping with each other's demands and problems? What particularly and how does it show itself? Who controls the housekeeping? Is the trouble with wasting the money on less essential items, inadequate planning, purchase of inappropriate goods or simply poverty? Who complains of poor housekeeping?
Who has difficulty with which children and their problems? How have they attempted to cope? Is the admission of difficulty to cope made directly and without hesitation or is there some evidence of shame and unwillingness to admit?

Observations The above questions form the basis of any observations that the assessment agent may be able to make. As the judgment of coping ability is largely inferential (apart from physical difficulties which are either obvious or easily ascertainable), care must be taken in interpreting observations. An important element in the judgment would be the statements by the parents or others close to them, that they cannot cope. The more evidence to this effect, the more trustworthy the eventual judgment is likely to be. Distinction should also be made in parents *not wanting* to as opposed to not being *able* to cope.

Action Guide See if you can do anything to increase parents' ability to cope. If not, decide how much this is likely to hurt the child and take appropriate measures.

---

10 Family Conflict

01 marital disharmony
02 verbal abuse
03 physical aggression
04 parental conflict with children
05 children's conflict with each other

The other major manifestation of adverse parental factors is the extent of conflict it generates within the home. Conflict can be both the cause and result of anxiety, stress and incompatible patterns of coping. It requires forms of adaptation which may be manifested in deviant behaviour either of the parents or of their children.

Assessment

Questions
Parents and others can be asked:

Do you often have arguments with each other?
What are these arguments about?

Do the arguments get very heated?
Is there anything you agree on with each other?
How much can you predict your husband's or wife's views and behaviour?
Are you often wrong?
Does he often swear at you? Is this normal in your arguments?
Do you mind it?
Does he ever beat you or otherwise hurt you physically?
Does he often have disagreements or trouble with the child?
Are these about something in particular or about anything?
Who do you think is responsible for these problems?
Do the children often fight, scrap, argue with each other?
Are these about a particular topic or about anything?
Are they usually limited or do they spill into wider conflicts with the rest of the family?

Observations In a home setting, observation of family conflict is likely to be difficult and incidental. All the above questions could be regarded as the basis of observing the interaction of members of the family with each other.

The ease and frequency of arguments between parents, the content and 'spread' of the arguments, whether their bodily stance to one another is belligerent or not, history or report of physical aggression and parents' arguments with the children, their content, extent and vehemence and similar aspects of children's conflict with each other, form a reasonable structure for commenting on the extent, intensity, duration and urgency of family conflict.

Action Guide See whether anything can be done to reduce family conflict or its impact on the child. In case of serious physical or psychological damage to the child, he may have to be removed.

---

11 Family Involvement

01 parental over-protection
02 parent ⟷ child indifference
03 parent ⟷ child rejection
04 siblings ⟷ child indifference/rejection

Although the existence of a home and of parents is crucially important, these would mean little if parents were either indifferent to the child or antagonistic towards him. The interest and involvement of members of a family with one another determine their level of motivation to provide support and help towards each other's healthy growth. Such involvement also determines whether and how much a child's behaviour can be controlled through an emotional relationship. It is widely shown in research that children with indifferent and rejecting parents are likely to be more problematic and less susceptible to corrective help.

Assessment

Questions

Do the parents deny that the child has any problems in order to protect him from the consequences? Do they express anxiety about these consequences?

Do the parents become aggressively possessive and protective when it is suggested that their children may have problems and that they should receive some special form of help?

Do the parents treat the child as much younger than his years?

Do the parents try to fight the child's battles for him at school or with peers?

Is it felt that parents' attitude to the children's problems prevents the children learning that they have done wrong and that their acts have certain unpleasant consequences?

Do the parents and child appear to coexist in parallel without making much impact on each other? Is there evidence of past or present lack of concern with each other?

Do either party claim that the other is indifferent?

Do either parents or the children shun each other?

Do they express the wish to be parted or not to have anything further to do with each other?

Do the parents refuse to have the child live with them or see them or write to them? Or vice versa?

Is there any history of the child having run away from home and/or expressing unwillingness to return home?

Is the child's life style and his reasons for that life style in explicit negation of parental demands?

Do the same considerations apply to the relationship of siblings with the child?

Observations

In their physical encounter with the child do they stand close to the child, turn their body towards the child or make any other gestures such as putting an arm around him which suggests protectiveness?

Is this protectiveness more than you consider warranted by the realistic demands of parenting, society or the circumstances?

Do they speak to each other in a manner as if the reaction of the other person did not matter?

Is their encounter devoid of excitement or any other normal sign of emotional significance?

In situations of physical encounter do they turn away from each other or make gestures of dismissal?
Is the content of their verbal or physical encounter dismissive and uncaring?
Do any of the siblings behave towards the child in this manner or vice versa?

Tests Family Relations Test, Repertory Grid and specially constructed Sentence Completion tests can be used to augment information about the degree of family involvement.

Action Guide Decide whether and how it is possible to improve the quality of family involvement and whether its paucity is likely to damage the child so much that special measures are necessary.

---

12 Emotional Support

01 parents ⟷ child overdependent
02 parent(s) intolerant
03 parent ⟷ child hostile

The degree and quality of family involvement is both the basis and result of the quality of emotional relationship between the parents and child. The two are frequently intertwined and inseparable. Emotional support given by parents is, however, distinct from the quality of their involvement. Parents may be closely involved, but in a hostile rather than supportive manner. The closer the degree of emotional support the more children will find it easy to cope with stress and overcome temporary disadvantage because they are able to share this anxiety with and gain succour from parents. The degree and quality of emotional support can either be overpowering or alternatively too little to meet the needs of the child during his growth.

Assessment

Questions
Ask the parents to talk to you about how much they rely on their child for anything that is significant to them.
How much do they speak of the child having helped them cope with certain problems?
How much do they appear to rely on the child to either fulfil any deficiencies in their life or to carry out tasks which should have been dealt with by other people?
Is either party known to have suffered in the absence of the other?
What does the child say about his dependence on parents?
Do the parents express intolerance of the child's attitudes and behaviour?

Do the parents express hostility to the child?
Is the manner and content of speech suggestive of lack of love?
Is this different from other families you know in this social class and culture?
Do parents say that they will have nothing to do with the child regardless of what is likely to happen to him?
Do they express a wish for the child to be taken away or to be locked up or to die? Or vice versa?
Does either party complain of lack of love and caring on the other's part?

Observations
Do either parents or child become tearful or otherwise emotional when possibility of their separation is mentioned?
Do parents and child speak in warm and sympathetic terms about each other?
Do either parents or children speak or behave in dismissive or hostile manner towards the other?
Do they say or do things to each other which are hurting or undermining?
Are their actions obvious or subtle?
Are they used to this or do they still react strongly?

Tests The same two tests above as well as a number of evaluative tools such as Semantic Differential or specially constructed Sentence Completion Tests can be used to evaluate the depth and pervasiveness of affectional bonds between family members.

Action Guide Evaluate how serious the impact of poor emotional support on the child is in order to determine whether it is worth expending the skills and expensive resources in trying to improve it.

---

13 Parental Guidance

01 denies the need	03 inconsistent
02 inadequate	04 deviant

In order to turn a randomly developing child into a socially competent individual, parents must provide intensive guidance and correction over a prolonged period. This guidance involves not only demonstration of what is expected and acceptable within the family setting but also highlighting and enforcing of the wider social boundaries. There is considerable literature to show that delinquent and disordered children have received frequently inadequate or inconsistent guidance. Such guidance is not only preventive but is also parental acknowledgement that the child's behaviour is unacceptable and, therefore, in need of correction.

Assessment

Questions

Do the parents acknowledge that the child has any problems?
Do they express the belief that the child's problems will sort themselves out?
Do their expressions regarding the child's problem appear feeble, irrelevant or inappropriate?
Do their accounts of the content and quality of their guidance tally with each other's or with their actions?
Are they known to have taken any measures to curb the child's problems?
Do the parents suggest that it is someone else's job – teachers, the police or others – to provide such guidance?
Do the parents' attitudes and actions suggest that they may be inculcating deviant views and norms in their child?
If the parents are themselves deviant, do their expressions of how they want their child brought up significantly differ from their own actions?
Does the child's account of parental guidance suggest that either parent or both are inadequate, inconsistent or deviant?
Are the parents known to have inculcated deliberately deviant views and forms of action in their children?
Do the parents speak as if they approve of the children's deviant or problematic behaviour?

Observations Other than in specially devised situations, it is not possible to observe the quality of parental guidance. In such situations, the above questions can form the basis of an observation schedule.

Action Guide If the parents are ignorant of the child's need for guidance, educate or train them until they know. If they know but cannot or will not give it, decide whether effect is so serious that you need to remove the child.

---

14 Parental Control

01 inadequate
02 inconsistent
03 harsh
04 through bribes
05 through collusion against other parent
06 through collusion against outside authority

In the course of normal growth every child behaves from time to time in a manner which is unacceptable either from the parents' point of view or judged by the wider norms of society. Most children grow up and out of this with minimal intervention. Parental response to such behaviour is indicative not only of the parental qualities earlier discussed but also of the kind and extent of control they exert and the methods they use to do so. Ultimately it is the extent and quality of parental control which determines whether the child's problems escalate to such an extent that external intervention and, hence, the need for assessment arises.

The extent and closeness with which parents supervise their children's behaviour in and out of the home determines how much they notice deviant behaviour which, if not corrected, may become persistent. Parental control can be exerted to correct unacceptable behaviour which is manifested in any setting from the family to the school to the wider society. It is the parents' acknowledgement and ability to exert such control which is eventually reflected in the degree of self-control manifested by the child. If the extent and quality of parental control is inadequate, then the child is likely to get caught in an ascending spiral of problems. This is so serious as to have been included as a major test of whether a child should be taken into care.

Assessment

Questions

How closely do the parents and child say he is supervised? Just in the home or outside it as well?

How much do they know of where he is, who his companions are and what they are doing? Have you checked that this knowledge is accurate?

Do the parents know of any undesirable association the child has and have they done anything to curb the contact?

Do the parents say that they cannot control their child? What methods have they used and with what results?

Do they speak as if they have given up or are likely to give up controlling their child?

Are the views expressed by parents about the control of the child's behaviour inconsistent either internally or between one another?

Do they express disapproval of each other's methods of control?

Do they express approval of one form of control while exercising a different one?

Are parental expressions of control disproportionately harsh?

Do they speak of their child's behaviour as if it were more seriously problematic than it is and therefore justifies their preference for more punitive methods of control?

Do the parents talk as if they feel that giving their children more of their own way is likely to alleviate the problem? Does anyone else say that parents have attempted to control their child through harsh measures or bribes?

Do parental expressions suggest that one parent attempts to control the child's problem behaviour by disguising it or denying it to the other?

Do the parents ignore some behaviours but attend to others?

Do they ignore some behaviours at one time but pick them out at another?

Are the parents known to have used harsh physical punishment as a means of controlling their child's behaviour?

Have either the parents or the child complained of harsh punishment?

Does the child behave in a frightened manner when speaking of parental punishment?

Is there any evidence that parents have given in to all the child's demands within their means in order to control his behaviour?

Does the child or anyone else say that he was 'bribed' to stop the trouble?

Observations Other than through watching parent-child interaction over a period and variety of settings, it is difficult to observe the extent and quality of parental supervision and control. In any situation, however, the above questions would form the major axis of an observation schedule.

Action Guide See what can be done to improve the quality of parental supervision and control. If little or nothing, evaluate the pros and cons of removing the child from home.

---

15 Child Abuse

01 pawn between parents
02 emotional blackmail
03 scapegoating
04 physical
05 sexual

The public have become increasingly shocked at the number of children and adolescents who are subjected to physical and mental cruelty by parents. This is sometimes accidental and an unfortunate result of inept parental attempts to control a child's behaviour. Often the physical hurt of the child and its consequences so frighten the parents that the form of control is not exerted again. In some instances, however, punitive over-reaction to the child's problems becomes habitual and in still more serious cases it becomes a ritual of torture almost for its own sake. But overt physical hurt of the child is only one form of abuse to which he can be subjected. Others have more subtle effects but, equally seriously, impede the normal physical and psychological development of the child and predisposes him to faulty growth.

The assessment of parental abuse of adolescents is more difficult than that of young children. This is because adolescents' activities spread over a wide area, have no close network of agencies to oversee their development, and do not present the same linked clues about their maltreatment as do younger children.

Assessment

Questions

Do the parents say that in their conflicts the child takes one side rather than the other? Is the child closer to one than the other? Do the parents say anything which suggests that they use the child as a way of controlling or affecting their partner's behaviour?

Does either parent threaten the child that if he continues his behaviour something horrible will happen to them?

Does either parent speak of leaving the home or sending the child away?

Does either parent appear to frighten the child inappropriately about the effects of his behaviour on either parents or other members of the family?

Do the parents readily place the blame on the child for their troubles with one another or with the other children or with the wider society? Is this untrue and inappropriate?

Does the child appear to 'pay' for the aggravation caused by either parents, other siblings or problems with the community?

Does the child or anyone else accuse parents and siblings of wrongly blaming him for the problems of the family?

Does either parent or the child speak of physical hurt inflicted on the child? Is there any evidence of child having been hurt in the home?

Is the parents' explanation of injuries inadequate, discrepant, or excessively plausible?

Do any of the social agencies suspect that the parents are likely to inflict injury on their child?

Is there a history of violence in the family or injury to the other children?

Does the child have a history of violence and destructiveness to other children, animals or property?

Has the child ever attempted self-destructive acts at the behest of the family?

Has either parent or the child ever accused a parent of sexual abuse?

Is the child known to have been sexually assaulted or engaged in (damaging, forced) sexual acts with either parents or siblings?

Observations
Is the accidental injury reported to a hospital?
Has there been much delay between the injury and the reporting?
Is there evidence of earlier injury?
Do the parents exhibit unusual disturbance or concern at the child's injuries?
Does the child exhibit any fear of or apathy to parents?
Does the child show unusual fear of people, situations or of objects?

Action Guide Reduce risk by intensive, appropriate help to parents; otherwise, remove the child.

---

16 Adverse Sibling Factors

01 physical defect
02 mental disorder
03 alcoholic/heavy drinker
04 prostitution
05 in care
06 offender
07 DC/borstal/prison
08 residential establishment

Although the parents are regarded as the main source of influence on their children, there is considerable evidence to suggest that siblings are also powerful shapers of each other's behaviour. For this reason it may be worthwhile to look at the other children and any adverse factors that may affect them. Such adversities may also point to the existence of probable difficulties in the home which may not yet have manifested themselves in the case of the particular child under scrutiny.

Assessment All these adverse factors are similar to those of parents discussed previously in this chapter. The same methods and content of assessment apply.

Action Guide Try and reduce the impact of these characteristics on the child. Evaluate whether risks are so great, singly or in conjunction with other adversities as to point to more drastic action.

---

17 Deviant Identification

01 with parents
02 with siblings
03 attitude and behaviour to self
04 attitude and behaviour to others

A child's conception of the world emerges as a result of his interaction with his parents and subsequently his peers and wider social agencies. Parents are the chief source of the gratification and the child's medium for the earliest interpretation of the world to him, As such they are the main sources of his identification. A child who sees himself as being like parents who are deviant or who sees himself as being dramatically different from parents who are normal is likely to experience and present problems in the wider society. More crucially, a child's conception of himself and his attitudes and expectations develop in response to how his parents see and value him. A child who is devalued by parents is unlikely to have much self-respect and finds it difficult, therefore, to respect and value others.

Assessment

Questions

Both parents and children should be asked to describe themselves and to say how much they believe they are like each other.

Are these statements and judgments very similar?
Does either parent claim that the child is particularly like him/her?
Does the child or anyone else say that he is like the parents?
Do the same questions apply with one or more of the siblings?
Do the parents' statements suggest that the child accepts the negative or deviant view they may have of him?
Does the child say that his attitudes and behaviour towards himself reflect parental attitudes to him?
Do the parents' and child's view of others, particularly society and authority, closely match?
Does either parent say of the other that he encourages the child to have the wrong attitude or to behave in a deviant fashion?
Does the child or anyone else say that he is encouraged to think or behave in a particular way towards others?

Observations

Does the child's behaviour appear to follow the pattern of his parents?
Do the parents seem to encourage the child in his deviant attitudes and behaviour by what they do to and/or with him?
Do any of the above considerations apply to the other siblings?
Is there any evidence that the child's view of himself reflects those of the parent or siblings to him?
Is there any evidence that parents and/or other siblings have encouraged him to hold a deviant view of himself such as a criminal, a sex offender, 'good for nothing'?

Tests Repertory Grid and Semantic Differential techniques, as well as a variety of projective measures such as the Children's Apperception Test can be used to test the closeness of deviant identification between the child and parents or siblings.

Action Guide Determine how powerful the deviant identification is and how serious its consequences are before engaging on the very difficult and time-consuming business of changing it. Otherwise, explore ways of reducing the family impact on the child.

---

18 Child's Attitude to Home

01 runs away
02 wanders away
03 steals from
04 stays out late
05 destructive/violent

The way a child is treated at home centrally affects the development of his personality and his reactions to the outside world. It also shapes his view of the home itself. In turn, this view determines how he perceives and reacts to influences exerted by the home. The home which is viewed positively is likely to be more effective in controlling the child's behaviour and guiding the direction of his social development. One that is viewed negatively is likely to be avoided, opposed, and eventually dismissed as a basis of the child's conscious development and self-determination.

Assessment

Questions

Does the child have a history of running away?
When did this commence and how episodic or recurrent has it been?
Did he just fail to come back home or did he run away?
Did he take food, money, clothes, etc. which suggested that he was going to go away?
Were these in response to any particular stresses at home?
Did he wander, how far, and for how long?
Has he stolen from home? If yes, how long? From everyone or just from one person or thing?
What happened when discovered and how did he react to the discovery?
How frequent is the staying out late?
Is this because parents are over-restrictive?
Does he say why? Are his reasons cogent?
Is he destructive or violent in the home? To whom/what and under what circumstances?
Are these precipitated by particular events or are they apparently random?
What does he do after the act?
What does the family do?
Is he at all like this outside the home?

Why do the family say he is like this?
What does he say?

Observations and Tests are not practicable or relevant in this area.

Action Guide If the problem is intolerable to parents, attempt to improve their tolerance. If the child is otherwise out of control and thereby at greater risk, find ways of curbing his behaviour either at home or elsewhere.

Selected Reading

Anthony, E. J. & Bene, E. 'A technique for objective assessment of child's family relationships', *J. Ment. Sci.*, 103: 541–555, 1957.

Depart. of Health & Social Security. Circulars on Non-Accidental Injury to Children, LASSL (74) 13, 76 (2).

Cooper, J. D. (Chairman). *The Family in Society; Dimensions of Parenthood*, London: HMSO; 1973.

Hoffman, L. W. & Lippit, R. 'The measurement of family life variables' in Mussen, P. H. (Ed), *Handbook of Research Methods in Child Development*, New York: John Wiley, 1960.

Howells, J. G. & Lickorish, J. R. *The Family Relations Indicator*, London: National Foundation for Education Research, 1962.

Kellmer Pringle, M. L. *The Needs of Children*, London: Hutchinson, 1975.

Kempe, R. S. & Kempe, C. H. *Child Abuse*, London: Fontana, Open Books, 1978.

Lickorish, J. R. 'The psychometric assessment of the family' in Howells, J. G. (Ed), *Theory and Practice of Family Psychiatry*, Edinburgh: Oliver and Boyd, 1968.

Priestley, P., McGuire, J., Flegg, D., Hemsley, V. and Welham, D. *Social Skills and Personal Problem Solving, A Handbook of methods*, London: Tavistock Publications, 1978.

Rutter, M. & Madge, N. *Cycles of Disadvantage*, London: Heinemann, 1976.

Wedge, P. & Prosser, H. *Born to Fail?*, London: Arrow Books, 1973.

9/Social Skills Problems

A CHILD HAS A PROBLEM when his dealings with other people, whether adults or children, are fraught, full of conflict or devoid of satisfaction, for him or others. Most of these difficulties can and still often are construed under the rubric 'relationships'.

Relationship, however, is a confused and confusing term invested with wide-ranging emotional overtones. It is so frequently used and in such diverse circumstances that it has become almost devoid of any clear meaning. For this reason it is avoided in a book which advocates the clear description of children's problems.

In any case, relationships are the end product of the exercise of certain social skills. Any attempt to improve the social interaction of the child with those around him must seek to put right those *individual* elements which may be responsible for the child's and others' dissatisfaction with his social functioning.

Of all the problem areas described in this book, problems of social skills are given the lowest priority both by referral and treatment agencies. This is partly because social skills problems are mainly manifested in small group settings when the members are, for a variety of reasons, close enough to be affected. Members of small groups do not complain about each other's social skills unless these are severely deficient and then manifested in obnoxious or destructive behaviour.

Social agencies are not particularly concerned with children's interpersonal problems unless these are associated with or thought to cause other problems such as absconding or fighting.

Social skills difficulties are also deeply culture-bound. On the whole, middle-class people appear to be more concerned with and prone to evaluating others in terms of their social skills than are other classes. Although 'airs and graces' are sometimes pejoratively regarded as 'bourgeois', manners and basic social skills appear to be necessary for peaceful and rewarding coexistence with almost any group of people, however disordered, regardless of class. We have, therefore, concentrated on those social skills deficiencies and peculiarities which create problems for the child and/or those around him in tolerant settings.

In the United Kingdom 'social skills' and 'social training' have become associated with 'social problem solving', such as experiencing normal sexual relations or successfully completing a job interview. But these situations encapsulate and put to the test many different social skills. For this reason, we have brought together such situations as apply to children and young people as 'specific situational problems'.

Characteristically, difficulties in this area arise from deficient or peculiar socialisation experiences. A child who has been brought up in a culturally alienated and disordered family is likely to acquire skills for survival within his family which may place him at odds with those from more 'normal' (in this sense meaning 'usual' rather than 'correct') families.

Other children may develop social skills problems because of basic personal abnormalities such as severe extraversion or withdrawal and yet others because they lack the necessary intellectual or linguistic competence to understand or learn from social interactions.

In the assessment of social skills, because of the probability of cultural biases, it is particularly important to be specific about the circumstances in which the child has a problem in order to draw general conclusions about his difficulties. Depending on the importance to be attached to the assessment and certainly before any treatment commences, it may be necessary to closely follow the format of questions set out in Chapter 5.

The assessment of social skills relies more on observations than any of the other problem areas. When the opportunity is not available the framework of observations can be translated into a series of questions which those close to the child – parents, teachers and other children – may answer.

The opinions of peers regarding a child's specific problem behaviours are particularly noteworthy and may be elucidated by the 'Guess Who' game. In this game descriptions of a child's behaviour – 'He always says hurting things', 'He never has a pencil' – are read out and the children asked to guess who is being described. Good and bad points are included to avoid a feeling of victimisation and the questions of interest to the assessor should be disguised by questions on other children. The ease with which a child is spotted by the description of the behaviour indicates the degree to which his difficulties impinge on and are noticed by other children.

The following paper and pencil measures are generally available and provide information on a child's social relationships:

Bristol Social Adjustment Guide:
Age Range 5–14 years
Rogers Personal Adjustment Guide:
Age Range 9–13 years
Mooney Problem Checklist:
Age Range Junior High School – Adult

---

01 Presentation

01 dirty, odorous
02 odd body movement or posture
03 odd facial features
04 odd speech rate/volume
05 poor eating habits

How a person looks and sounds is the first thing another notices about him. First impressions can bring into play many preconceived ideas and colour the whole of subsequent interactions. These may in turn give rise to further problems. It is, therefore, important to note the child's self-presentation skills and where they are deficient, seek to improve them.

Assessment

Questions
Do parents and others comment on his presentation?
Are there any suggestions or reports that others may have found him offputting?
Does the child notice anything odd about himself?
How does he appear to feel about it?

Observations
Do people shy away from him because of his smell, looks or manner?
Are there any oddities of posture, coordination, muscular control (including tics and twitches) or walking gait?
If so, do they restrict his physical activities only or games and other social activities as well?
Is there anything offputting about his facial features – usually open mouth, drooling or covered in sores?
Is his speech aggressive and querulous?

Are eating habits properly formed? Do other people object to his eating habits?
Does he take notice of any feedback given to him in these areas?

Action Guide Remove any physical problems if possible. Give intensive feedback to child regarding his impact on others. Teach manners.

---

02 Basic Interaction Difficulties

01 odd visual contact
02 misuse of facial expression
03 inappropriate use of gesture
04 stands too close/too far
05 touches people inappropriately

Eye contact, facial expression, gestures and bodily distance are all involved in even the most basic social contact. In the course of their growth and according to cultural patterns, children learn to adopt the appropriate use of these modalities. They become a form of implicit body language to which other people respond.

Their 'correct' use is necessary not only in order to make and maintain normal social contact, but also to convey accurately any emotional tone which may or may not be communicated verbally. If the verbal and bodily messages are incongruent or inappropriate, this may give rise to conflict with adults and lead to the labelling of child as 'peculiar', 'odd' and socially inept.

These interaction skills are so basic that any deficiency is usually indicative of either very poor social training or alternatively of other functional disorders.

Assessment

Questions
Are there any reports from school or other sources speaking of the child's oddness? Do they give instances?
Do the parents notice any difference between this child and others?
In what terms? Do they relate the 'oddness' to any particular factors?
Does the child show any awareness of how others regard him?
Do the parents and others comment on any of the above behaviours?

Observations
Does the child stare? Is the stare blank? Is it always there or does it vary with his mood and circumstances?
Does he look you in the eye when talking? Does he avert gaze whenever eye contact is made? Does the contact shift and flicker rapidly? Are his facial expressions appropriate to the mood and matter of the moment?

If relatively unvarying, what emotion does it indicate?
Is his facial expression marked by a habitual tic or grimace?
Does he use a lot of gestures? Are they appropriate to what he is talking about or are they pervasive and relatively unvarying?
Does he have a characteristic gait and body posture? Are these adopted for effect?
Does he stand so close or so far as to make others uncomfortable?
Does he touch people too often? Is the touch suggestive?
Of what? Does he maintain contact for long?
Is the child a 'fidget'? Does his fidgeting impair interaction or communication?
Does it follow a stereotyped pattern?

Action Guide Rule out possibility of visual defect. Attempt correction by giving child immediate feedback on the effects of what he is doing. Otherwise institute a relatively easy, longer term social training programme.

---

03 Conversation Skills

01 makes noises while others speak
02 interrupts
03 persistent, inane questioning
04 lies
05 constantly complains

Conversation is the chief medium of social interaction. Even in young children, speaking to each other is the chief form of gaining information and coordinating actions. It is, therefore, important that as well as learning the language which permits communication, children master the skill of conversing. The subjects a child talks about must interest others if they are to gain enjoyment in talking to him and he, in turn, is to gain social acceptance. A child whose conversation is boring or offensive will have difficulty in making friends.

Poor conversational skills result from many sources, but are usually associated with very poor and primitive levels of social training. Because of this and associated problems, they are likely to create the kind of social dissatisfaction and distance which pushes the child toward more unusual forms of achieving attention and satisfaction.

We have included lying in conversational problems because of its negative impact on the listener, like other behaviours in this group. Lying has, of course, many other aspects and is a major source of distress to those who have to deal with the child. Anti-social and moral aspects of lying are dealt with in the next two chapters.

Assessment

Questions

Do people complain that the child cannot hold a sensible conversation?
Does he complain that no one ever listens to him?
Does he either irritate others in the way he starts conversations or fails to gain attention when he appears to want it?
Do people seem to take an interest in talking to the child?
Have people said that the child is a nuisance in discussion groups or impossible to talk to?
Has he been referred to as 'stupid' or 'immature' on the basis of what he says rather than what he does?

Observations

Does the child start conversations by hanging round aimlessly until spoken to; grabbing people physically; shouting across the room; just barging in?
Does the child wander off while still being spoken to?
Does the child habitually make a noise or go on chattering while others are speaking?
Does he interrupt frequently?
Does he reply when people are talking to him? Does he seem to ignore what people are saying? Is there any suspicion of hearing loss?
Is the child verbose, take hours to reach his point, repeat himself, gabble away without giving others a chance to speak?
Is his speech monosyllabic or over-curt?
Are his comments usually related to what is being talked about?
Does he wander off the topic frequently?
Does he persistently ask inane questions?
Is his silliness amusing or irritating? Does he acknowledge that he is being silly or does he seem to be in a world of his own?
Does the child frequently tell lies? Are these small lies or fantastical tales? Is it done to the extent where no one believes a word he says? Does he insist they are true when challenged?
Is the child forever complaining or whining? What about? Is it justified?

Action Guide Use direct teaching and simulation methods to give him better conversational skills. In extreme cases, refer to a psychologist for an opinion as to the child's mental and emotional state and advice as to social skills training.

04 Social Discomfort

01 shy and uneasy
02 easily embarrassed
03 avoids social contact
04 shows anxiety in interaction
05 inept attempts to make friends

These difficulties suggest that the child's social relationships are not satisfactory or that he is uncomfortable in social settings. They include fears concerning social contact and complaints of dissatisfaction. These can, in themselves, further reduce social acceptability by making others feel ill at ease. Similarly, constant inept attempts to make friends may indicate that the child is lonely and socially unskilled and such failures may further promote unease and unhappiness in relationships.

Assessment

Questions

Do reports from school suggest social unease or other difficulties in this area?
What would the teachers say if questioned about this area?
Do the parents say anything about their child's difficulty in social settings?
Does the child himself complain?
Can he relate his difficulties to particular settings or types of company?
Does he say whether he has tried to do anything about it?
Does he spend most of his time alone?
Does he stay at home most of the time?
Does he seem anxious or worried in social situations?

Observations

Does the child seem shy?
Does he seem suspicious of other children's approaches?
Does he seem quiet?
In his approach to others is he tentative and ready to withdraw?
Does he seem to fear being in the limelight?
Is he easily flustered by people?
Does he appear muddled and confused about what to do in company?
Is this true of a particular type of company?
Does he try to work by himself when possible?
Does he ignore the fads or crazes of the group?
Is he reluctant to take part in group activities?
Does he rarely speak?
Does he avoid break or free time activities in school?
Does he join groups then leave quickly (Scouts, Youth Clubs)?
Does the child try to make friends but fail?

Does he try to make friends mostly with younger or less able children?
Does he try to buy friendships with gifts or promises?
Does he swamp newcomers with attention?
Does he pester other children?
Does he get over excited when friendship seems to be developing?
What do other children think of this?

Tests Of those generally available, the Social Inferiority Scale of the Rogers Personal Adjustment Guide, and the School or Residential edition of the Bristol Social Adjustment Guide give information about child's social discomfort. It may also be useful to peruse the Personal Problem section relating to Anxiety State (Chapter 11).

Action Guide Reduce distress by any obvious means. If the problem is acute refer for wider clinical assessment to a psychologist or psychiatrist prior to taking remedial action.

---

05 Unpopularity

01 ignored by others
02 disiked by others
03 bullied by others
04 scapegoated
05 taunted by others
06 has no friends
07 friendships shortlived

'Unpopularity' is the most general and pervasive indicator of a child's difficulty within a small social group. If his unpopularity is relatively widespread, it may indicate deficient social skills. But a child's unpopularity is a problem in its own right because it reduces the rewards he gains from his social interactions and may lead to social isolation and victimisation. As a result of constant rejections by others, a child may become hostile, unhappy and willing to do anything, including law-breaking, to gain acceptance and attention. Lack of satisfactory contact with other children may also impede the social maturation of a child by narrowing the range of his experiences.

Assessment

Questions
Does the child have difficulty in finding people to play with outside school?
Do other children call for him?
Are his siblings unwilling to go out with him because of others' reactions?
Is the child friendless?

Does he lay claim to friends who do not act like friends?
Do parents say the child is taunted or picked on?
Do parents and others say he is unpopular or friendless?
Does the child himself complain of isolation and unpopularity?
What reasons does he give?
Does he have difficulty in making and keeping friends?

Observations
Is he usually forgotten or the last to be chosen for teams, games, etc.?
Does he leave classes or school all by himself?
Does he approach others far more often than they approach him?
Do other people ignore him when he talks?
Does the child seem to be disliked by most other children?
Does the child seem to be disliked by most adults?
Do other children seem reluctant to work or play with him?
Do others seem to avoid him?
Do others complain about him?
Is the child bullied?
What form of bullying is used: verbal, physical or extortion?
Is the child subjected to excessive teasing?
Do other children play practical jokes on him that could really hurt?
Does he have a variety of derogatory nicknames?
How does the child react to the teasing?
Does the child ever appear tearful, bruised or unhappy on his return from a gathering of his age mates?

Tests Sociometry can be used to assess ignoring, dislike, and friendlessness. Each child in a group is asked to choose who they would most like to be with them for certain activities and who they would least like to have with them. The pattern of choices can be analysed to give information on the child's standing within that specific group.

Action Guide Reduce child's distress to tolerable levels. Further investigate any factors associated with his difficulty as a prelude to taking remedial action. Encourage others to take a more positive view of him.

---

06 Attitude to Children

01 unattached
02 manipulatory
03 domineering
04 antagonistic
05 submissive
06 overdependent

How a child gets on with other children will determine how happy or miserable he is going to be in the major part of his social life. Children's attitudes to their peers, like all other attitudes, are acquired in the course of their growth. They are shaped by the outcome of their cumulative experiences with others and the influence of significant models in their lives.

All children show elements of negative attitudes, depending on the circumstances. It would be inappropriate to regard these as problematic. However, when a child appears to adopt a primary mode of response to others and this mode of response is not altered to suit the circumstances and leads to conflict with other children or adults, it becomes maladaptive. Such modes of response, here called attitudes, are essentially behavioural and may or may not be associated with expressions of appropriate beliefs and feelings.

Assessment

Questions

Do school reports suggest that the child is unattached to any grouping?
Are there any other reports which speak of child's loyalty and attachment to others?
Do parents speak of their child's lack of attachments?
Does he try and get children to do things which profit him?
Do other children believe he makes use of them?
Is the child said to be 'bossy' or 'domineering'?
Have such words as 'antagonistic', 'provocative', or 'disruptive' been used about him? Are they based on any reported instances?
Do parents and others describe him as a 'follower', 'meek', 'gullible', 'easily led' or other such things?
Is there any evidence that he has previously done what others have suggested without much resistance or thought for the consequences?
How does he describe his own attitude to other children?
Is this much at variance with their descriptions of him?

Observations

Does the child tell tales or divulge 'secrets' about other children ('grassing') without much persuasion?
Does his movement among other children suggest the absence of any emotional ties?
Is he crafty in his dealings with other children? To his own benefit and their distress?
Does he set about organising others against their will?
Does he taunt or bully others into accepting his status? What are the consequences?
What does he do with those children who resist his attempts to dominate?
Do his dealings with the other children frequently end in conflict?
Do the other children complain of him as a tease or a bully?

Is his teasing cruel or beyond reasonable fun?
Is he involved in more squabbles than other children?
Do most children react to him in this way or only a touchy minority?
Is he the butt of other children's teasing?
Is he an early choice for anyone who wants a follower or a fall guy?
Do other children take advantage of him?
Is he easily taken in, dared to do silly things or tricked into doing others' work?
Does he complain of being mistreated?
Does he resist others' attempts to dominate him?

Tests Cattell's Children's Personality Questionnaire and High School Personality Questionnaire contain scales relating to submissiveness – dominance and group dependency – self-sufficiency. The 'Guess Who' game can be played with the whole group as a means of gaining confirmatory information from other children.

Action Guide Little can be done other than through long-term attitude change or social skills training to modify these basic response modes. Concentrate instead on reducing distress to child and others.

---

07 Attitude to Adults

01 untrusting
02 defiant
03 hostile
04 over familiar
05 over dependent

As the child grows older and goes to school he will come into increasing contact with adults other than his parents. The child's attitudes to adults, it is believed, are shaped by and are an extension of his attitude to his own parents or their surrogates. If the attitude is trusting, open and controlled, the child is likely to act in a similar manner to the adults he encounters outside his home. If not, the child will generalise to the adults whatever negative experiences he may have had with his own parents.

But adults are not just passive recipients of the child's attitudes. They also have specific response modes to children according to their own perceived roles and experiences. Their consequent response to children will, in turn, elicit reactions which are likely to be self-reinforcing and generating. Because adults are empowered to decree that certain of children's conditions are unacceptable, problem children's contact with and attitudes to adults is likely to be negative. This is particularly true of authority figures who are able to make powerful judgments about children with consequences that the latter do not like.

Because assessment agents are also adults, it is important to guard against the possibility of personal reactions and biases to a child, who, by virtue of his past experiences, may react to them in a manner they do not like.

Assessment

Questions

Have previous reports from schools and other authority figures suggested any difficulties of the above kinds?
If yes, do they specify difficulties with particular type of person?
Do parents speak of difficulties with a particular person?
How does the child express his attitude to adults?
Does he say he gets a rough deal from adults?
Have you ruled out the possibility that his response may be determined or distorted by the circumstances in which he finds himself?
What does he say about the reason for or experiences associated with his reactions?

Observations

Does the child look or behave warily towards adults?
Does he believe what you tell him or check it out with other children if the opportunity arises?
Does he keep out of adults' way? Does the length of his acquaintance with or the gender/position of the adult make any difference?
Does he come into frequent conflict with adults because he does not do what he is asked?
Does he openly question adult authority?
Does he challenge adults to carry out threatened sanctions?
Does he behave similarly to most adults regardless of age, position or ability to deal with him?
Are his challenges pursued to a showdown or does he retract? Under what conditions?
Does he do anything to 'get at' any adults?
Is this for an obvious reason? How generalised is this?
Are his actions public or covert?
Do the tone and content of his conversations with adults betray any hostility?
Does he use adults' first names even if they object?
Does he quiz them on their personal lives?
Are the jokes he exchanges risque? Does he banter and make supercilious comments?
Is he constantly asking adults for help?
Does he hang round them?
Is there any obvious sign of anxiety at their departure or delight at their return?

Tests The Bristol Social Adjustment Guide (residential) has scales relating to hostility, human unconcern and overdependence. Additionally, an adjective checklist consisting of a range of negative and positive adjectives may be used as a standard measure of children's view of adults. Such adjectives can also be used in the form of 'Semantic Differential' scales.

Action Guide Provide intensive feedback to the child regarding the unacceptability of his behaviour. If it is so serious as to get him into trouble, seek advice about setting up a programme of retraining.

---

08 Sensitivity

01 undersensitive to cues
02 misinterprets cues
03 ignores cues
04 does not alter behaviour to fit social environment

Sensitivity is used here to refer to the child's perception of the feelings, mood and reaction of others particularly as expressed by physical signals of facial expression, voice tone and gesture.

Some environments (such as courts, libraries, football crowds) have atmospheres either because of the mood of people in them or because of their function. These require certain responses. Some children fail to respond to these and, therefore, can make social gaffes.

In order to coordinate his actions to the feelings of the others in any situation a child must first notice the cues they give, such as facial expression, he must understand the meaning of such signals and then he must alter his behaviour to fit the situation. Problems of how a child reacts to others' feelings rather than how he perceives them are dealt with in the last chapter.

Assessment

Questions

Do parents and others speak of tactless or unfeeling behaviour?
Is there any suggestion that the child is not aware of the feelings of others?
Does he constantly behave in a way which is opposed to the mood of the group as a whole?
Does he describe people's reactions or feelings towards him in a way that suggests he has misunderstood what is happening?
Would you call him 'tactless' or 'thick skinned'?
Does he frequently behave in a way which is inappropriate to his environment?
What does he do?
How does he describe other people's reactions to him?

Observations
Is he good at judging other people or does he seem constantly surprised or indignant at their reactions to him?
Does he respond to frowns and other cues of annoyance or does he have to be ordered verbally to stop what he is doing?
Is there any particular mood to which he seems oblivious – tired, cheerful, irritable?
Does he ever apologise or show contrition when he has annoyed or hurt someone?
Does he ever comment on others' moods or feelings?
Does he respond to the atmosphere of different social environments, or is his behaviour constant?
Is the child aware of the need to behave differently according to others' moods or the place he is in?
Is he in these respects very different from other children in a normal setting? And those in your setting?

Tests Standardised tests of a child's sensitivity to the observable signals of others' feelings are not commercially available but procedures have been developed (e.g. Trower *et al*, 1978). These involve showing the child photographs of facial expressions and gestures conveying emotion and asking him either to name the emotion or choose which of given alternatives is being conveyed. Similarly, tape recordings can be used to test perception of voice cues. 'Undersensitivity' is indicated if a child persistently cannot label the materials correctly and 'ignores' if the child can say often how others feel but does not react appropriately in normal settings.

Action Guide As an immediate step provide the child with intensive feedback on how he makes others feel and what should be done in certain settings. In more serious cases, social skills training may be indicated. Refer to a psychologist for advice.

---

09 Sympathy

01 fails to help others
02 does not say nice things about others
03 does not show appreciation
04 does not show affection
05 unsupportive when others are troubled
06 shows no interest in others
07 does not share things
08 does not concede
09 does not cooperate

Sympathy or fellow-feeling is essential for social and biological survival of both the individual and the species. To help another human being in trouble, to provide support when someone is distressed, are qualities regarded as fundamentally human. This is so basic that anyone who is deficient in this area arouses deep anxieties and misgivings in his fellow human beings. Sympathy can be regarded as a collection of skills and personal qualities which include the correct reading and response to social cues, warmth and sensitivity.

Some of these qualities, such as warmth, appear to be inborn and related to wider aspects of personality. Others, such as sensitivity, appear to require not only certain cognitive and perceptual aptitudes but also a reasonably stimulating, caring and consistent social background. Children who are inadequately endowed with any of these may, as a result, show poor fellow-feeling.

The consequence of poor sympathy is that other people feel unwanted, superfluous, and 'object-like' in the company of the child. A further cause of concern is that children deficient in these skills, particularly those caught up in anti-social acts, are more likely to inflict serious hurt because they are incapable of gauging the effects of their behaviour on others' feelings.

Assessment

Questions

Do school and other reports suggest that the child is unfeeling toward or unconcerned with others?

Do parents say he was unaffected by distress in the family or that things did not seem to touch him?

Do adults use the adjectives 'selfish', 'uncaring', 'cold' or 'careless' when talking of the child?

Do other children refer to him as 'selfish' or 'greedy'?

Does the child possess a reasonable fund of information about people with whom he has daily contact?

Does he complain that people make him do more than his fair share of helping?

Does he complain unjustifiably that he always has to share or never gets his own way?

Does what he has to say about others suggest much depth of feeling?

Does he show any insight into what it might be like to be distressed?

Does he speak of others as if their feelings might guide his actions?

Observations

Does he help other people?

Does he complain or hinder when asked for help?

Does he ever remark kindly on others' appearance or achievement?

Does he notice or show pleasure at gifts of kindness?

Does he seem grateful for help when in difficulties?
Does he seem pleased to see people?
Does he muddle people's names or use stereotyped titles (Sir, Miss) even when he knows people well?
Does he show any conventional, physical sign of affection?
Does he smile at people or is his face always glum or blank?
Does he express positive feelings about anyone? What sorts and about whom?
Does he show any interest in people by watching them, talking and asking questions?
Does he keep sweets and possessions to himself?
Does he ever give something he values to others?
Does he take more than his fair share of food at meals or equipment in the classroom?
Does he do anything which shows he knows how others are feeling? Is the impression he gives that he doesn't know or does not care?
Does he insist on having his own way in spite of others' needs?
Does he simply conform to adult requirements without being 'touched' by them?
Does he cooperate with other children in work or play without bossing or quarrelling?
Does he apologise for hurting or offending others? Does he show any sign that he realises when he has done so?

Tests Restricted. The Bristol Social Adjustment Guide contains a Human Unconcern Scale.

Action Guide First, make sure others are not hurt by his acts. Attempt to give intensive feedback, in group setting, about his behaviour. In more serious cases undertake the necessarily long and difficult social skills training task.

---

10 Specific Situational Problems

01 being served in shops or cafés
02 speaking on a telephone
03 making dates with the opposite sex
04 talking to the opposite sex
05 visiting friends or being visited at home
06 interviews
07 skills for getting a job

These problems deal with specific types of situations. Some children seem to have difficulty in dealing with certain types of people or situations while getting on reasonably well in others. As can be seen from this list these problems do not usually arise until adolescence and this attribute usually applies only to older children although they encapsulate and put to the test many different social skills. Problematic behaviour can arise in specific situations for two main reasons: either the child has not learned the signals and/or rituals necessary to ensure smooth passage in these particular circumstances or they have notions about the situation which cause anxiety and discomfort.

The range of situations a child may have to cope with varies with cultural and socioeconomic factors. Therefore, the noted situations in which behaviour may be problematic is only intended as a guideline and assessors should compile lists appropriate to the children they are assessing. For instance, some adolescents may need to know how to behave in youth clubs while others need to know how to behave in a job setting.

Assessment

Questions Some guide to situations which cause a child particular difficulties can be gathered from asking about the situations in which a particular problem is most prominent (see Chapter 5). Otherwise adults and children should be asked simply whether any situation causes difficulty and the list of problems used as examples. The specific nature of the difficulties can then be further probed.

Older and more articulate children can then be asked what difficulties they find and why they are worried by the situation in question.

Observations Older children who acknowledge their own difficulties can be asked to keep a diary or log book of difficult situations or situations in which they did not feel comfortable. Situations causing the least difficulty can be compared to those causing most difficulty and examined to see if there is any obvious difference in circumstances or the child's behaviour.

Tests A scale devised for use with adults (Trower *et al,* 1978) may be helpful in suggesting problematic situations. The Mooney Problem Checklist also gives clues to specific situational problems.

Action Guide Determine what the specific social skills or other difficulties are in these situations and take appropriate measures as listed before.

Selected Reading

Argyle, M. *The Psychology of Interpersonal Behaviour*, London: Penguin Books, 1967.

Argyle, M. *Social Interaction*, London: Methuen, 1969.

Argyle, M. & Trower, P. *Person to Person*, London: Harper & Row, 1979.
Burland, J. R., Brown, T. W., Handham, R. P. *Steps to Self Sufficiency*, Barnstaple: Chelfham Mill School, 1977.
Cassell, R. N. *Test of Social Insight*, New York: M. Brace, 1976.
Cattell, R. B., & Beloff, H. *Handbook for the Jr – Sr High School Personality Questionnaire 'HSPQ'*, Illinois: IPAT (UK Distributors NFER), 1962.
Doll, E. A. *Vineland Social Maturity Scale*, Minnesota: American Guidance Service, 1965.
Eisler, R. M. 'The Behavioural Assessment of Social Skills', in Hersen, N. & Bellack, A. (Eds), *Behavioural Assessment, A Practical Handbook*, Oxford: Pergamon Press, 1976.
Evans, K. M. *Sociometry and Education*, London: Routledge and Kegan Paul, 1962.
Fensterheim, H. & Baer, J. *Don't Say Yes When You Want To Say No*, New York: David McKay & Co, 1975.
Goldstein, A. P., Sprafkin, R. P. & Gershaw, N. J. *Skill Training for Community Living: Applying Structured Learning Therapy*, Oxford: Pergamon Press with Structured Learning Associates, 1976.
Gronlund, N. E. *Sociometry in the Classroom*, New York: Harper, 1959.
Jesness, C. F. *The Jesness Inventory*, California: Consulting Press, 1966.
Liberman, R. P., King, L. W., DeRisi, W., & McCann, M. *Personal Effectiveness: Guiding People to Assert Themselves and Improve Their Social Skills*, Illinois: Research Press, 1975.
Mooney, R. L. & Gordon, L. V. *The Mooney Problem Checklists*, New York: The Psychological Corporation (UK Distributors, NFER), 1950.
Porter, R. B. & Cattell, R. B. *Manual for the Children's Personality Questionnaire* (CPQ) Illinois: IPAT, 1968.
Rogers, C. R. *The Personal Adjustment Inventory*, New York: Association Press (UK Distributors, NFER), 1961.
Stott, D. H. *The Social Adjustment of Children: The Manual of the Bristol Social Adjustment Guide*, 5th ed., London: Hodder and Stoughton Educational, 1974.
Stott, D. H. & Sykes, E. G. *Bristol Social Adjustment Guide: The Child in Residential Care; Bristol Social Adjustment Guide: The Child in School*, London: Hodder and Stoughton Educational, 1970.
Trower, P., Bryant, B., & Argyle, M. *Social Skills and Mental Health*, London: Methuen and Co., 1978.

10/Anti-social Behaviour

OF ALL THE PROBLEM AREAS tackled in this book, the present one arouses the deepest concern. This is because anti-social and disruptive acts are public and visible and affect a wide range of people. Anti-social acts are endemic and form the basis of extensive legislation and legitimise much official intervention in children's lives. This is because of the risk such acts are thought to present to the social fabric.

Whereas most other problems encountered in this book result in personal difficulty and private sorrow, anti-social acts directly threaten the safety of other people and their property, as well as some of the most cherished notions of what makes for an orderly, civilised society. Indeed, a child's other problems frequently come to light when he is identified as an offender. This is particularly so in the case of working-class children who constitute the majority of young offenders and who are referred for assessment.

Although the criminal justice system is primarily concerned with offences against person and property, these are not the only forms of anti-social behaviour or, in the long run, necessarily the most serious. Others include victimless offences such as drug taking and soliciting. Yet other socially disruptive and proscribed behaviours include truancy, absconding, temper tantrums, uncommon sexual interests and general aggression, which may not fall into the category of offences at all.

Also included in this area are self-destructive or 'parasuicidal' acts which, at their extreme, result in suicide. At first sight, it may seem peculiar that self-injury should be included in the category of anti-social behaviour. After all, suicidal acts are thought to be the result of such intense private sorrow or distress that self-destruction may be the only way out of an unbearable life. But extensive research and wide experience has shown that 'attempted suicide', particularly prevalent among young people, is qualitatively different from genuine suicidal acts. Although attempted suicides may result in death, they are more often thought of as socially disruptive, maladaptive, manipulatory acts which are intended to make their major impact not on the attempter but on his social surroundings. This is often evident among the more disturbed and disordered children who are referred for assessment. A genuine, persistent wish to die is usually associated with other conditions such as depression, which are dealt with under other headings.

The common characteristic of the wide gamut of behaviours covered in this area is that they make their major impact on the wider social setting. This warrants society's intervention, referral of the child for assessment, and frequently the eventual restriction of his liberty or other forms of sanction. Much of the evidence regarding past disruption and anti-social behaviour is gained through normal social enquiry methods of reading the available documentation and asking appropriate questions from such agencies as the police, probation, social services and others.

Although this is often undertaken as part of a routine, the significance of past evidence lies in its potential for helping to determine how far a child is likely to commit *further* anti-social acts. This is a particularly relevant area in which to illustrate a point made in the first part of this book. It is generally believed that as a child's history of past anti-social and disruptive behaviour increases in seriousness, he is more likely to continue untrammelled in the future and may, therefore, warrant special measures to reduce risk both to him and to the community.

In very general terms, research evidence has tended to emphasise that (1) anti-social behaviour is a normal, socialised response of disadvantaged, working-class youth during a particular phase of their development, or (2) some youngsters possess certain genetic, intellectual and personality characteristics which make them vulnerable to particular forms of social stress. Depending on one's political and empirical point of view, either explanation can be adopted. There are few indicators which point unambiguously one way or the other. For this reason, there is an increasing tendency to adopt a perspective which accounts for anti-social acts in terms of the interaction of a person with a specific set of environmental factors.

Because both social disadvantage and personal vulnerability tend to persist, the longer the history of anti-social acts, the more likely it is that the child will continue to present or to be at risk in the future. Assessment is, therefore, aimed at discovering the extent and intensity of both social disadvantage and personal vulnerability as an aid to predicting further risk potential.

In assessment, social enquiry reports, complemented by interview material and observations, provide much of the necessary information. The state of testing in the assessment of anti-social potential for research purposes is highly developed though of questionable practical utility in the majority of settings in which assessment is likely to be carried out. Further, the best tests are restricted for use by psychologists and psychiatrists and may, therefore, not be readily available. Where appropriate, such tests are mentioned.

---

01 Disruptiveness

01 stirs up trouble; disturbs others
02 allegations
03 temper tantrums
04 runs around
05 makes odd/inappropriate noises

In the previous chapter, comment was made on the skills required for adequate social functioning. Either because a child is inadequately skilled in this area or because he particularly wishes to upset a group, he may engage in a variety of disruptive acts. In group settings, children can be seen to fall on a continuum from the meek, submissive and compliant, to the dominant, assertive and disruptive. This quality assumes major importance for anyone who has to deal with children in groups because it raises problems of management which, unless tackled, can lead to the fragmentation and considerable discomfort for the individual and the rest of the group. Disruptive acts can be analysed as *instrumental*, a means of achieving another end, or *expressive*, undertaken for their own sake. A child may switch from one to the other depending on the circumstances. Although it may not be sensible to speak of a general quality of disruptiveness in children, a child who engages in such acts under one set of circumstances is more likely to do so in another than a child who is not disruptive. The degree to which this is a general characteristic of the child rather than his response to a particular unacceptable set of circumstances can be determined by removing him from one setting, such as a general class group to a 'sanctuary' unit, or from an open setting to a more structured one.

Assessment

Questions

Does the child have a history of troublesome behaviour at home?

Is there a history of conflict with siblings?
Do the parents say that he has caused trouble between them and/or between the family and others?
Is there a history of troublesome behaviour, particularly with other children at school or in other group settings?
Does the child say that he frequently gets into trouble with his peers?
Do the other children regard him as troublesome?
Do the staff and adults who come across him consider him ready to stir up trouble?
Is he said to make allegations and tell tales from one party to another?
Do these serve a particular purpose or are they for their own sake?
Are other people, both children and adults, disturbed by his presence?
Do either parents, members of the family or others, say that he has thrown temper tantrums?
Are these tantrums thought to be for particular ends or just general reactions to frustration?
Do these tantrums date from early childhood or relate to a particular period of the child's life?
Are these temper tantrums said to have occurred in any particular setting, such as home or school, or generally?
Were the tantrums brought to an end by any particular outcome or method?

Observations

Does the child verbally or physically aggravate others?
What particular ploys does he use to get others irritated?
Are these acts generally successful?
Does he pick particular types of children and adults with whom to make trouble or from whom to seek attention?
Can you identify any particular aspects in the situation, such as other people, setting and the child's state, which are associated with such acts?
Does the child behave in a fidgety, over-active, unsettled manner?
Does he upset other people's activities? Do you believe this is deliberate?
What happens when his victims react angrily?
Does he seem to learn from this and reduce his acts, remain unaffected, or increase them?
Does he run around, make odd noises and inappropriate gestures?
Does he make allegations? Against whom? Are these ploys obvious or subtle?
Does he goad others into retaliating?
Does he throw temper tantrums?
Are there any particular factors such as time, place, people or activity associated with such tantrums?
What consequences do his tantrums produce?

Action Guide Attempt to train others to tolerate or ignore his disruptive behaviour; teach him other ways of coping; or change his environment.

---

02 Truancy

01 does not attend school – occasional

02 does not attend school – persistent

03 school refusal

Both normal demands of socialisation and the law require that a child should be educated. The State spends a vast proportion of its resources on setting up an educational system to educate children and realise their academic potential. If a child does not participate in educational activities he is likely to be handicapped in the achievement of his potential. Also, research confirms that a strong association between truancy and offending exists. Over and above the acquisition of scholastic skills, attending school is thought to bring children under the beneficial influence of their educators and provide opportunities for appropriate social modelling.

Therefore, children who stay away from school are regarded as a cause for concern and become subject to early intervention by Education Welfare Officers, school psychological services and Child Guidance Clinics. This is in part to determine whether there are any special and adverse reasons driving the child away from school, such as bullying, inappropriate pressure towards scholastic attainment or whether there are factors in the environment, such as parental dependence for company or shopping, or the excitement of peer group escapades, that pull the child away.

This range of reasons is explored in appropriate chapters such as those relating to cognitive functioning, family, social skills and personal problems. In this chapter, only the problem of non school-attendance, its extent and intensity rather than its causation, is mentioned. The reason for non-attendance may range from persistent sickness through staying home to look after mother, school phobia to staying out to go fishing with mates.

Assessment

The most appropriate form of establishing the extent and intensity of truancy is through examining school records and questioning school staff. The school questionnaire presented in Chapter 3 suffices to answer most of the relevant questions in this area. Additionally, it may be worthwhile to discover whether and under what circumstances changes in the pattern of child's truancy have occurred.

Action Guide Try to improve attendance at the same school, at another, or, if not, evaluate costs and benefits of educating the child in a specialised setting.

---

03 Absconding

01 runs away from adults
02 plans and executes attacks on property to escape
03 hangs around doors and attempts to squeeze out
04 encourages others to abscond
05 runs away from home and other placements

Absconding only arises as a result of a child being placed in a setting which he does not, however momentarily, like to be in. It involves either running *away* from something, running *to* another, or the continuation of a habit as an end in itself, or as a means to something else. These forms of absconding are associated with different circumstances and almost invariably result from an interaction of the state of the child at a particular time with his perception of the environment.

Absconding applies strictly to children who are removed from their natural homes because they have presumably presented or experienced one or another of the problems in this book. As such, these children are already either subject to or a source of risk. Because of this and the fact that absconding puts them beyond the reach of the agents of control, absconding arouses deep anxieties in those responsible for the management of children's residential facilities. For this reason, absconding has always been prominent as a major source of disruption and received a good deal of attention. It is also known to be strongly associated with the commission of anti-social acts both as a means of keeping alive while on the run and as part of a wider pattern of deviant behaviour. For the sake of convenience, running away from home and associated places is included under this heading, although such running away cannot be called absconding.

Assessment

Questions

Is there a history of running away from home and other similar places?
Have there been abscondings from previous residential placements?
Has he run away from staff in open settings?
Is there a history of damage to property or attacks on other people in the furtherance of absconding?
Has the absconding taken place solo or with others?
Have there been any particular factors associated with these abscondings, such as personal upset or unhappiness?

Are the abscondings thought to have been planned or impulsive?
Are they thought to have been running away from something or running to something else?
What have been the past official and other reactions to absconding?

Observations
Does he talk about absconding?
Does he give the impression that he is 'casing the joint' in an attempt to abscond?
Are the attempts overt and easily detectable or subtle?
Does he appear preoccupied with the thought of and activities associated with absconding?
Are these easily discernible?
Are there any particular factors associated with the rise and fall of this preoccupation?
If put in a situation where he appears to be unsupervised will he attempt to abscond?
Does he encourage others to abscond?

Action Guide Determine whether the child actually should be where he absconds from. Having done so, evaluate whether you should tolerate the absconding; make it unproductive for him to run away and more rewarding to stay; tighten up his environment so he cannot run away.

---

04 Self-Destructiveness

01 takes overdoses or poisons
02 self-inflicted wounds
03 attempts to obtain offensive materials
04 tattoos
05 serious suicide attempts

The sanctity and continuity of life is the fulcrum around which all other social interests revolve. A person who puts his own or others' life in danger arouses the most intense reactions. All acts of aggression against oneself are regarded with pity and horror because such an act, particularly in a child, negates our most basic beliefs not only in the sanctity of life but also in the instinct of self-preservation. Such acts arouse deep guilt feelings in those surrounding the child because they question whether they could or should have done something (more) to make life less intolerable. These acts are frequently associated with serious forms of social disorder and personal disturbance which warrant decisive intervention.

There is some evidence that although actual suicide is decreasing, attempted or 'parasuicides' are on a dramatic increase. Over and above placing a young life at risk, however by default, self-destructive acts are regarded as particularly deviant modes of attention-seeking and gaining ends which may not be obtainable by other means. They cause severe disruption in any social setting whether the family, the school or a residential facility.

Under this rubric are included all acts such as tattoos, which involve the infliction of physical hurt on the self. In the extreme reaches it is not very easy to distinguish genuine self-destructive acts from persistent attention seeking attempts. In any case, it is not prudent to be very confident that a person is a parasuicide rather genuinely intending to kill himself. Serious professional intervention is therefore warranted.

Assessment

Questions

Is there a history of the child having talked about taking his own life?
Has he ever attempted or succeeded in taking overdoses or poisons?
Are these thought to have been impulsive or premeditated?
Has he attempted to obtain offensive weapons or poisons for which there are no adequate alternative explanations?
Has he been involved in other self-destructive acts such as running in front of a bus, jumping from a high point, or self-strangulation?
Has he received hospital or other specialist treatment for these acts?
Are these acts thought to have been reactions to a particular set of circumstances or not?
What was the outcome of the previous acts?
Did the child receive much positive attention or other desired ends?
Is the setting in which the child attempts such an act so intolerable as to justify it?

Observations

If the child does not have a history of self-destructive behaviour, does he do anything that makes you concerned? What?
Does the child threaten that he will kill himself?
Does he do so only under particular circumstances or as a ready response whenever frustrated?
Does the child do so in adult hearing or does this come to adult ears via other children?
Are there any other indications such as notes, diaries or gestures which indicate possible self-destructive intentions?
Are these acts and gestures made with bravado or quietly?
Is the child on the lookout for potentially dangerous instruments?
Is the child ready to use such instruments or turn others into weapons for this purpose?

Is this done quietly when the child cannot be observed or publicly and when he is readily discoverable?
Does the child appear to be impervious to painful physical stimulation?
Is the child so despondent and unhappy that you think he may seek to injure himself?
Does he open wounds or scars?
Does he pick scabs or other parts of body so as to produce damage?

Tests Tests for the measurement of depression, anxiety, personal instability, introversion and other factors variably associated with self-destructive acts may be worthwhile in isolating those personality attributes which are likely to contribute to the repetition of further acts.

Action Guide Determine whether you would do any or all of the following: refer for medical/psychiatric assessment to rule out serious mental or emotional disorder and possible treatment; teach the child other ways of getting attention; change his circumstances to reduce experience of intolerable stress; increase vigilance and structure to reduce potential; ask a psychologist to devise an appropriate treatment programme.

---

05 Verbal Aggression

01 criticises	04 swears
02 antagonises	05 gestures/snarls
03 threatens	06 screams abuse

Aggression is a generic term indicative of the use of force, verbal or physical, which is used either to ventilate frustration or to inflict deliberate hurt. In social encounters, verbal aggression not only indicates the mood but also the intent of the aggressor and as such provokes retaliatory action. It arouses anxiety, defensiveness and hostility and is, therefore, liable to provoke similar behaviour from the victim.

The significance of verbal aggression lies in its potential for antagonising others and spiralling into further conflict. It is not necessarily associated with physical aggression though those who are ready to be verbally aggressive also appear to be more ready to use physical force.

Assessment

Questions
Is the child regarded by parents and siblings as verbally aggressive?
Is he said to swear, verbally antagonise others, needle, threaten, snarl, or make aggressive gestures or use abusive language?
Is he said to be so only with one or more members of the family?

Do they regard him as generally like this or only under particular circumstances?
Is the same thing said of him at school and by other people who know him?
Has he been cautioned, or disciplined by his teachers and others, for use of abusive language?
Do his peers regard him as verbally aggressive?

Observations
Does he antagonise, threaten, swear and engage in other such verbal behaviours that you would regard him as aggressive?
Compared with the population you deal with would you regard him as verbally aggressive?
Does he frequently get into conflict with his peers and adults because of his bad language?
Does he use such language habitually or only when he is aroused to anger?
Is it easy to bring such language under control?
Does he use aggressive language habitually or as a means to an (obvious) end?
Do you believe him to have the ability to control his language if he wants to?
Is this the sort of behaviour which is likely to antagonise others so that they might retaliate?

Action Guide Encourage others to tolerate or ignore his bad language; if serious, punish verbal aggression and reward socially acceptable discourse.

---

06 Physical Aggression

01 nips
02 hits/punches
03 kicks
04 spits
05 bites
06 throws objects as missiles
07 physically assaults
08 head butts
09 bullies
10 violent to animals
11 injures others deliberately

Sanctity of the person is the crux of social order in Western societies. Any threat directed against others arouses strong feelings of anxiety and hostility. Because of this, it is the single most critical form of social behaviour.

In any grouping of children and indeed in the course of a child's growth, aggressive acts are normal and occur from time to time as one means of establishing a network of group relationships and social hierarchy. Whether this is done in play or in earnest depends on many circumstances. Such 'normal' aggression, which is indeed essential for normal social development, is accepted until the child grows away from the need to exercise it. There is, additionally, a latitude of social tolerance which can accommodate a good deal of episodic aggression. This human characteristic, like many others, ranges from the minimal and negligible to the persistent and gravely serious. When aggression becomes either habitual or serious, it becomes the subject of severe social intervention aimed at curbing its escalation into grave acts of violence.

Even more than verbal aggression and other forms of anti-social behaviour, physical aggression appears to be a response to personal anxiety, frustration and anger. It acts as a safety valve which releases tension and allows a person to regain some equilibrium. It is also frequently used instrumentally as a means of escape, gaining dominance in a peer group, or in the furtherance of other acts, such as extortion. To a lesser extent, it is sometimes employed as the basis of personal identity or 'machismo'.

Western societies are currently experiencing a dramatic surge in offences of violence. Although statistics on this issue are hard to interpret, it appears nevertheless that the public's awareness of physical violence is vastly increased and reflected in portrayal of this problem by the media. The evaluation of aggressive potential of a child is, therefore, likely to become a matter of increasing concern to politicians, the judiciary, social agencies and the people who have to handle aggressive children.

Assessment

Questions

Does the child have a history of what his parents and siblings would describe as 'aggressive' behaviour?

What particular form have such aggressive acts taken: nipping, biting, spitting, kicking, hitting, punching, throwing objects, head butting or injury to animals?

How young was the child when he first started manifesting such behaviour?

Has the behaviour continued unabated or has it only been manifested periodically?

If periodic, are these said to have been associated with particular events or phases in the child's life?

If continuing, has the problem become better, worse or remained the same?

Has this behaviour been manifested at school, in the playground and similar settings with other children?

Are the same things said of it as they were at home?
Is the aggression said to have been directed mainly at other children or adults? Was there any sex preferences?
Is there any evidence that it was triggered off by particular acts or situations?
Is the child said to have engaged in such behaviour for its own sake or in order to gain a particular outcome?
Is he said to have been sorry and to have tried to make amends, to have been unaffected or to have derived positive enjoyment from his acts?
Is he said to have been deterred for any period or from tackling a particular type of person by the effects of any retaliation?
Does the child describe himself as aggressive?
Whether 'yes' or 'no', what are his reasons and bases for comparison?
What feelings does he express regarding his acts?
Is there any warmth, contrition or guilt?
What does he say about personal and social consequences of being aggressive?
Has he ever been severely beaten? By whom? What are his recollections and feelings about it?

Observations
Does the child engage in any of the aforementioned behaviours and others like them?
Would you regard him as particularly aggressive compared with the other children?
Would you regard his aggressiveness as a general response characteristic or only something he shows when provoked or in a tight spot?
Can you identify any particular circumstances in which he is aggressive?
Is there any discrimination in terms of whom he is aggressive to, how and under what circumstances?
Does he use aggression as a way of gaining particular social or material ends?
How is he affected by the outcome of his aggressive acts?
Does he seem exhausted and sad after an aggressive act, indifferent or flushed and excited?
Does he hurt others or are his aggressive acts superficial assertions and acts of bravado?
How well does he appreciate that he is hurting his victim?
Does the child do anything which makes you believe he is capable of grave violence to other people? If so, what is your reason?

Tests There are numerous tests, either specifically concerned with hostility, aggressive potential or other items related to aggression. The Rosenzweig Picture Frustration Study, Caine & Foulds Hostility and

Direction of Hostility Questionnaire, the Jesness Inventory, the P Scale of the EPI, can all be used to throw some light on aspects of aggressive behaviour. However, because of the grave risks to society of underestimating aggressive potential and risk to the aggressor of overestimating it, it is particularly important not to place any great reliance on test results by themselves as a basis for describing the aggressive potential of youngsters. These tests are of primary value in throwing further light on the results of questioning and observing. They may help to determine whether aggression has a central place in the child's adaptation to the normal variations of social experience and is supported by relevant attitudes and personality characteristics.

Action Guide If the aggression is a response to specific situational stress, change the situation by either varying the characteristics or the child's responsiveness to it. It may be worthwhile to refer the child for more specific assessment of his aggressive potential. If the reaction is thought to be general and serious, you should protect the public by creating conditions where he is not provoked and his response patterns can be altered.

---

07 Uncommon Sexual Interests

01 transvestism
02 fetishism
03 exhibitionism
04 homosexuality

Sexual standards are in a continuous state of transition and change. There are also dramatically divergent sexual mores and practices both between and within cultures. Society's tolerance of sexual behaviour and standards is very wide and only determinable by enquiry in a particular social setting.

However, there is widespread anxiety about the sexual behaviour of children among all social classes, particularly when these are exemplified by uncommon sexual interests. Heterosexual behaviour is what is common, usual and, therefore, 'normal'. Almost anything outside this is regarded as uncommon. Children on the whole do not manifest many unusual sexual interests. When they do, it is not easy to determine whether the matter is serious and warrants intervention or whether it is part of the passing ferment of puberty and adolescence from which the child will grow away. In this sense, most of children's sexual problems are, in reality, problems of adult discomfort and anxiety, which have their own explanations. Of the numerous forms of uncommon sexual behaviour only a small number are included here.

Assessment

Questions

Do the parents complain of or comment on any unusual sexual behaviour or interests?

What form is this interest said to take?

When did such behaviour first become apparent?

Did the child show this interest openly or did he hide it?

Are/were there any other members of the family or immediate acquaintances of the child known to have engaged in such behaviour? Did the parents regard this matter with serious concern or only as mildly unusual?

Do teachers and others recollect or express concern about the child's wearing of clothes belonging to the opposite sex, particular sexual response to specific articles, exposure and flashing, or abnormal interest in members of the same sex?

Were these manifestations readily discernible or only discovered by accident?

Observations

Does the child express preference for dressing in clothes of the opposite sex?

Is this over and above what would be regarded as normal 'unisex' style of clothing? Has this preference existed over a period?

Does he seem to derive particular (sexual) pleasure from handling and touching an object or a particular item of clothing?

If given the opportunity will he steal or secrete away an item of clothing belonging to the opposite sex? How do you know?

Does the child ever expose himself?

Is this under special circumstances or indiscriminate?

Is it subtle and stealthy or fairly open?

How much do you believe your particular strictures and styles of management inhibit or facilitate such behaviour?

Is the child called a 'poof' or similar names by his age mates?

Is this because of certain characteristics—soft voice, manner and style of walking—or because of more suggestive acts?

Can he be observed to seek proximity to or handhold, touch and engage in more overt sexual acts with a member of his own sex?

Action Guide Determine whether in the context of the child's other problems, this is sufficiently serious to warrant intervention. If yes, then the risk can only be reduced by specialised treatment which may require removal of the child from his normal setting.

08 Sexual Misbehaviour

01 attempts to masturbate others without consent
02 attempts to persuade others to engage in sexual activity
03 talks a lot about it
04 over-indulgence in sexual contact
05 no control of sexual urges
06 soliciting

Increasingly in the course of the present century, it has been recognised that sex play and sexual exploration are part of normal development of children and adolescents. Extensive research shows that many 'normal' youngsters engage in a variety of sexual behaviours which, although still frowned upon by adults and viewed with concern, must be regarded as the base against which any evaluation of sexual *misbehaviour* should be made. Many children are still referred for assessment by a variety of agencies because parents and other people are worried about their sexual behaviour.

Even within this population the problems of sexual misbehaviour are widely varied. These range from the tendency of the child to talk a lot about sex through collecting pornographic and sex related materials to engaging in public sexual behaviour which is, nevertheless, not a breach of the law. It is such behaviours, defying, as they do, adults' and often other children's sexual strictures, that raise the possibility that the child may be in danger either of putting others at risk or being himself put at risk from 'moral danger'.

'Moral danger' is a euphemism for various sexual acts, such as soliciting, which either because of the age of the child or the surrounding circumstances, are regarded as harmful but are not dealt with as offences. Nevertheless, given the present state of society, they are regarded with alarm and attempts are made to curb them. If the child has sexual problems this is usually gleaned from referral information and background history. It is critical in this area to ensure that the personal morality of the assessment agent does not become the standard by which he judges the child's problems or the problems he presents to others. Even more than some other areas in the totality of a child's problems, this attribute should be based on evidence.

Assessment

Questions

Has the child ever been referred for sexual problems?
If yes, have they occurred at home and/or in other settings?
What form is it said to have taken?
Have the parents complained of or shown concern about such behaviour?
Is he said to talk a lot about sex?

Has he collected pornographic material or other sex related objects?
Is this behaviour abnormal for the family or his cultural setting?
Has he been known to have publicly masturbated?
Has he attempted to masturbate others without their consent?
Is there a history of soliciting or engaging in sexual activities?
For money, goods or other reasons?
Is this unusual in the child's family or cultural setting?

Observations
Does the child talk a lot about sex?
Is the talk exaggerated, including fantastic stories of exploits, or is it about the present reality?
Is the talk suggestive of what he wishes to do or be done to?
Is it accompanied by gestures and illustrative acts?
Does he engage in subtly or overtly suggestive acts?
Is this directed at others without their consent?
Is this behaviour triggered off and maintained by any obvious aspect of his surroundings, including other people?
Does his behaviour embarrass, anger or amuse others?
What is his reaction?
Does he expose himself or masturbate publicly?
Does he flaunt his sexuality? Mainly to adults or other children?
Is this more than can be regarded as a 'normal' search for sexual identity?
Does he use his sex as a bargaining or bartering counter?
Do you believe these behaviours to be deliberate or beyond the child's control? What is your evidence for either conclusion?

Action Guide Determine whether misbehaviour is so serious and intolerable as to warrant intervention. If yes, the child may need to be placed in a controlled environment where his opportunities are curtailed and where, if appropriate, he may be treated.

---

09 Sexual Offences

01 indecent exposure
02 sexual assault on a younger person
03 sexual assault on others of the same sex
04 sexual assault on others of the opposite sex
05 sexual assault on an older person
06 rape

Sexual offences are relatively uncommon even among persistent and disordered young offenders. They fall at the more serious end of offences against the person and, according to the circumstances, tend to be treated as a matter of grave concern by social services, the police and judiciary. However, what constitutes a sexual offence is much more ambiguous than might appear. These range from sexual exploratory behaviour and fondling between an older and younger child to sexual assault involving force and urgency at the other extreme. As with other offences, the task is mainly one of using the child's history and present characteristics as a means of evaluating his propensity for committing further offences. Inevitably notions of risk to the public are implicated. For this reason and because of the severe stigmatising effect it would have on the child's future, it is important to look particularly cool-headedly at the circumstances in which the offence took place, the degree of deliberateness of the act, the extent and severity of the offence, and the child's subsequent response.

Assessment

Questions

Has the child committed any sexual offences?
Has there been only one episode or have there been others even if not legally processed?
Are they of recent origin or spread over a period?
Have they become worse?
Has the offence been committed against a particular category of victim, or does it appear to have been relatively indiscriminate?
Was the offence committed solo or jointly?
Was the offence planned or apparently committed on impulse?
Are there any particular circumstances that could account for it?
Was the offence associated with another act or an end in itself?
Was it committed in a relatively public place or a secluded area?
How is the child said to have reacted during and after the commission of the offence?
Is the act regarded as totally unexpected and out of character or something that might have been expected?
Is there any history of such offences in the family?
How did those in the child's immediate environment react to his behaviour when it became known?
If the offence has been repeated, whether more or less serious, are the circumstances surrounding the new offence the same or different from the previous one?
What are the child's comments and feelings about the offence?
Does he show any appreciation of or insight in the seriousness of his behaviour?
What does he say about his victim's feelings?
What does he say about sex offences generally?

Are there any signs of guilt or contrition? Are these more than 'crocodile tears'? What is your evidence for the answer?
How does he evaluate the chances of a repetition of the offence?
How does he react to the probable consequences?

Observations
Does the child force or draw attention to his own sexuality?
Does he force sexual contact on others of opposite or same sex?
Do children or adults of the opposite sex feel uncomfortable or threatened in his presence? Do they try to avoid him?
Is his behaviour manifested only under specific circumstances or fairly generally?
Is it particularly affected by its outcome or reactions of others?
Does he engage in a lot of sex talk?
Does he brag about his sexual activities?
Do you feel he is capable of committing a serious sexual offence?
If yes, what is your evidence?

Action Guide If the offence is serious and an examination of circumstances suggests that the child is likely to commit it again, he will need to be placed in a setting where his opportunities are curbed and where he may be able to mature and, if possible, receive treatment.

---

10 Property Offences
01 aiding and abetting
02 theft
03 motor theft
04 burglary
05 robbery
06 robbery with violence
07 destroys property
08 damages property

Next to offences against the person, property offences attract the most hostile public reaction. The 'territorial imperative' of which possession of property is a major part is regarded as almost a biological principle necessary for the survival of species and any acts against it are treated harshly. This is particularly so in Western societies where property ownership is closely tied with power and social standing. There is some acceptance of mild, petty thieving, particularly by children. This is because children are regarded as morally ignorant until they reach a particular age. In any case, the courts could not deal with all thefts, even if the police managed to apprehend all the thieves. But persistent and serious property offending is a different matter.

Delinquency primarily concerns group participation of boys in acts of theft. As such it is an international phenomenon and something most children grow out of as they move towards adulthood. However, there are wide variations in the rate and quality of property offences not only between countries but also among different social classes and different areas of the same country. Persistent thieving occurs mainly as a means of obtaining goods which are not otherwise available to the relatively impoverished working class youth and it is they who are seen as an intolerable threat and a nuisance by the rest of society and dealt with accordingly. There is extensive legislation and a complex structure of judiciary and quasi-judiciary response to this form of behaviour.

Young people under 18 are now thought to account for roughly two-thirds of all recorded offences and a considerably higher proportion of acts of petty theft. This is also the most frequently invoked reason for taking youngsters into care under Sections 2 or 7 of the 1969 Children and Young Persons Act. It is, therefore, a matter of concern to magistrates, social workers, probation officers and others to assess not only the history of property offences but also the circumstances surrounding such acts and hence the probability of the child's continuing to engage in such behaviour.

Assessment

Questions

Has the child committed any property offences?
What did this entail?
Were the offences committed jointly, solo or both?
Does he have a long history of offending (more than two years) or a relatively short one?
Does the pattern of offending suggest that they have become more extensive and serious in the course of time?
Can the offences be seen as having been a means of obtaining particular goods that the child needed or wanted or do they appear to have been indiscriminate?
Is there any evidence that the offences were premeditated and planned or impulsive?
What was done with the child when offences were first discovered and how did this affect him?
Is there any evidence that the child had been forced into offending?
Do parents speak of stealing from the home and other places?
How do they say they reacted?
Was there any stealing at school?

Observations

How ready is the child to talk about his offences?
Is there any evidence of guilt, shame or remorse?
Are his accounts of the offences accurate, underestimated or exaggerated?
What does he say about his offence history?

Why does he say he committed them?
Does he try to exonerate himself? How? Does he shift the blame?
What does he say about his chances of committing further offences?
What feelings does he express regarding the probable outcome?
Does he seem to derive much self or public esteem from his accounts of his offences?
Is he ready to steal or appropriate other people's property?
Is this indiscriminate or are his victims well chosen?
Are there any particular circumstances associated with his thefts?
Is his theft for something he badly wants, or does it seem to be an act of taking for its own sake?
Does he steal as a way of taking 'revenge' on another child or adult?
Is he ready to receive what he knows to have been stolen from others?
Does he show embarrassment or does he bluff when discovered to have stolen something?
Would you regard him, compared with your population, as having the potential for becoming a more serious and determined property offender?
If yes, what is your evidence?
Does he incite others to steal in order to give him the property?

Tests There are no particularly good tests available for discovering the thieving potential of a young person. Such tests as the PD Scale of the MMPI or the Socialisation Scale of the CPI or the P Scale of the EPI may be used to provide some evidence of the existence of psychological characteristics normally associated with persistent, more serious thieving.

Action Guide Other than by changing the child's basic response pattern by costly, socially questionable methods, the only remaining alternatives are either to tolerate the offences or curb his opportunities for commission of further acts.

---

11 Arson

01 lights fires
02 assembles and sets bombs
03 attempts to obtain flammable materials

In terms of its gravity, arson falls somewhere between serious property offences and physical violence against persons. Indeed, arson, though directed at property, has potential for the infliction of severe hurt on people. For this reason offences of arson are regarded as 'grave crimes' and treated as such. Whether an act of fire setting is designated as one of 'arson' or treated otherwise, such as 'malicious damage', depends on the circumstances of the offence, the child's situation, and the particular police officer's views and his department's policy.

Fire seems to have a profound and almost mystical significance for all human beings. Its importance for children is probably no less but not as well understood. It is commonly observed that most children, at some time in the course of their growth, play with fires, engage in fantasies about it, experiment with its properties and take delight, mixed with fear, in its obvious destructive properties, warmth and beauty. It is difficult to distinguish between a child who lights fires accidentally or for fun and one who sets them deliberately either as a means of destruction or in order to satisfy some unknown yearning. Because of the potentially serious consequences, not only for the fire raiser but also of property damage and severe injury to others, all acts of fire raising are treated seriously.

Official agencies are particularly concerned to evaluate a child's potential for and preoccupation with fire raising. Statistics suggest that damage to property as a result of fire is on dramatic increase. It is suspected both by the police and insurance companies that most of these are associated either with criminal arson by adults or fire setting by youngsters as acts of revenge or as a means of gaining some other satisfaction. As with other offences, the evaluation of the child's past history of fire raising is achieved through normal social enquiry methods and the perusal of police, probation, social services and other documents.

Assessment

Questions

Has the child committed any offences of fire raising?

Was this offence of recent origin (within two years) or does it go back earlier than that?

Are there reports of other acts of fire raising not dealt with by the police?

Were these committed jointly or solo?

Do they appear to have been premeditated or impulsive?

Is there any evidence that they were aimed at gaining particular ends (such as destroying a disliked school) or for no particularly apparent reason?

Was the fire raised at night or during the day?

Was it of a public or private property, secluded or open to view?

Was it deserted or occupied and was this condition known to the child?

What were the consequences of his fire raising?

How did the parents and others react to the fire and the consequences?

How did he react to the fire and the consequences?

Are there any parental and other reports about preoccupation with fire?

What form do they say this took?

What does the child have to say about the fires?

Why did he say they were raised? What feelings does he express?
Does he try to exonerate himself?
What does he say about the possible consequences? For others?
For himself?

Observations
Does the child talk about fire and fire raising?
Is he more ready to talk about it than are other children?
Is he seen to be drawn to fires, lights or materials which could be used for this purpose?
If such materials are 'accidentally' left around does he pick them up?
Does he hide them or use them openly?
Does he volunteer for making a fire or doing something which involves the use of fire, heating or lighting materials?

Action Guide If the information suggests preoccupation with fire raising, the risk may be so great as to warrant removal of the child to a facility where his tendency may be curbed and eventually eliminated.

---

12 Management

01 defies staff
02 tests out limits
03 forces confrontation
04 unreasonably seeks attention
05 demands counselling/medication/services for no good reason
06 provokes frequent conflicts
07 wears out staff

Although for society at large a child's offences against person and property are the most important, to those who actually have to handle the children such acts are much less serious than a child's response to management.

A child is referred to a particular facility because of his problems. Whatever the task undertaken by that facility—care, education, assessment or treatment—an essential prerequisite is the drawing and enforcement of boundaries of acceptable behaviour and some degree of stability without which it can achieve none of its other aims. Depending on the nature of the particular population, the staff expect to spend a certain amount of effort and resource in achieving adequate control over the children's behaviour. When the children fail to respond to what is regarded as normal effort, they are regarded as 'management problems' requiring special resources or handling skills which may not be readily available.

This arouses apprehension, anxiety, anger and, occasionally, fear among the particular staff. This not only has repercussions for the child and his future, but is also likely to lead to his stigmatisation as a particularly problematic child who may require more serious forms of intervention. This may lead to his rejection by one facility after another. Under these circumstances the child soon learns that he is uncontrollable, and as such continues to test out to the limits any new facility which attempts to cope with him. There comes a point at which fairly dramatic steps have to be taken to exert control over his behaviour.

It is crucial to recognise that the management difficulties presented by a child are not only indicative of his past history and response potential but also a direct reflection of the coping competence of the particular environment. This problem supremely illustrates the 'interactive' nature of many of children's social difficulties.

Assessment

Questions

Has the child been regarded as particularly difficult in any facility?
If so, how many facilities have attempted to cope and how?
Why did they find him difficult?
Was the child regarded as difficult generally or only under particular circumstances such as after a parental visit or at nights or with individual members of staff?
Was this difficulty experienced by everyone or just by particular persons?
Did the other children find him difficult and, if so, what were their reasons?
Did the parents and/or teachers find the child difficult to manage and why?
Did they find that some styles of management were more successful than others?
Was the child excluded from any setting because of the management difficulties he presented?
Does the child believe he is difficult to manage?
What are his reasons for saying so?
Are his statements 'factual' or turgid with either sorrow or boasting?
What does he believe to be the effects of his behaviour on others? On himself?
How does he see his future? Is he concerned?

Observations

Does the child present any major management problems?
Are these difficulties experienced in response to the staff's instructions and requests or generated by him?
What form do these management difficulties take?

How would you place him in comparison with the rest of your group?
Are you satisfied that the difficulties are not a reasonable response to unreasonable pressures?
Is the child more or less difficult to manage under particular circumstances?
Do particular persons find it more or less difficult to manage him?
Does a pattern of age, sex and authority relationship seem to account for this?
Is the child aware of the difficulties he presents?
Does he relish them or is he remorseful about them?
How does he respond to attempts to bring him under control?
Is he a drain on staff patience, tolerance, sympathy and courage?
Would the staff be happy to get rid of him?

Action Guide Evaluate whether you can improve staff competence and tolerance; improve his behaviour by the use of rewards and sanctions; find another setting in which his behaviour will be better managed.

Selected Reading

Bandura, A. *Aggression: A Social Learning Analysis*, Englewood Cliff, N.J.: Prentice-Hall, 1973.

Caine, T. M., Foulds, G. A. & Hope, K. *Manual of the Hostility and Direction of Hostility Questionnaire (HDHQ)*, London: University of London Press, 1967.

Clarke, R. V. G. & Martin, D. N. *Absconding from Approved Schools*, London: HMSO, 1971.

Eysenck, H. J. & Eysenck, S. G. *Manual of the Eysenck Personality Questionnaire, Junior and Adult*, London: Hodder and Stoughton, 1975.

Feldman, M. P. *Criminal Behaviour: A Psycho-Analysis*, Chichester: John Wiley and Sons, 1977.

Gough, H. G. *California Personality Inventory*, San Francisco: Consulting Psychologists Press, 1956.

Hathaway, S. S. & Monachesi, E. D. (Eds). *Analyzing and Predicting Juvenile Delinquency with the MMPI*, Minneapolis. Univ. Minnesota Press, 1953.

Herbert, M. *Conduct Disorders of Childhood and Adolescence*, Chichester: John Wiley and Sons, 1978.

Hoghughi, M. S. *Troubled and Troublesome – Coping with Severely Disordered Children*, London: Burnett Books in association with André Deutsch, 1978.

Jesness, C. F. *The Jesness Inventory: Development and Validation*, Sacramento: California Youth Authority Report No. 29, 1963.

Kreitman, N. *Parasuicide*, London: John Wiley and Sons, 1977.

Rosenzweig, S., Fleming, E. E. & Rosenzweig, L. *The Picture Frustration Study (form for children)*, Provincetown, Mass.: (UK Distributors, NFER Publishing Co. Ltd., Windsor), 1948.
Tutt, N. (Ed) *Violence*, London: HMSO, 1976.
Tyreman, M. J. *Truancy*, London: University of London Press, 1968.
West, D. J. *The Young Offender*, Harmondsworth: Penguin, 1967.
West, D. J. *Present Conduct and Future Delinquency*, London: Heinemann, 1969.
West, D. J. & Farrington, D. P. *Who Becomes Delinquent?*, London: Heinemann, 1973.
West, D. J. & Farrington, D. P. *The Delinquent Way of Life*, London: Heinemann, 1977.

11 / Personal Problems

THIS AREA REFERS TO the individual characteristics and ways of functioning that determine a person's unique adjustment to the environment. It includes his personality structure, his motives, habits, attitudes, feelings and value systems. Personal problems are not exclusively problems of personality, although personality factors do contribute to a person's failure to cope successfully with the demands of life.

Numerous definitions, theories, typologies and diagnostic systems of personality have been formulated but, however complex and valid, they are largely irrelevant in the Problem Profile Approach advocated here; the latter invokes no diagnostic, aetiological or explanatory factors but focusses on problems that, because of their nature, extent and severity, are deemed unacceptable either by the person himself or by those around him.

Traditionally, people experiencing personal problems have been the concern of psychiatrists and clinical psychologists who have employed various classifications and categories to describe them. Many of the traditional terms and labels, therefore, are retained here, partly because no better terminology is currently available, and partly to act as a communication bridge between traditional nosology and the problem approach advocated here.

Personal problems manifest themselves within maladaptive behavioural patterns and seem to arise from three main sources:

One is deviations in personality structure and trait. Personality is the cluster of distinctive characteristics of an individual. Without excluding from consideration those features which are universal human traits, personality emphasises those qualities, or combinations of qualities, which set one person apart from another. A person's personality is not defined by his being human, or possessing speech, or being gregarious, but more by how his own personal formula operates to identify him as an individual in his social context. Problems can arise if the individual's characteristics deviate massively from what is generally regarded as normal.

Variations of emotional tone, adaptation and control make up another group and include those functional disorders traditionally classified as neurotic reactions, in which anxiety and distortions of mood occur, often accompanied by maladaptive patterns of behaviour, such as phobic reactions.

Personal identity and self-concept refers to the individual as he is known to himself: his conception and appraisal of the kind of person he perceives himself to be.

The assessment of personal problems is relatively well developed. There are numerous tests and techniques available for the evaluation of personality and rather fewer for problems of personal adaptation. However, because of the range of skills involved in administering and interpreting them, their use is confined to trained specialists. Our suggestions are, therefore, confined to commonly available tests or questions and observations, the response to which determines those judgments which become subjects of tests and clinical judgments by specialists.

---

01 Extraversion

01 seeks company to excess
02 constantly seeks excitement
03 talkative to excess
04 tells all to others
05 seeks group recognition to excess
06 over-exuberant
07 dependent on others for stimulation

Extraversion is a major dimension of personality. It means, literally, 'turning outwards'. The extraverted person is one who is dependent on external stimulation for the determination of his behaviour. But extraversion, like most other human characteristics, is a matter of degree.

The extravert tends to be more sociable and to appear to make easy relationships and to move from one to the other without much misgiving. He tends to be heedless, impulsive, and less concerned with the consequences of his actions than seeking participation. He responds better to reward than punishment, becomes easily bored, and has more difficulty in learning from past experience. The extreme extravert tends to 'act out' under all conditions, and hence is often identified as a 'nuisance' or 'pest' or 'show off'. Only at its extreme is extraversion a problem when it is associated with serious maladaptation.

It is important to note that most children sometimes behave in a highly extraverted fashion. There are also apparent differences with age. Extraversion appears to be inborn, though it is obviously subject to modification in the course of growing up. Along with one or two other factors in personality, this dimension has received the most extensive attention and its assessment is most efficiently achieved by appropriate tests.

Assessment

Questions
The child and others who know him can be asked:
Does he enjoy being in groups?
Does he like to be the centre of attention?
Does he move from one 'friend' to another?
Does he enjoy excitement?
Does he decide to do things on the spur of the moment?
Does he get into the same sort of trouble repeatedly?

Observations
Does the child show off?
Does he spend little time alone?
Is he always 'into' things?
Does he get easily bored and flit from one person or activity to another?
Does he take long chances?
Does he do things without forethought?
Does he enjoy being, and actively seek to be, the centre of attention?
Do other children refer to him as a 'bighead' or 'show off'?
Does he readily volunteer for group activities?
Does he attempt to 'organise' groups?
Is he often the first to offer to 'help'?

Tests This characteristic is best assessed by psychometric methods. Unfortunately, all are in the 'restricted user' category.

Action Guide Little can be realistically done to change personality structure; attempt should, therefore, be made to reduce the impact of the least desirable behaviours. Specialist psychological assessment may be indicated before a treatment programme is implemented.

---

02 Introversion

01 avoids groups
02 prefers quiet routine
03 secretive
04 loner
05 introspective
06 inexpressive (keeps himself to himself)
07 actions/thoughts directed inward
08 prefers own company

Introversion lies at the opposite pole of extraversion as a main axis of personality. At its extreme, it is the attribute describing children who are often referred to as 'loners'. They are more likely to respond to criticism than extraverts but learn more readily from experience.

Extreme introversion may isolate the child almost totally from the mainstream of daily living. Stresses are more likely to be transformed into inner conflicts compared with the extravert, who acts them out. The term 'introvert' should be used cautiously and should not refer to a person who engages in episodes of elective solitude. The same caution and general remarks made about extraversion apply here.

Assessment

Questions
Do parents and others say that he has always been a quiet child?
Do they speak of him as self-sufficient?
Is he said to prefer to be alone?
Is he described as shy and withdrawn?
Is he regarded as a 'deep' child?
Does he see himself as 'withdrawn'?
Does he express any discomfort at his own company?

Observations
Does he spend a great deal of time alone?
Does he prefer a quiet, steady routine?
Is he very careful about decisions?
Does he dislike being the centre of attention?
Does he actively reject group activities?
Is he slow at volunteering?
Do other children refer to him as a 'loner'?
Are his pastimes 'solo' pursuits?
Does he appear uneasy in company, particularly of strangers?
Tests are as for extraversion.

Action Guide As for extraversion.

---

03 Egocentricity

01 uses others for own ends
02 never helps others
03 selfish
04 greedy, over demanding
05 envious
06 interested primarily in self
07 indifferent to others
08 no genuine interest in feelings and welfare of others
09 seeks to achieve personal sense of superiority

Egocentricity means literally 'self-centredness' or extreme selfishness.

An egocentric child is interested in himself and his own concerns to such a degree that he regards himself as 'number one' in all situations, often to the detriment of the welfare of others. Other people are regarded mainly as means to the child's own ends.

In its extreme form, egocentricity functionally prevents the child from engaging in a harmonious and social life style. His emphasis on 'take' and neglect of 'give' exposes him to others' resentment and will lead to early rejection and social isolation. It should be stressed that all children, particularly in their earlier years, have periods or areas of selfishness which become gradually modified in the course of growing up.

Assessment

Questions

The child and others could be asked:
Does he like giving presents to people, whether purchased or made/collected?
Does he believe in doing favours for people? If so, why?
How does he feel when his favourite team loses heavily?
Does he very much mind losing in any games or competitions?
Does he ever give presents, bought or found, to others?
Does he ever do favours for others unasked?
Does he ever give up any thing or opportunity to someone else who may seem to need it more?
Does he express any appreciation of other people's points of view?
Does he say he is affected by them?

Observations

Do his relationships with others tend to be superficial and ephemeral?
Does he invariably thrust himself forward when 'goodies' are distributed?
Does he ever offer anything, such as food on the table, before helping himself?
Is he easily roused to jealousy?
When given choices, does he take the lion's share?
Is he generally unmoved by the misfortune of others?
Does he frequently seek to manipulate situations to suit his own ends?
Does he offer assistance when he sees others struggling?
Does he open a door, place chairs, etc. for others?
Does he tend to put his own interests before those of others?
Does he give any sign that his behaviour is affected by considerations of others?

Tests Questionnaires yield little data purporting specifically to measure egocentricity. Examination of certain factors identified in such questionnaires as the High School Personality Questionnaire, Children's Personality Questionnaire, Eysenck Personality Questionnaire, provide useful data.

Action Guide Protect others, if necessary, against the extremes of child's selfishness. Establish social skills training programme to encourage the child to show a greater interest in others.

---

04 Immaturity and Precocity

01 engages in behaviour appropriate to a younger child
02 engages in behaviour appropriate to an older child
03 prefers company of others mostly older or younger than self

Immaturity refers to the presence in a child of bodily and mental biases, attitudes, modes of expression and patterns of responses usually associated with a much younger child. Precocity refers to such manifestations usually observed in an older child. Levels of maturity involve behavioural, cognitive and social aspects.

Deviations in emotional development suggest that the child's behaviour and attitudes are not commensurate with those usually seen in someone of his chronological age. His behaviour, therefore, tends to place him at odds with his peers, and adults tend to label his behaviour 'babyish', or, on the other hand, accuse him of trying to 'behave like an adult'. Either mode of behaviour causes problems for the child though more in the former than the latter. Level and style of maturation appear to reflect primarily the way a child has been brought up.

Despite its frequent usage, it is evident that 'immature' is much more an evaluative than a descriptive term. It is, as such, deeply bound up with cultural and individual biases regarding what constitutes mature behaviour. This is because there is little consistent information available about the attitudes, values and behaviours of youngsters in different age groups against which judgments of maturity can be made with any great confidence. Caution should, therefore, be exercised in making such judgments.

Assessment

Questions
Is he described as 'mature' or 'babyish' by parents and others?
Is he said to spend most of his time with younger or duller children?

Is he said to be able to do things on his own without relying on other people, or without supervision?
Do parents or others express concern about the rate at which he is growing up?
How does he see himself in relation to his age mates – more or less grown up?

Observations
Does he seek the company of younger/older children most of the time?
Is he happy with his choice?
Does he respond to praise and criticism in a manner usually seen in a much younger or older child?
Does he share things with his friends?
Does the child behave independently at times?
Are his demands on adults and other children very different from those of his age mates?
Has he a sense of give and take?
Is he reasonably aware of his physical, social and intellectual limitations and capabilities?
Does his sense of imagination fall within the limits of reality?
Are his interests and behaviours appropriate for a child of his age?

Tests The Manchester Scales of Social Adaptation and the Bristol Social Adjustment Guide yield valuable data on which judgments of the level of maturity of the child may be based.

Action Guide Attempt to improve maturity by encouraging or shaping more appropriate behaviour.

---

05 Frustration tolerance

01 lacks patience
02 cannot tolerate delay of gratification
03 shows tantrums/aggression if does not get own way immediately
04 easily disappointed
05 easily disheartened
06 easily gives up on tasks

Frustration tolerance is the ability to postpone or delay the reaching of a goal, or to respond reasonably to a thwarted wish or desire.

In the nature of society, not all goals, needs or wants can be immediately satisfied. A young child has little appreciation and demands immediate fulfilment. As he grows older he learns increasingly to control his demands and to accept their delayed gratification. In the course of growing up, the child also has to learn that daily living is a mixed bag of pleasant and unpleasant events. Early explosive responses to unpleasant experiences have to be gradually moderated if the child is to find an acceptable place in society.

There is some evidence that frustration tolerance may be a basic and inborn personality trait. Even so, like other personality traits, frustration tolerance is fundamentally shaped by socialisation experiences. Demanding, petulant and self-willed children are usually seen to have been brought up by parents who seem to have been unable to set and enforce boundaries for their children and have given in to all their demands as a means of encouraging their good behaviour.

Assessment

Questions

Do reports suggest that the child has always been demanding?
What do they say of his response to frustration?
Did he always try to get his own way immediately?
Did he give up easily if he hit snags in anything he was doing?
Have the parents and others tried to do anything about the child's poor tolerance and with what results?
How does the child rate his own tolerance?
Does he say he would be annoyed if he had to wait for something he wanted?
Does he accept that he is bound to have frustrating experiences?
Does he say his ability is changing? For better or worse?
Does he see himself as having conflicts because of his poor tolerance?
Does he restrict these to a particular area?

Observations

Can the child wait for something he wants?
How does he react if he has to wait? Is there a pattern of reaction relating to particular forms of frustration?
Do these involve particular people or child's moods?
Are the reactions in any way unusual or extreme compared with other children's?
Does the child generally lack patience?
Does he make unnecessary mistakes due to impatience?
Does he give up easily when success is not immediate?
How noticeable are these characteristics in relation to the rest of your population?
Does the child get into trouble with adults and other children because of this tendency?

Tests Among the tests available, Porteous Maze and the Rosenzweig's Picture Frustration Study are valuable. Specific sentence completion schedules may be constructed to give a more standardised measure of this characteristic, although the results would not be any the less easy to interpret than those to the above questions.

Action Guide If seriously worrying, refer to psychologist to consider use of behaviour modification techniques to alter behaviour.

---

06 Personality Disorders

01 extreme egocentricity
02 extreme coldness
03 calculating
04 no remorse or guilt
05 does not learn from mistakes
06 lacks feeling for others
07 high need for excitement and variety
08 cannot defer gratification
09 lacks inhibitions
10 hostile
11 cheats, lies, steals
12 views others as enemies

As is evident from the range of behaviours above, this is a rag-bag or dustbin category of problems. It includes all those behaviours which do not neatly cluster together in any other way or present a clear picture of disturbance which can be classified in the traditional disease model of psychiatry.

The underlying premise is that no one can present the above difficulties without suffering from *some* form of pathology. And yet, frequently, such people are free of other obvious psychiatric disorders. In view of this, they are assumed to be suffering from a fundamental kink in their make up – a disorder of personality structure or trait – which is responsible for their socially unacceptable behaviour.

The social basis of psychiatric diagnosis, subject of so much recent debate, is nowhere more clear than in the category of anti-social or 'dissocial' personality disorders. Almost all the behaviours in this area are severely or persistently anti-social and remorseless. No 'normal person' is assumed to behave in this way. The subject is, therefore, said to suffer from a form of psychopathology. This form of pathology has been variously referred to as 'moral insanity', 'psychopathy', 'sociopathy', 'character disorder', 'conduct disorder' and a number of other exact-sounding names.

This diffuse and jumbled set of disapproved behaviours has been elevated to the status of a disease with the diagnostic feature of 'disorder of the mind', and included as a basis for certification in the Mental Health Act of 1959. It exercises such power and so neatly encapsulates social fear and legitimises action, that something very nearly like it, is retained in the recommended revision of the Act.

Despite their usefulness as means of communicating negative value judgments as administrative shorthands, the scientific and clinical stature of such terms as 'psychopath' and 'personality disordered' even with qualifications like 'aggressive' or 'inadequate', remain seriously doubtful. The groups so termed have as many dissimilarities as likenesses. The findings regarding their characteristics and their origins remain either inconsistent or insignificant. This is not to say that there are no common features among sub-groups, but that these shift according to the criteria employed and the criteria do not remain constant.

More seriously, current formulations of the disorders do not have any specific treatment implications. Where they do, it is in relation to specific behaviours, such as aggression.

Most crucially, the behaviours usually subsumed under this heading fall into a number of other problem areas, such as anti-social behaviour. There is no need to infer a personality disturbance in order to assess or treat it. In our own intensive daily dealings with severely disordered children we do not find the terms helpful and, therefore, do not employ them and do not in any way feel handicapped by the loss. We believe the stigmata attached to a youngster from the application of such terms is too great a price to be paid for the perpetuation of a term which has no therapeutic implication and has outlived its usefulness.

Assessment

The assessments of the most important behaviours in this category are presented under other headings.

Action Guide See the guides for other relevant attributes.

---

07 Impulsivity

01 acts without thought, volition or deliberation
02 does not control self
03 restless
04 easily bored
05 no resistance to temptation
06 immediate reaction to stimulus

Impulsivity is characterised essentially by sudden tendencies to act, without deliberation or volition, on the mere presentation of a stimulus or situation.

Poor impulse control embroils the child in numerous and varied trouble-laden situations. The sudden translation of ideas or perceptions into overt acts does not allow the child to consider the ramifications of his actions. Further, such disinhibited behaviour is disliked in cultures which value serenity and caution. The process of socialisation is seen by many to be primarily characterised by increasing self-control, to guide one's actions after due weighing up of pros and cons, to resist temptation to do wrong and to take an ever longer view of the consequences of one's actions. These cultural ideals are largely manifested by the majority of adults who are valued in society. The fact that practically everyone behaves impulsively from time to time, that spontaneity is the name we give to the same characteristic in the people we like, and that we distrust people who are always well-controlled, does not diminish our distrust of impulsive behaviour.

The origins of the characteristic are believed to be inborn but, like others, are subject to substantial shaping by the environment.

Assessment

Questions

Do parents and others refer to the child as impulsive or thoughtless?
Do they say he has been in trouble because of it? What trouble?
Do they say he is like any other member of the family?
What particular aspects of his impulsiveness have worried them?
What have they done about it?
Is he noticeably different from other children in this respect?
Does the child say he tends to do things on the spur of the moment?
What does he say he would do if another boy fooled him during a favourite activity?
Does he say he would fight first and ask questions afterwards?
What would he do if he found himself in a shop and the clerk was in the back room?
Does he say he is easily bored?
Does he regard himself as quick tempered?
What does he say about the consequences of being impulsive?

Observations

Are his reactions quick or slow and deliberate?
Does he engage in thoughtless behaviour which he subsequently recognises?
Does he admit to thoughtlessness? Does this affect his subsequent behaviour?
Does he give in readily to temptation?
Is he more susceptible to some temptations than others? Are these affected by circumstances?
Is he easy 'bait' for the other children?
Does he quickly lose his temper when provoked? Does he show any insight into his responsiveness?
Do the other children regard him as unpredictable?

Has he done anything that could have been serious and which he should have foreseen?
Is he very different from the rest of your population in this respect?

Tests Such tools as the British Social Adjustment Guide, Porteous Maze, Nufferno Speed Test, may yield useful information, as would a number of more specific measures developed for research (e.g. Shaffer *et al*, 1974).

Action Guide If possible, reduce risk to the child and others through impulsive behaviour. Reduce impulsivity through the use of direct teaching, modelling and feedback. In more serious cases, refer to psychologist for specialist assessment and possible treatment.

---

08 Emotional Lability
01 cries/laughs easily
02 gets over-excited
03 sulky, petulant
04 over-reacts to stress
05 has pronounced mood swings
06 superficial shallow emotions
07 bland, never shows emotions
08 emotionally cold
09 fearful, scared

Emotions are the spice of life. Changes in emotions reflect variations of experience both internally and externally stimulated. Changes in emotions are expected. When such changes are dramatic and beyond what is acceptable, or alternatively, when they do not occur at all, we become uneasy and become worried or suspicious.

Emotional lability is characterised by instability or quick changeability of feelings, their biological bases and their expressions in behaviour. In short, emotional responses are readily triggered off, either by environmental stimuli or by processes within the child.

The emotionally labile child often becomes a management problem because of the unpredictability of his behaviour. Adults, for example, say that they 'don't know where they stand' with such a child. Such unpredictability of response also leads to isolation from peers.

Emotional 'warmth' is a more difficult quality to define because it is so bound up with a child's perception of to whom he is reacting. Many children, because of the hurt and damage they have sustained, become emotionally cold or bland as a defence against further hurt. Whether for this reason or others, some children are characteristically colder to both peers and adults than is warranted by the immediate circumstances. The origins of emotional lability are not known with any confidence, but appear to include a large measure of genetic inheritance and usually a pattern of unfavourable life experiences.

Assessment

Questions

Do parents and others recount a history of noticeable moodiness?
Can they associate these with particular periods or events?
Did they become evident in different settings?
Was (is) moodiness a problem at school?
Do adults usually know 'where they are' with the child?
Has the child shown any evidence of emotional callousness? What is the evidence?
Has such callousness been evident since childhood?
Has it worried the parents or others?
Have they done anything about it?
Is the child like another member of the family?
Does the child see himself as moody?
Does he say he laughs or cries very easily?
How does he rate his own self-control?
If not well, does he mind it? Does he say he tries to control his mood and temper?
Is he aware of things or events that excite or depress his mood? Is he concerned about his emotional tone? Do the other children describe him as 'moody' or 'cold'?

Observations

Does the child lose control easily when under pressure?
What does he do?
Is he subject to mood swings? Are these moods precipitated by particular events?
Are they periodic or cyclical? Are they better in the morning or later in the day?
Is he emotionally over-sensitive? Is he easily hurt, or easily pleased?
Does he show little emotional response, even under adverse conditions?
Do other people, including children, regard him as a 'cold fish'?
Does it appear as if he is trying to control his emotions or that he experiences no emotion?
Do people feel as if he is emotionally distant and beyond reach?
How does this distance manifest itself?
Do children and adults express unease about him?
Do they avoid him?

Action Guide Reduce any environmental features which seem associated with the instability. If seriously worried, refer to psychiatrist or psychologist for more specialised evaluation and help with management.

09 Depression

01 excessively and continually unhappy
02 self-deprecation
03 appetite loss
04 sleep disturbance
05 preoccupation with self
06 persistent lethargy and apathy
07 unusual pallor
08 poor muscular tone
09 gross under-activity
10 guilt feelings
11 suicidal ideas
12 self-pity
13 weeping with little or no provocation
14 lack of attention to others

Depression has been defined clinically as an emotional state with retardation of psychomotor and thought processes, a depressive emotional reaction, feelings of guilt or criticism and delusions of unworthiness. It can refer to a physiological mood state, a subjective feeling, a collection of clinical signs or a disease entity. To tell these apart and separate a deep and appropriately depressed reaction from a possible physiological, morbid change, requires high levels of clinical experience and is, even then, often difficult.

Clinical depression must not be confused with the normally occurring state of being 'fed up', which is a transient and expected part of day-to-day living. A genuine clinical depression is an intense and almost palpable state that has a debilitating effect on the individual which, to all intents and purposes, isolates him from the mainstream of life. Clinical depressions are rare in children, but recent events, such as separation, bereavement, may induce a transitory or longer term depression in the child, which warrants management, care and attention.

Assessment

Questions

Have the parents or others commented on the child's depression? Have equivalent words been used to describe him?
Has he previously been referred to a G.P., clinic or psychiatrist for any of the above behaviours?
Is parental worry and the behaviour of long standing or of recent origin?
Is the behaviour associated with any recent events? If yes, what?
Has the child's deterioration been slow or rapid?
Does the child comment on his own mood?
Does he recognise it as unusual?

Observations

Does the child go around with a hangdog expression?

Can he be induced to laugh or smile easily?
Have you ensured that nothing in the immediate environment is making him miserable?
Is the child noticeable by virtue of any of the above behaviours?
Do the other children comment on his state?
Does anything happen which seems to lift the child's mood?
Is there any variation according to time of day or the activity involved?

Tests Restricted.

Action Guide Refer to psychiatrist for appropriate assessment and treatment.

---

10 Anxiety

01 tense, unable to relax
02 restless
03 over-active
04 apprehensive
05 indecisive
06 needs constant reassurance
07 irritable, jumpy
08 tics and tremors
09 feelings of impending disaster
10 sleep disturbance
11 palpitations or pallor
12 excessive perspiration
13 nausea
14 constipation or bedwetting
15 seems impervious to stress

Anxiety may be defined as an unpleasant emotional experience, varying in degree from mild unease to intense dread. It leads to physiological and behavioural changes, very similar to those of fear. It shares certain features of depression. Levels of anxiety are influenced by personality traits (trait anxiety), as well as personally significant stresses (state anxiety). Anxiety may be general and all-pervasive (free-floating) or alternatively, specific to a particular topic (focal).

If a child is reported to be anxious, several considerations must be taken into account. Firstly, it should be recognised that anxiety may be a normal or an appropriate response under some circumstances, such as before examinations or after removal from home. Anxiety has considerable biological significance for survival in terms of increased alertness and awareness, or as a response to threat and unfamiliarity. Secondly, anxiety is often a symptom of other psychiatric, psychological and physical disturbance and may, therefore, indicate other possible disorders which should be investigated. Thirdly, anxiety levels are protean, and different children will show different responses to ostensibly the same anxiety-inducing situations.

Although low anxiety levels may be regarded as a blessing, a particularly low level of anxiety will deprive the child of that aspect which acts as an early warning system and an indicator of undue stress. A child who does not react with appropriate anxiety is likely to get into scrapes and other forms of trouble which are avoided by a person with a normal complement of anxiety. This has been proffered as an explanation of some criminal careers by some researchers.

When investigating a child's level of anxiety (high *or* low), possible constitutional factors, patterns of early socialisation, and current life experiences should be evaluated.

Assessment

Assessment of an abnormal level of anxiety should be ultimately the responsibility of a trained clinician. However, non-specialists may be able to provide clues that will assist in describing an individual's level of anxiety.

Questions

Do parents and others speak of the child as anxious and worried?
Has he always been like this or only recently? Do any events account for this?
Has he been referred to anyone for this problem and with what consequences?
How does the child describe himself in this context?
Does he say he often has 'the shakes' in his hands?
Does he sweat a lot, even when sitting quietly?
Does his heart often 'thump'?
Does he have difficulty going to sleep?
Does he have something worrying him? Is he afraid of something? Does he know what it is?
Does he often feel that something terrible is going to happen?
Does he worry a lot? Does he try to reduce his anxiety? Does he have what he considers good reasons for his state? Does he think he needs help?

Observations

Is the child excessively fidgety?
Does he appear to be 'on edge'?
Is he often bilious for no apparent physical reason?
Is he often indecisive even over small matters?
Does he often complain of feeling sick?
Does he complain of difficulty in going to sleep?
Is he edgy and over-sensitive? Is this regardless of time, place and events?
Is he 'always on the go'? Is this with a purpose or does it appear to be just time filling?

Does he seem to lack confidence? Is this better or worse with particular people and situations?
Does he frequently visit the toilet?
Does he often seek help, company and counsel for small matters?
Have you ensured that his care requirements are being met?

Action Guide Reassure and provide protective care. If anxiety appears excessive and debilitating, refer to psychiatrist for evaluation and treatment.

---

11 Obsessive-compulsive Neurosis

01 rigid conformist
02 strictly conventional
03 orderly
04 insists on perfection
05 scrupulous
06 intolerant
07 inflexible
08 does the same things over and over again
09 over-preoccupied with daily routines
10 unspontaneous
11 uncreative
12 self-righteous
13 complains of persistent, irrational thoughts, impulses and actions

When obsessions and compulsions coexist, the condition is referred to as an obsessive-compulsive neurosis. Obsessions consist of (unpleasant) words, thoughts, ideas and impulses that a person is unable to exclude from his mind, however hard he tries. Despite common usage to the contrary, an obsession is *not* a preoccupation with ideas or principles, whose pursuit may result in an orderly, efficient, and happy life style. Compulsions usually overlap with obsessions but they involve specific, repetitive acts, such as hand washing and getting out of bed to check things for safety. Obsessive-compulsive behaviour should not be confused with habit patterns, but can be distinguished by the child's slavish adherence to behaviour patterns which may be unpleasant and not directed at his greater happiness. Much of this behaviour is normally related to particular levels of individual development and unlikely to cause severe distress.

Obsessive-compulsive behaviour becomes debilitating when it takes over and dominates the individual's day-to-day routines, to such an extent that it serves no constructive purpose, and is often distressing to the individual and impairs his functioning. The child's behaviour often contains signs and symptoms indicative of an above average level of anxiety. Obsessive-compulsive behaviour patterns, rare in children, are believed to be maladaptive attempts at reducing anxiety. They should be carefully evaluated because they may be masking psychotic symptoms.

Some children, however, may be described as having an obsessive-compulsive type of personality, known as an anankastic personality, in which traits of rigidity, conscientiousness, reliability, punctuality and moral scrupulousness are found. Such a child is often described as 'finicky'.

Assessment

Questions

Do parents and others report behaviours of the above type?
Do their descriptions suggest that they noted anything wrong?
Did they try to do anything about it? If yes, what and with what results?
Are there other family members with the same behaviour patterns?
Does he say he checks over and over again things he has already completed?
How does he feel if he doesn't recheck something?
Does he like to touch or count things over and over again?
Does he avoid walking on certain things or does he avoid certain routes or paths? Does he say he tries to stop himself from doing things but can't?
Does he say he gets lots of awful thoughts coming into his head?
What are these thoughts? Why does he regard them as awful?
Does he try to push the thoughts out of his mind? How and with what results?
Does he think his state is unusual?
Is he worried about his state?
Does he think he needs help?

Observations

Does the child repeat things over and over again? Both words and actions?
Does he engage in precise and predictable behaviour patterns repeatedly? What?
Are these related to what is required of him? How frequently does he do these?
How does he respond to a change in established routines?
Is he preoccupied with always doing things in a strict, orderly manner?
Does he have very regular habits?
Does he have stereotyped expressions and mannerisms?
Is the child meticulously slow when doing something?
Does he often appear scowling and preoccupied? Does he take the opportunity to snap out of these thoughts?
How does the child react to minimal failure?
Do the other children regard him as odd?

Tests Restricted.

Action Guide Refer to psychologist and/or psychiatrist who, after specific evaluation, may proceed to appropriate treatment.

---

12 Phobic Reaction

01 fear of animals
02 fear of situations
03 fear of persons
04 fear of places
05 fear of objects

Fear of dangerous or unfamiliar objects and situations is biologically necessary for survival. Fear or apprehension associated with a wild animal or a potentially hazardous situation is not a neurotic phobia. Neither is an isolated, specific, fear of say, heights, dogs or air travel – these are idiosyncratic reactions or personal preferences. In contradistinction, a fear must be irrational, intense, persistent, and characterised by a high level of anxiety and debilitating before it can be called a phobia. Many children experience fears, some of them intense, in the course of their growing. They eventually grow out of them and do not require any particular help, especially if these fears do not impede their progress.

An intense fear becomes maladaptive when it so disturbs the individual that he is unable to lead a normal, healthy life. For example, if a person is so seriously disturbed by crowds that he is unable to use public transport, go to work or enter shops, then a phobic neurotic reaction is indicated. His irrational and intense fear will be reflected in his anxiety and persistent attempts to avoid anything to do with the feared stimulus. Phobias are regarded as instances of overlearning from an overreaction to a particularly fearful experience.

Assessment

Questions
Are there reports of particular fears?
Were these regarded as unusual either in kind or degree?
How did the fear manifest itself?
Was he ever referred for help?
Are there any other members of family with intense fears?
Does the child say he has strong fear?
Does he avoid certain things or places because he knows they will make him feel uneasy?
Does he feel very uncomfortable if he is in contact with a particular animal, object, place, etc.?

Is he afraid of the dark?
Can he think of anything that gives him the 'jitters'?
Is he unhappy about his fear? How does he explain it?
Does he try to cover it up? How?
How does he rate himself in relation to other children?
Does he think he needs help?

Observations
Does the child specifically avoid certain situations, objects, places or people?
Does the child show signs of high anxiety in specific places, at certain times, or when in the presence of certain people or animals?
Is his avoidance or fear reaction obvious or subtle?
Does his reaction interfere with normal life?
Do the other children know of his fear?
Is he likely to be penalised because of it?

Action Guide If the fear is not debilitating, leave it alone. If it is, refer to a psychologist or psychiatrist for specific treatment.

---

13 Hypochondriasis

01 exaggerated concern with physical and/or mental health
02 over-sensitive and over-responsive to the normal fluctuations of health
03 uses extreme measures to safeguard health
04 frequently complains of minor ailments
05 numerous visits to sick bay/surgery with spurious complaints

Hypochondriasis is the name given to a collection of behaviours characterised by persistent and exaggerated worry about bodily health, when there is nothing demonstrably wrong with the child. In spite of reassurance, the child remains convinced that he is suffering from a disability or disease. The behaviours are regarded as neurotic because they are thought to be generated by anxiety and maintained by the attention the hypochondriac receives. Distinction should be made between hypochondriac behaviour and phobia of a specific disease, such as cancer.

As with any neurotic reaction, hypochondriasis causes discomfort in the individual and interferes with his ability to cope with the day-to-day demands of life. Simultaneously, the hypochondriac, because of his behaviour, tends to be regarded as a pest and a nuisance.

It is believed that hypochondriac reactions, which are much more common among adults than children, are learned through family experiences and modelling on a hypochondriac person in the child's immediate life space.

Assessment

Questions
Do parents and others say that the child has been a worrier about his state?
Are the parents worried about the child's health?
Have they sought frequent help to sort out the ills?
Do the parents' and child's worries have a good foundation? Why?
Does the child worry about his health?
Does he very often think he is ill more than other people?
What does he do when he is not well?

Observations
Does the child frequently request to see a doctor or nurse?
Does he frequently complain about his poor health?
Does he make a fuss if he is suffering from some minor ailment?
Is he described as 'always having something wrong with him'?
Is he considered a pest because of his complaints?

Action Guide If at all possible, ignore or tolerate the behaviour and advise others to do the same. If you cannot and you think it warrants the use of scarce resources, refer him to a psychologist for treatment.

---

14 Hysteria

01 loss or disorder of sensory functions
02 loss or disorder of motor functions
03 loss of voice
04 sleepwalking
05 loss of memory
06 disorders of eating
07 disorders of excretion

Hysteria, in spite of its popular usage as a specific condition, remains another clinical dustbin. Speculations as to its nature are legion and have abounded for centuries among diagnosticians, although little evidence exists to suggest that such a condition exists as a discrete disorder. For the purpose of this book, however, the *term* will be retained but its *behavioural* components will be emphasised.

Hysteria, whatever it means, should be distinguished from a histrionic personality. Attention-seeking behaviour, liveliness, shallowness, flirtatiousness, self-centredness, dependency and emotional exaggeration characterise the histrionic type personality. Hysterical symptoms (behaviours) can occur in numerous psychiatric conditions and often stem from the person's inability to cope with life, or as reactions to some unbearable stress, often spilling over into symptoms of conversion or dissociation.

We would strongly suggest that a *diagnosis* of hysteria be avoided, not only because the term is clinically pejorative, but also because it is tantamount to ruling out the possibility of treatment. Instead, it may well be sufficient to isolate the problem behaviour and, having ruled out other problems, concentrate on its treatment.

Assessment

Questions

Are there any reports of loss of function without good physical reasons?
Have parents and others sought help for it? If yes, with what results?
Are there reports of histrionic behaviour?
Does the child say he loses the use of an arm or leg for no apparent reason?
Does he say he has 'fits' or has difficulty keeping his balance?
Does his skin ever go numb so that he cannot feel a nip or a pin prick?
Does he sometimes suffer from blurred vision, or feel that there is something wrong with his eyes?
Does he get pains in his chest or back?
Does he ever do things in a sort of 'dream' without remembering afterwards what he did?
Does he sometimes think he is deaf?
Does he ever lose his voice?
Does he sometimes lose his memory?
Does he sometimes find himself in places without quite knowing how he got there?
How does he explain and feel about his problems?
Does he appear indifferent and seem to be content to let you get on with solving his problem?

Observations

Does the child stumble, limp, or faint without any discernible physical cause?
Does he complain of loss of feeling in his skin?
Does he complain of deafness or being unable to speak?
Does he appear lost at times?
Does he turn up in inappropriate places and is unable to account for his being there?
Does he engage in exaggerated behaviours of the type you would call histrionic?

Action Guide If possible, tolerate the behaviour, otherwise refer to psychologist for protracted treatment.

---

15 Self-concept

01 does not agree with how others see him
02 unrealistic
03 inflated
04 fluid
05 confused
06 self-reproaching
07 negative

Self-concept concerns the individual's perception of himself; it includes his attitudes towards himself, his needs, fears, aspirations and expectations. It can best be construed as a child's answers to such questions as 'Who am I?', 'Who cares for me and whom do I care for?', 'What am I worth?', 'What is my place in my universe?'.

Quite obviously not many children, nor many adults, actually pose such questions to themselves and try to answer them. But self-concept is thought to emerge from the child's interactions with his human environment. His attitudes to himself will largely reflect those of others. This is the main reason why children who are unloved believe themselves to be unlovable and eventually turn out unable to love.

All purposive behaviour of a child has to be mediated by his perception of the consequences of his action for himself. The concept of 'self' is, therefore, widely implicated in behaviour. If the concept is unrealistic, confused or negative, the actions mediated by it are likely to suffer and result in the child being at odds with his environment. Although a child's 'ideal' self may be different from his 'actual' self, both must be sufficiently clear and 'realistic' to facilitate socially and personally satisfactory behaviour.

It should be noted, however, that children's self-concepts are liable to change with their maturation and exposure to new experiences. Because of the relatively scant attention to this area by researchers, it is more than usually difficult to know when a self-concept is sufficiently abnormal to be commented on.

Assessment

Questions

Are there any reports to the effect that the child seems to live in a fantasy world?
Is his view of himself particularly confused or negative?
What does he think of himself?
What does he say about his difficulties, his hopes and his aspirations?
How does he describe his ideal person in terms of personality characteristics, behaviour towards others, and pursuits?

What would he choose if allowed to have any three wishes?
How would he describe himself in relation to his ideal?

Observations
Does he have difficulty in answering such questions as the above?
Is this difficulty more noticeable than other children's?
Is the difficulty more than you would expect for a child of his ability?
Are his accounts beyond anything that might be regarded as reasonably realistic?
Are they confused, contradictory and frequently changing?
Are his accounts accompanied by any particular emotional reactions?
Does he emerge from his statements as a purposive child, in control of what is happening to him, or a puppet controlled by events?
Does he see himself as inexorably progressing into more trouble?
Does he express concern about the consequences?

Tests Sentence Completion schedules with short stems such as 'I', 'I hope . . .', 'I wish . . .', etc. are a particularly fruitful, standardised means of collecting information about self-concepts, individually and in groups. Similarly, Semantic Differential proformas can be devised which enable the evaluation by the child of himself and others. Other forms of adjective checklists and rating scales can be used to advantage to augment the results of interviews. Particularly valuable techniques such as the Repertory Grid, although not restricted, require high levels of specialised training for administration and interpretation.

Action Guide Intensive individual and group counselling may be helpful in alleviating negative features of self-concept and enhancing its positive aspects.

---

16 Moral Development

01 cannot correctly label right and wrong
02 only distinguishes acts on fear of external punishment
03 minimal concern for the impact his behaviour has on others
04 ignores rules/obligations
05 identifies with and emulates delinquent standards
06 anti-authority attitudes and proclivities, no guilt or shame

Moral development refers to progressive changes in individuals in the degree and manner they are capable of resisting temptation to do what is pleasurable or profitable, though regarded as wrong.

In this case, an immoral person is one who fails to inhibit such impulses but pursues the immediate gratification of his desires. Morality may also refer to the control of one's behaviour by reference to 'internalised' standards, rather than by reference to the possible consequences of the behaviour for the actor. The motives and intentions of the actor must be considered, because taking action solely on the basis of its consequences is not deemed to be moral, whereas actions not taken because of moral prescriptions or prohibitions are. Finally, morality may be indicated by behaviour that is carried out by reference to rules or principles rationally accepted for reasons understood to be legitimate; moral behaviour follows a moral decision, and the behaviour is carried out because it is considered to be 'the right thing to do'. Immoral behaviour, therefore, is behaviour carried out in the pursuance of self-gratifying ends, in spite of the fact that the behaviour or ends conflict with the requirements of moral rules or principles.

Moral development implies that the child has internalised concepts of the differences between right and wrong, and indicates to what degree he subscribes to widely accepted principles and rules. It also includes the child's ability to understand and observe the rights of others, the manner and the degree to which he can resist temptation, and the manner in which his actions correspond with his verbal intentions. The child's level of moral development is determined by his familial and cultural background and these factors must be considered when estimating his level of morality.

Moral development, or under-development, has cognitive, affective and behavioural implications for the life style of a child. As such, it refers to a knowledge and understanding of rules and obligations, the feelings a child has pertinent to what he regards as right or wrong, and the behavioural manifestations relating to the development of a moral code. Deviations in moral development, therefore, expose the child to situations, formal and informal, in which he is likely to experience social and personal turmoil.

Children's expressions of moral standards and attitudes should be judged with considerable caution, particularly when children are in trouble. This is because of their tendency to give socially desirable responses as a means of exculpating themselves or giving a good impression.

Assessment

Questions to the child

These are either direct or couched in situations with a 'moral' element which the child is asked to explain or interpret.

What would you do if you found £1 in the street?
Which is worse – someone who deliberately smashes a glass or one who accidentally drops a whole trayful of glasses? Why?

Which is worse – a father breaking a promise to his son, or the son breaking a promise to his father? Why?
Who are your favourite book or TV characters?
Do you try to copy them?
Can you put yourself in someone else's place and understand their point of view?
Do you ever think about your own behaviour? In what way?
Do you ever feel sorry for anyone else? If so, who and when?
Do you care if other people are very pleased or disappointed by your behaviour?
Do you ever think about the consequences of your behaviour? Why? How?
Do you think of other people's behaviours in terms of right and wrong?
What kinds of things do you think are right and what wrong?
List five of each.
Do you have some rules of your own that you always stick to, no matter what happens? What are they?
Do you keep your word? Do you do what you say you will do?
What do you feel and do if you have done something wrong or harmed somebody?

Observations
Does the child usually admit to being wrong or acting badly?
Does he attempt to minimise the severity of his undesirable behaviour?
Does he usually blame someone or something else for his misdemeanours?
Does the child identify with disreputable TV, film or book characters?
Does he ever spontaneously talk about 'right' and 'wrong'?
Can he put himself in someone else's shoes?
Does he ever comment on his own (mis)behaviour in moral terms?
Does he sympathise with or comment sympathetically upon another child's misfortune?
Does he appear to have any personal rules or principles?
Is he trustworthy?
Is he a confidant of the other children?
How well can he resist temptation? Does this vary in different situations?
Does he express sorrow, remorse or guilt after doing something wrong?
Do these appear to be sincere or are they demanded by the circumstances?
Does he do anything to remedy whatever wrong he has done?

Tests Kohlberg's elaborate and searching techniques in which children are questioned about moral dilemmas may be used to determine the level of a child's moral development.

Action Guide Improve moral sense by tuition, example, regulated social behaviour or more specific clinical techniques.

Selected Reading

Blackham, G. J. and Silberman, A. *Modification of Child and Adolescent Behavior*, Belmont, California: Wadsworth, 1975.

Caine, T. M., Foulds, G. A. and Hope, K. *Manual of the Hostility and Direction of Hostility Questionnaire (HDHQ)*, London: Univ. of London Press, 1967.

Cattell, R. B. and Beloff, H. *Handbook for the Jr–Sr High School Personality Questionnaire* (HSPQ), I.P.A.T., Illinois, 1962.

Eysenck, H. J. and Eysenck, S. B. G. *Manual of the Eysenck Personality Questionnaire – Junior and Adult*, London: Hodder and Stoughton, 1975.

Fransella, F. and Bannister, D. *A Manual for Repertory Grid Technique*, London: Academic Press, 1977.

Furneaux, W. D. *The Nufferno Tests of Speed, Accuracy and Level*, London: University of London Press, 1955.

Gathercole, C. E. *Assessment in Clinical Psychology*, Harmondsworth: Penguin Books, 1968.

Hare, D. *Psychopathy*, New York: John Wiley and Sons, 1970.

Herbert, M. *Conduct Disorders of Childhood and Adolescence*, Chichester: John Wiley and Sons, 1978.

Jesness, C. F. *The Jesness Inventory: Development and Validation*, Sacramento: California Youth Authority Report No. 29, 1963.

Kohlberg, L., Colby, A., Speicher-Dubin, B. & Lieberman, M. *Standard Form Scoring Manual*, Cambridge: Moral Education Research Foundation, 1975.

Lickona, T. *Moral Development and Behavior*, New York: Holt, Rinehart & Winston, 1976.

Marks, I. M. *Fears and Phobias*, London: Heinemann, 1969.

Mischel, W. *Personality and Assessment*, Chichester: John Wiley and Sons, 1968.

Mittler, P. (Ed), *The Psychological Assessment of Mental and Physical Handicap*, London: Methuen and Co., 1970.

Osgood, C. E., Suci, G. J. and Tannenbaum, P. M. *The Measurement of Meaning*, Illinois: University of Illinois Press, 1957.

Page, J. D. *Psychopathology*, Chicago: Aldine Atherton, 1971.

Porteous, S. D. *The Porteous Maze Test Manual*, London: Geo. G. Harrap & Co., 1967.

Potter, R. B. and Cattell, R. B. *Manual for the Children's Personality Questionnaire* (CPQ), I.P.A.T., Illinois, 1968.

Rogers, C. R. *Personal Adjustment Inventory*, New York: Association Press, 1961.

Rosenzweig, S., Fleming, E. E. and Rosenzweig, L. *The Picture Frustration Study (form for children)*, Provincetown, Mass.: The Journal Press, 1948.

Rutter, M. and Hersov, L. (Eds), *Child Psychiatry – Modern Approaches*, Oxford: Blackwell, 1976.

Savage, R. D. *Psychometric Assessment of the Individual Child*, Harmondsworth: Penguin Books, 1968.

Shaffer, D., McNamara, N. and Pincus, J. H. 'Controlled observations on patterns of activity, attention and impulsivity in brain damaged and psychiatrically disturbed boys', *Psychol. Med.*, 4, 4–18, 1974.

Taylor, J. A. 'A Personality Scale of Manifest Anxiety', *J. Abnormal Soc. Psych.*, Vol. 48, No. 2, 1953.

Wolman, B. B. *Handbook of Clinical Psychology*, New York: McGraw Hill, 1965.

Wolpe, J. and Lang P. J. 'A Fear Survey Schedule for Use in Behaviour Therapy', *Beh. Res. Ther.*, 2, 27–30, 1964.

Wright, D. *The Psychology of Moral Behaviour*, Harmondsworth: Penguin Books, 1971.

References

Advisory Council on Child Care. *Care and Treatment in a Planned Environment*, London: HMSO, 1970.
Anthony, E. J. & Bene, D. 'A technique for objective assessment of child's family relationships', *J. Ment. Sci.*, 103; 541–555, 1957.
Argyle, M. *The Psychology of Interpersonal Behaviour*, Harmondsworth: Penguin Books, 1967.
Argyle, M. *Social Interaction*, London: Methuen, 1969.
Argyle, M. and Trower, P. *Person to Person*, London: Harper & Row, 1979.
Bandura, A. *Principles of Behavior Modification*, New York: Holt, Rinehart & Winston, 1969.
Bandura, A. *Aggression: a social learning analysis*, Englewood Cliffe, N.J.: Prentice Hall, 1973.
Bannister, D. & Mair, J. M. M. *The Evaluation of Personal Constructs*, London: Academic Press, 1968.
Barker, R. C. *Ecological Psychology*, Stanford: Stanford University Press, 1968.
Becker, H. S. *Outsiders: Studies in Sociology of Deviance*, New York: Free Press, 1963.
Bellack, L. *The T.A.T. and C.A.T. in Clinical Use*, New York: Grune and Stratton, 1954.
Blackham, G. F. & Silberman, A. *Modification of Child and Adolescent Behavior*, 2nd ed. Belmont, California: Wadsworth, 1975.
Block, N. & Dworkin, G. (Eds), *The IQ Controversy: Critical Readings*, London: Quartet Books, 1977.
Brain, Lord *Speech Disorders*, London: Butterworths, 1961.
British Association of Social Workers. *The Social Work Task*, Birmingham: BASW, 1977.
Bruch, H. *Eating Disorders*, London: Routledge, Kegan Paul, 1973.
Buehler, R. E., Patterson, E. R. & Furniss, J. M. 'The reinforcement of behaviour in institutional settings', *J. Behav. Res. & Therapy*, Vol. 4; 157–167, 1966.
Burland, J. R., Brown, T. W. & Handham, R. P. *Steps to Self Sufficiency*, Chelfham Mill School, Barnstaple: Viaduct Publications, 1977.
Buros, O. K. *The Seventh Mental Measurement Year Book*, Highland Park, N.J.: The Gryphon Press, 1972.

Caine, T. M., Foulds, G. A. & Hope, K. *Manual of the Hostility & Direction of Hostility Questionnaire (HDHQ)*, London: University of London Press, 1967.

Cannell, C. F. & Kahn, R. L. 'Interviewing' in Lindzey, G. & Aronson, E. (Eds), *The Handbook of Social Psychology*, Vol. III, Reading, Mass.: Addison-Wesley Publishing Co., 1968.

Cassell, R. N. *Test of Social Insight*, New York: M. Brace, 1976.

Cattell, R. B. *The Scientific Analysis of Personality*, Harmondsworth; Penguin Books, 1965.

Cattell, R. B. & Beloff, H. *Handbook for the Jr – Sr High School Personality Questionnaire (HSPQ)*, Illinois: I.P.A.T., 1962.

Chazan, M., Moore, T., Williams, P. & Wright, J. *The Practice of Educational Psychology*, Harlow: Longmans, 1974.

Child, D. *Psychology and the Teacher*, London: Holt, Rinehart & Winston, 1973.

Clarke, R. V. G. & Martin, D. N. *Absconding from Approved Schools*, London: HMSO, 1971.

Cone, J. D. & Hawkins, R. P. *Behavioral Assessment*, New York: Brunner/Mazel, 1977.

Cooper, J. D. (Chairman) *The Family in Society : Dimensions of Parenthood*, London: HMSO, 1973.

Cottrell, L. S. 'Interpersonal interaction and the development of the self' in Goslin, D. A. (Ed), *Handbook of Socialisation Theory and Research*, Chicago: Rand McNally, 1969.

Cox, A. & Rutter, M. 'Diagnostic appraisal and interviewing' in Rutter, M. & Herson, L. (Eds), *Child Psychiatry*, Oxford: Blackwell, 1976.

Daniels, J. C. & Diack, H. *The Standard Reading Tests*, London: Chatto & Windus, 1972.

Dept. of Health and Social Security. *Community Homes Design Guide*, London: HMSO, 1971.

Dept. of Health and Social Security. Circulars on Non-Accidental Injury to Children, LASSL (74) 13, 76, (2).

Doll, E. A. *Vineland Social Maturity Scale*, Minnesota: American Guidance Service Inc., 1965.

Eisler, R. M. 'The Behavioural Assessment of Social Skills' in Hersen, M. & Bellack, A. S., *Behavioural Assessment*, Oxford: Pergamon Press, 1976.

English, H. B. & English, A. C. *A Comprehensive Dictionary of Psychological and Psychoanalytic Terms*, New York: Longman, Green & Co., 1958.

Evans, K. M. *Sociometry and Education*, London: Routledge & Kegan Paul, 1962.

Eysenck, H. J. & Eysenck, S. B. G. *Manual of the Eysenck Personality Questionnaire – Junior and Adult*, London: Hodder & Stoughton, 1975.

Feinstein, A. D. 'A critical overview of diagnostic psychiatry' in Rakoff, V. M., Stancer, H. C. & Kedward, H. B. (Eds), *Psychiatric Diagnosis*, New York: Brunner/Mazel, 1977.

Feldman, M. P. *Criminal Behaviour: A Psychological Analysis*, Chichester: John Wiley & Sons, 1977

Fensterheim, H. & Baer, J. *Don't Say Yes When You Want To Say No*, New York: David McKay & Co., 1975.

Fiske, D. W. *Measuring the Concepts of Personality*, Chicago: Aldine Publishing Co., 1971.

Fransella, F. & Bannister, D. *A Manual for Repertory Grid Technique*, London: Academic Press, 1977.

Furneaux, W. D. *The Nufferno Tests of Speed, Accuracy and Level*, London: University of London Press, 1955.

Garrison, K. C. & Magoon, R. A. *Educational Psychology: An Integration of Psychology and Educational Practices*, Columbus, Ohio: Merrill, 1972.

Gathercole, C. E. *Assessment in Clinical Psychology*, Harmondsworth: Penguin Books, 1968.

Geschwind, N. *Selected Papers on Language and the Brain*, Boston: Reidel, 1976.

Gittins, J. S. *Approved School Boys*, London: HMSO, 1951.

Gittins, J. S. 'The Observation and Assessment of Children and Young Persons in the Light of the 1969 Children and Young Persons Act in Residential Care and Treatment', London: Advisory Council on Child Care, 1970.

Goldstein, A. P., Sprafkin, R. P. & Gershaw, N. J. *Skill Training for Community Living. Applying Structured Learning Therapy*, Oxford: Pergamon Press with Structured Learning Associates, 1976.

Gough, H. G. *California Personality Inventory*, San Francisco: Consulting Psychologists Press, 1956.

Gray, M. 'The myth of objective assessment', *Comm. Care*: 1 March, 1978.

Gronlund, N. E. *Sociometry in the Classroom*, New York: Harper, 1959.

Gulick, W. L. *Hearing, Physiology and Psychology*, London: Oxford University Press, 1971.

Gunzburg, H. C. *Progress Assessment Charts and Manual*, Birmingham: SEFA Publications Ltd., 1975.

Hare, D. *Psychopathy*, New York: John Wiley & Sons, 1970.

Hargreaves, D. H. *Social Relations in a Secondary School*, London: Routledge & Kegan Paul, 1967.

Harris, D. & Hyland, J. (Eds), *Rights in Residence*, London: Residential Care Association, 1979.

Hathaway, S. R. & Monachesi, E. D. (Eds), *Analyzing and Predicting*

Juvenile Delinquency with the MMPI, Minneapolis: Univ. Minnesota Press, 1953.

Haynes, S. N. *Principles of Behavioral Assessment*, New York; Gardner Press Inc., 1978.

Heaton, J. M. *The Eye*: Phenomenology and Psychology of Function and Disorder, London: Tavistock Publictions Ltd., 1968.

Herbert, M. *Problems of Childhood*, London: Pan Books Ltd., 1975.

Herbert, M. *Conduct Disorders of Childhood and Adolescence*, Chichester: John Wiley & Sons, 1978.

Hersen, M. & Bellack, A. S. *Behavioural Assessment*, Oxford: Pergamon Press, 1976.

Hobbs, N. *The Futures of Children*, San Francisco: Jossey-Bass, 1975.

Hoffman, L. W. & Lippit, R. 'The measurement of family life variables' in Mussen, P. H. (Ed), *Handbook of Research Methods in Child Development*, New York: John Wiley & Sons, 1960.

Hofman, F. G. *A Handbook in Drug and Alcohol Abuse*, London: Oxford Univ. Press, 1975.

Hoghughi, M. S. 'A conceptual model for a comprehensive child care system', *Child Care*, Vol. 25, 2, 41–57, 1969.

Hoghughi, M. S. 'Assessment: purpose & practice', *Child In Care*, Vol. 11, 1, 10–16, 1971.

Hoghughi, M. S. *Conceptual Model of a Treatment System for Problem Children*, Aycliffe: Aycliffe Studies of Problem Children, 1975.

Hoghughi, M. S. *Organising for Treatment*, mimeo, privately circulated, Aycliffe: 1977.

Hoghughi, M. S. *Monitoring Treatment in the Special Unit*, mimeo, privately circulated, Aycliffe: 1978a.

Hoghughi, M. S. 'Diagnosis of Children's Disorders – a Critique', Paper read to the Irish Branch of the Association of Child Psychology and Psychiatry, 1978b.

Hoghughi, M. S. *Troubled and Troublesome* – Coping with Severely Disordered Children, London: Burnett Books in association with André Deutsch, 1978c.

Hoghughi, M. S. 'Assessment – myth, method and utility', *Social Work Today*, Vol. 10, No. 29, 11–17, 1979a.

Hoghughi, M. S. 'Residents' Rights or Pleas for Decent Care?' in Harris, D. & Hyland, J. (Eds), *Rights in Residence*, London: Residential Care Association, 1979b.

Hoghughi, M. S. 'What Do We Do with Disturbed Youngsters', Paper presented to the Third International School Psychology Colloquium, York University, 1979c.

Hoghughi, M. S. 'Oh, Occam where art thou?', *Int. J. Law & Psychiat.*, (in press), 1979d.

Hoghughi, M. S. & Porteous, M. A. *Manual of Aycliffe Data Card – Mark II*, Aycliffe: Aycliffe Studies of Problem Children, 1976.

Horrocks, J. E. *Assessment of Behavior*, Columbus, Ohio: C. E. Merrill Books, 1964.
Howard League for Penal Reform *'Unruly' Children in a Human Context*, Chichester: Barry Rose, 1977.
Howells, J. G. & Lickorish, J. R. *The Family Relations Indicator*, Windsor: National Foundation for Educational Research, 1962.
Hunter, I. M. L. *Memory*, Harmondsworth: Penguin Books Ltd., 1964.
Hutt, C. *Males and Females*, Harmondsworth: Penguin Education, 1972.
Jesness, C. F. *The Jesness Inventory: Development and Validation*, Sacramento: California Youth Authority Report No. 29, 1963.
Johnson, O. G. & Bommarito, J. W. *Tests and Measurements in Child Development: A Handbook*, San Francisco: Jossey Bass, 1971.
Johnson, D. J. & Myklebust, H. R. *Learning Disabilities: Educational Principles and Practices*, New York: Grune and Stratton.
Jones, R. R., Reid, J. B. & Patterson, G. R. 'Naturalistic observation in clinical assessment' in McReynolds, P. (Ed), *Advances in Psychological Assessment*, San Francisco: Jossey Bass, 1975.
Kellmer Pringle, M. L. *The Needs of Children*, London: Hutchinson, 1975.
Kempe, R. S. & Kempe, C. H. *Child Abuse*, London: Fontana/Open Books, 1978.
Kerlinger, F. N. *Foundations of Behavioral Research*, New York: Holt, Rinehart & Winston, 1964.
Kohlberg, L., Colby, A., Speicher-Dubin, B. & Lieberman, M. *Standard Form Scoring Manual*, Cambridge: Moral Education Research Foundation, 1975.
Kreitman, N. (Ed), *Parasuicide*, London: John Wiley & Sons, 1977.
Lachman, S. J. *Psychosomatic Disorders: A Behavioral Interpretation*, New York: John Wiley & Sons, 1972.
Lezak, M. D. Neuropsychological Assessment, New York: Oxford University Press, 1976.
Liberman, R. P., King, L. W., DeRisi, W. & McCann, M. *Personal Effectiveness: Guiding People to Assert Themselves and Improve their Social Skills*, Illinois: Research Press, 1975.
Lickona, T. (Ed), *Moral Development and Behavior*, New York: Holt, Rinehart & Winston, 1976.
Lickorish, J. R. 'The psychometric assessment of the family' in Howells, J. G. (Ed), *Theory and Practice of Family Psychiatry*, Edinburgh: Oliver & Boyd, 1968.
Livingston, S. A. 'Psychometric techniques for criterion-referenced testing and behavioral assessment' in Cone, J. D. & Hawkins, R. P. (Eds), *Behavioral Assessment*, New York: Brunner Mazel, 1978.
Lunzer, E. A. *Manchester Scales of Social Adaptation (Manual)*, Windsor: NFER, 1966.

McReynolds, P. *Advances in Psychological Assessment*, San Francisco: Jossey Bass, 1975.

Marks, I. M. *Fears and Phobias*, London: Heinemann, 1969.

Mercer, J. R. 'Psychological assessment and the rights of children' in Hobbs, N. (Ed), *Issues in the Classification of Children*, San Francisco: Jossey Bass, 1975.

Millham, S., Bullock, R., Hosie, K. *Locking Up Children*, Farnborough: Saxon House, 1978.

MIND *Assessment of Children and Their Families*, London: National Association for Mental Health, 1975.

Mischel, W. *Personality and Assessment*, London: John Wiley & Sons, 1968.

Mittler, P. (Ed), *The Psychological Assessment of Mental and Physical Handicaps*, London: Methuen, 1970.

Mooney, R. L. & Gordon, L. V. *The Mooney Problem Checklist*, New York: The Psychological Corporation (UK Distributors NFER), 1950.

Morganstern, K. P. 'Behavioural interviewing' in Hersen M. & Bellack, A. S. (Eds), *Behavioural Assessment*, Oxford: Pergamon Press, 1976.

Munro, A. & McCulloch, W. *Psychiatry for Social Workers*, Oxford: Pergamon Press, 1969.

NFER National Foundation for Educational Research, Test Department, Darrville House, 2 Oxford Road East, Windsor, Berks.

Nethercott, S. M. N. 'The Development of a Problem Index', paper delivered at the Third International School Psychology Colloquium, York University, 1979.

Oppenheim, A. N. *Questionnaire Design and Attitude Measurement*, London: Heinemann, 1966.

Osgood, C. E. & Miron, M. S. *Approaches to the Study of Aphasia*, Illinois: University of Illinois Press, 1963.

Osgood, C. E., Suci, G. J., and Tannenbaum, P. M. *The Measurement of Meaning*, Illinois: University of Illinois Press, 1957.

Page, J. D. *Psychopathology*, Chicago: Aldine Atherton, 1971.

Passmore, J. *Philosophical Reasoning*, London: Duckworth, 1961.

Phillips, L., Draguns, J., & Bartlett, D. 'Classification of behavior disorders' in Hobbs, N. (Ed), *Issues in the Classification of Children*, San Francisco: Jossey Bass, 1975.

Pincus, A. & Minahan, A. *Social Work Practice: Model and Method*, Itasca, Illinois: F. E. Peacock Publishers, 1973.

Polsky, H. W. *Cottage Six: The Social System of Delinquent Boys in Residential Treatment*, New York: John Wiley & Sons, 1962.

Popper, K. *The Logic of Scientific Discovery* (Third Edition), London: Hutchinson, 1972.

Porteous, S. D. *The Porteous Maze Test Manual*, London: Geo. G. Harrap & Co. Ltd., 1967.

Porter, R. B. & Cattell, R. B. *Manual for the Children's Personality Questionnaire (CPQ)*, Illinois: IPAT, 1968.

Priestley, P., McGuire, J., Flegg, D., Hemsley, V. & Welham, D. *Social Skills and Personal Problem Solving: A Handbook of Methods*, London: Tavistock Publications, 1978.

Prugh, D. G., Engel, M., & Morse, W. C. 'Emotional Disturbance in Children' in Hobbs, N. (Ed), *Issues in the Classification of Children*, San Francisco: Jossey Bass, 1975.

Rains, P. M., Kitsuse, J. I., Duster, T., Freidson, T. 'The labeling approach to deviance' in Hobbs, N. (Ed), *Issues in the Classification of Children*, San Francisco: Jossey Bass, 1975.

Reinach, E., Lovelock, R., Roberts, G. *First Year at Fairfield Lodge*, Portsmouth: Hampshire Social Services Dept., 1976.

Renfrew, C. E. *Speech Disorders in Children*, Oxford: Pergamon Press, 1972.

Rogers, C. R. *Personal Adjustment Inventory*, New York: Association Press (UK Distributors NFER), 1961.

Rosenheim, M. (Ed), *Pursuing Justice for the Child*, Chicago: University of Chicago Press, 1976.

Rosenzweig, S., Fleming, E. E. & Rosenzweig, L. *The Picture Frustration Study (form for children)*, Provincetown, Mass.: (UK Distributors NFER Publishing Co. Ltd., Windsor), 1948.

Rotter, J. B. 'External control and internal control', *Psychology Today* 5, 37–42, 58–59, 1971.

Rutter, M. *Helping Troubled Children*, Harmondsworth: Penguin Books, 1975.

Rutter, M. 'Classification' in Rutter, M. & Hersov, L. (Eds), *Child Psychiatry*, Oxford: Blackwell, 1976.

Rutter, M., Graham, P. & Yule, W. *A Neuropsychiatric Study in Childhood*, London: Spastics International Medical Publications in assoc. with Heinemann Medical Books Ltd., 1970.

Rutter, M. & Hersov, L. (Eds), *Child Psychiatry – Modern Approaches*, Oxford: Blackwell, 1976.

Rutter, M. & Madge, N. *Cycles of Disadvantage*, London: Heinemann, 1976.

Ryback, R. S. (Ed), *The Problem Oriented Record in Psychiatry and Medical Care*, New York: Grune & Stratton, 1974.

Savage, R. D. *Psychometric Assessment of the Individual Child*, Harmondsworth: Penguin Books, 1968.

Savage, R. D. 'Intellectual assessment' in Mittler, P. (Ed), *The Psychological Assessment of Mental and Physical Handicaps*, London: Methuen, 1970.

Shaffer, D., McNamara, N. & Pincus, J. H. 'Controlled observations on patterns of activity, attention and impulsivity in brain damaged and psychiatrically disturbed boys', *Psychol. Med.*, 4, 4–18, 1974.

Shapiro, M. B. 'Assessment interviewing in clinical psychology', *Brit. J. Soc. Clin. Psychol.*, 18, 211–218, 1979.
Shearer, A. 'Tragedies revisited', *Social Work Today*, 9, 16, 23 Jan., 1979.
Sherif, M. & Sherif, C. *Reference Groups*, New York: Harper & Row, 1964.
Shouksmith, G. *Assessment Through Interviewing*, London: Pergamon Press, 1968.
Social Work Service Group *Assessment of Children*, Edinburgh: Scottish Home & Health Dept., 1971.
Social Work Service *Use and Development of Observation & Assessment Centres for Children*, London: DHSS, 1977.
Spitzer, R. L., Sheehy, M., Endicott, J. 'DSM–III: Guilding Principles' in Rakoff, V. M., Stancer, H. C. & Kedward, H. B. (Eds), *Psychiatric Diagnosis*, New York: Brunner/Mazel, 1977.
Stott, D. H. *The Social Adjustment of Children: The Manual of the Bristol Social Adjustment Guide*, 5th edn., London: Hodder & Stoughton Educational, 1974.
Stott, D. H. & Sykes, E. G. *British Social Adjustment Guide – (a) The Child in Residential Care; (b) the Child in School*, London: Hodder & Stoughton Educational, 1970.
Taylor, J. A. 'A personality Scale of Manifest Anxiety', *J. Abnormal & Soc. Psych.*, Vol. 48, No. 2, 1953.
The Diagram Group *Man's Body. An Owner's Manual*, New York: Paddington Press, 1976.
Thorndike, E. L. *The Thorndike Junior Illustrated Dictionary*, London: University of London Press, 1947.
Trower, P., Bryant, B., & Argyle, M. *Social Skills and Mental Health*, London: Methuen, 1978.
Truax, C. B. & Mitchell, K. M. 'Research on certain therapist interpersonal skills in relation to processed outcome' in Bergin, A. E. & Garfield, S. L. (Eds), *Psychotherapy and Behaviour Change*, London: John Wiley & Sons, 1971.
Tutt, N. (Ed), *Violence*, London: HMSO, 1976.
Tyreman, M. J. *Truancy*, London: University of London Press, 1968.
Warnock, H. M. (Chairman). *Special Educational Needs – Report of the Committee of Enquiry into the Education of Handicapped Children and Young People*, London: HMSO, 1978.
Wedge, P. & Prosser, H. *Born to Fail?*, London: Arrow Books, 1973.
Weed, L. L. *Medical Record, Medical Education and Patient Care*, Cleveland: Case Western Reserve Univ. Press, 1969.
West, D. J. *The Young Offender*, Harmondsworth: Penguin Books, 1967.
West, D. J. *Present Conduct and Future Delinquency*, London: Heinemann, 1969.

West, D. J. & Farrington, D. P. *Who Becomes Delinquent?*, London: Heinemann, 1973.

West, D. J. & Farrington, D. P. *The Delinquent Way of Life*, London: Heinemann, 1977.

Wing, J. K., Cooper, J. E. & Sartorius, N. *The Measurement and Classification of Psychiatric Symptoms,* Cambridge: Cambridge University Press, 1974.

Wingate, P. *The Penguin Medical Encyclopaedia*, Harmondsworth: Penguin Books, 1976.

Wolman, B. B. *Handbook of Clinical Psychology*, New York: McGraw Hill, 1965.

Wolpe, J. & Lang, P. J. 'A fear survey schedule for use in behaviour therapy', *Beh. Red. Ther.*, 2, 27–30, 1964.

Wright, D. *The Psychology of Moral Behaviour*, Harmondsworth: Penguin Books, 1971.

Wright, H. F. 'Observational child study' in Mussen, P. H. (Ed), *Handbook of Research Methods in Child Development*, New York: John Wiley & Sons, 1960.

Yarrow, L. J. 'Interviewing children' in Mussen, P. H. (Ed), *Handbook of Research Methods in Child Development*, New York: John Wiley & Sons, 1960.

Index

Index